Tuscany and Beyond

Keith Hern

First published in 2013

Paperback ISBN13 978-1-78092-398-7

epub ISBN 978-1-78092-399-4

PDF ISBN 978-1-78092-400-7

Published in the UK by MX Publishing,

335, Princess Park Manor, Royal Drive, London, N11 3GX

www.mxpublishing.co.uk

Cover by www.staunch.com

Introduction

In spite of having been interested in travel since the late 1970s I had never actually made it to Tuscany, that is until 2004, although I had seen the photographs many a time and wondered if it could really be that impressive. Then, in February 2004 there was on offer from a local property agent to go and have a look at a development they were marketing near Palaia, with the obvious requirement to listen to the talk about owning an apartment there, not that that was an option, but the idea appealed.

At the end of the four days when the offer to buy was politely declined, the discussion turned to a hitherto unmentioned 'membership club', and having been well and truly taken in by the area were interested. Duly signing up for the lowest cost timeshare-style arrangement for a twenty year period with the entry-level five night a year deal at the Borgo di Colleoli, the base for exploring Tuscany was now there.

Apart from a couple of financial scares when the whole project was at risk, I have been able to visit Tuscany twice a year ever since 2004, visits that have always been hugely enjoyable, as everything that is Italy continues to charm and entice. Whether it's the scenery, the weather, the culture and architecture, the food and wine, just the lifestyle, or any or all of these it's provided a base to explore Tuscany, and latterly further away as a few days have now been added to one of the trips each year to see further afield and nowhere has disappointed.

The photographs selected for this book aim to show what some of the smaller, lesser known places and areas look like, hence there are only a few shots of the likes of Pisa, Siena and Florence. The 'beyond' element includes shots from a range of locations from Lake Maggiore north of Milan, to the stunning Cinque Terre on the west coast, down through Bologna and Parma to Elba. This years' extension is likely to see a return trip to Parma.

Personal update

This is my third travel photography book, the others being 'Zimbabwe In Pictures' and 'Guatemala In Pictures', with hopefully more to come. All are available through the main online retailers in both printed paperback hard copy as well as Kindle versions, and can also be ordered from my website www.keithhern.com . If you like the photography then please follow my blog at www.keithhern.com/blog and you'll also be able to find me on twitter, LinkedIn, Facebook and Youtube (the channel is Keith Hern Photography).

In addition, I have started giving illustrated travel talks, something began a couple of years ago. During a promotional trip to Zimbabwe I was asked to speak at the Sanganai Tourism Conference in Harare, which led to being invited as guest speaker to a large travel event run at their London Embassy during the World Travel Market, from which I gained the confidence to further develop this new line.

At about the same time I had received an extraordinarily powerful testimonial from a cancer patient who had read my book 'Bangers & Mash', written during my own journey through throat cancer in 2007. Details of the book, and the associated photographs from my treatment can be found at my website www.journeythroughcancer.co.uk . Boosted by the confidence of the Embassy talk I turned the book into an inspirational presentation which I have now given to a wide variety of audiences, the largest to date being some 600 at a national conference. A whole new area of opportunity is now opening out in the speaking world, with video recordings of both 'Handling Adversity & Opportunity' and 'Have Camera, Will Travel' up on Youtube.

Looking forward life is full of exciting new opportunities and challenges, but one thing is assured, namely that I will continue to travel and take photographs from whichever places I am fortunate enough to get to.

Personal dedication and thanks

There has to be one massive thank you to a whole group of people to whom this book is dedicated – all of those in the medical and alternative medicine world with whom I have had the pleasure to work over the last six years, as I have the dubious honour of being struck down by cancer on no less than three occasions.

Without your tireless work, effort and encouragement I simply wouldn't be here, so a heartfelt thank you to every one of you. This book is dedicated to your fantastic work that has enabled me to continue following my passion of travelling, camera in hand.

Last but not least, a huge thank you to family (particularly my wife Madeleine, and daughter Jess) and friends who have been so incredibly supportive and encouraging when I most needed it, and for probably suffering from my various career changes!

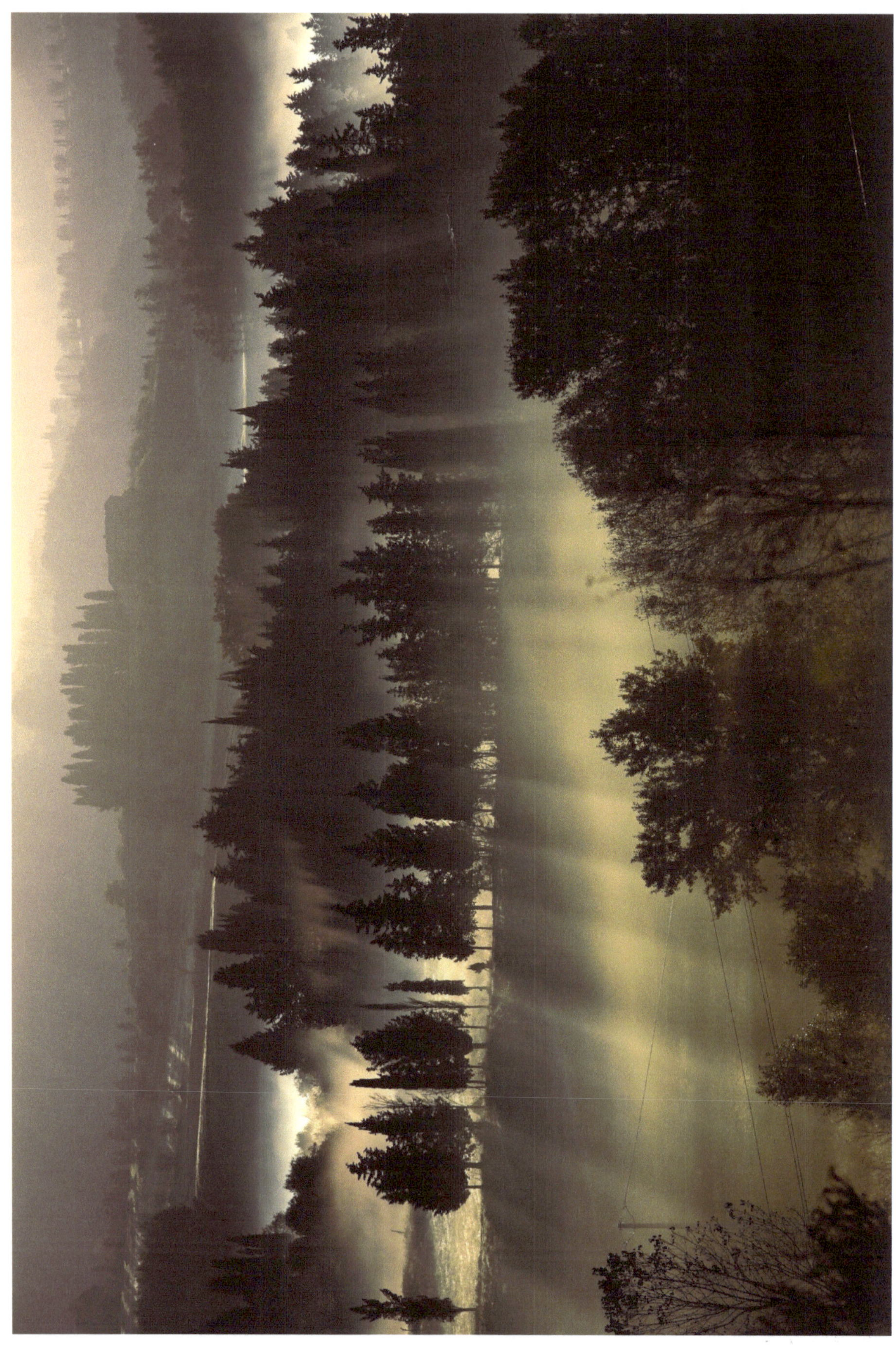

Wonderful early light near Castelfalfi – it only lasted about five minutes.

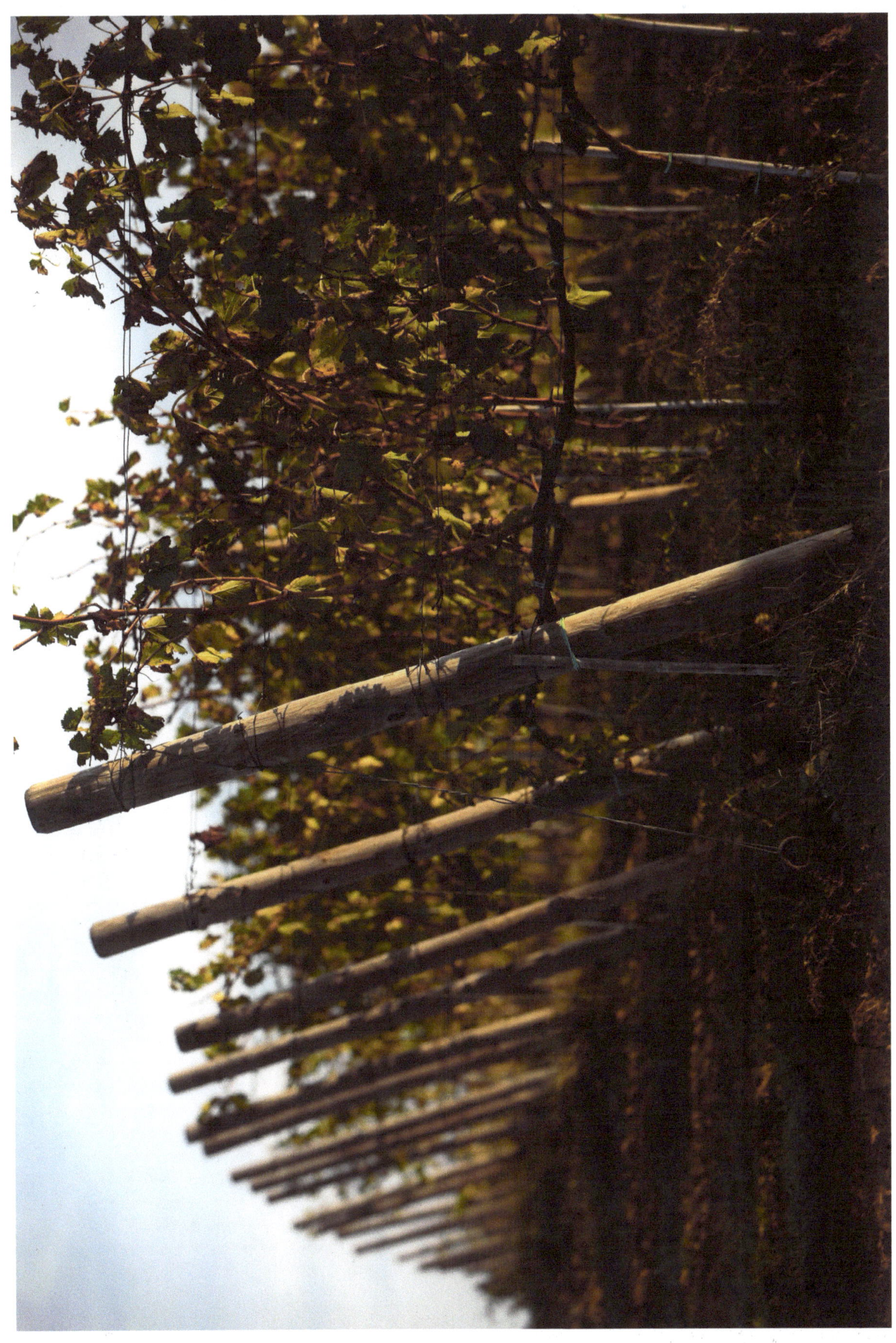

Shallow depth of field and early golden light on these vines near Castelfalfi.

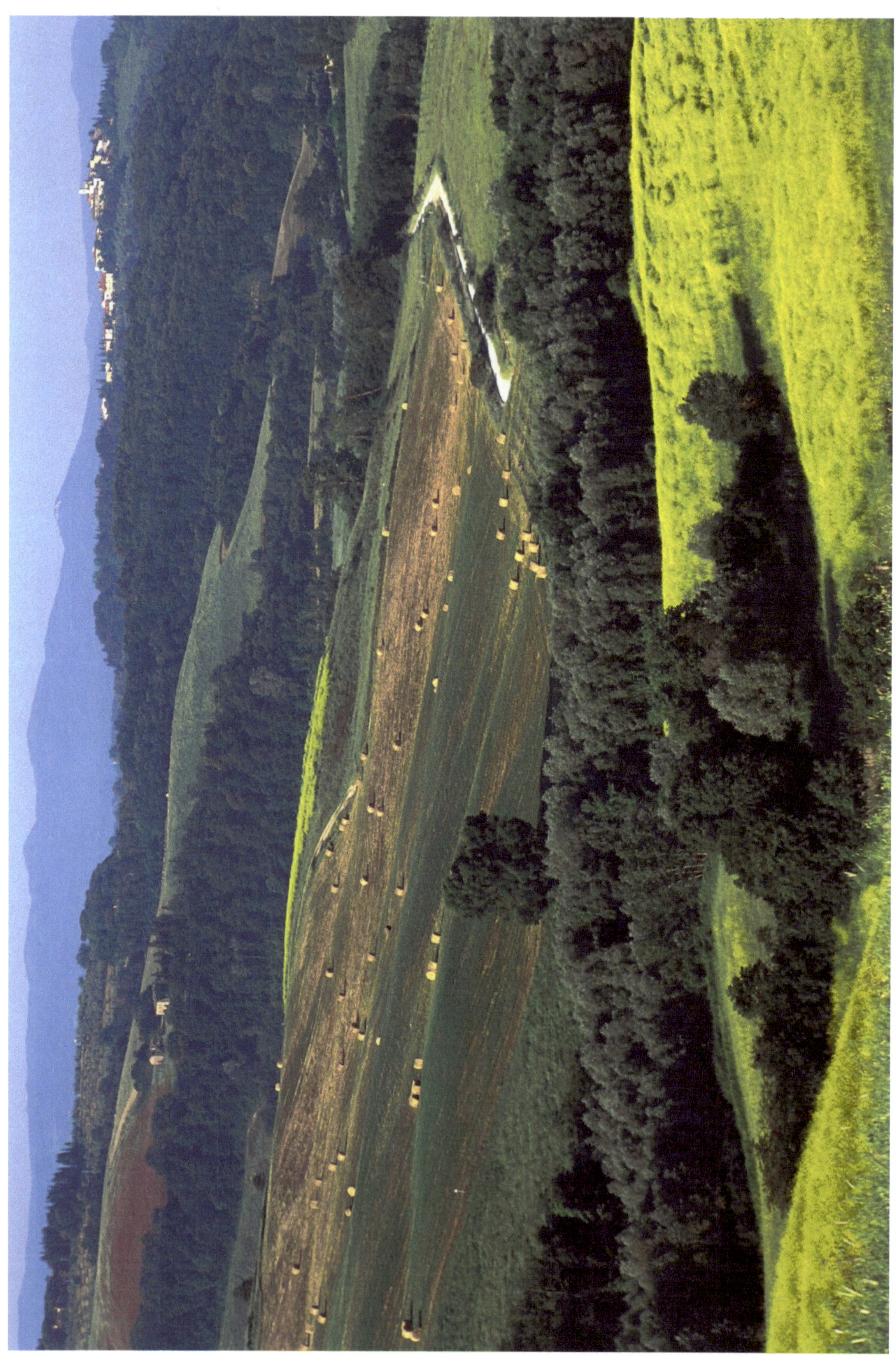

South-westerly view from the road between Montefoscoli and Castelfalfi.

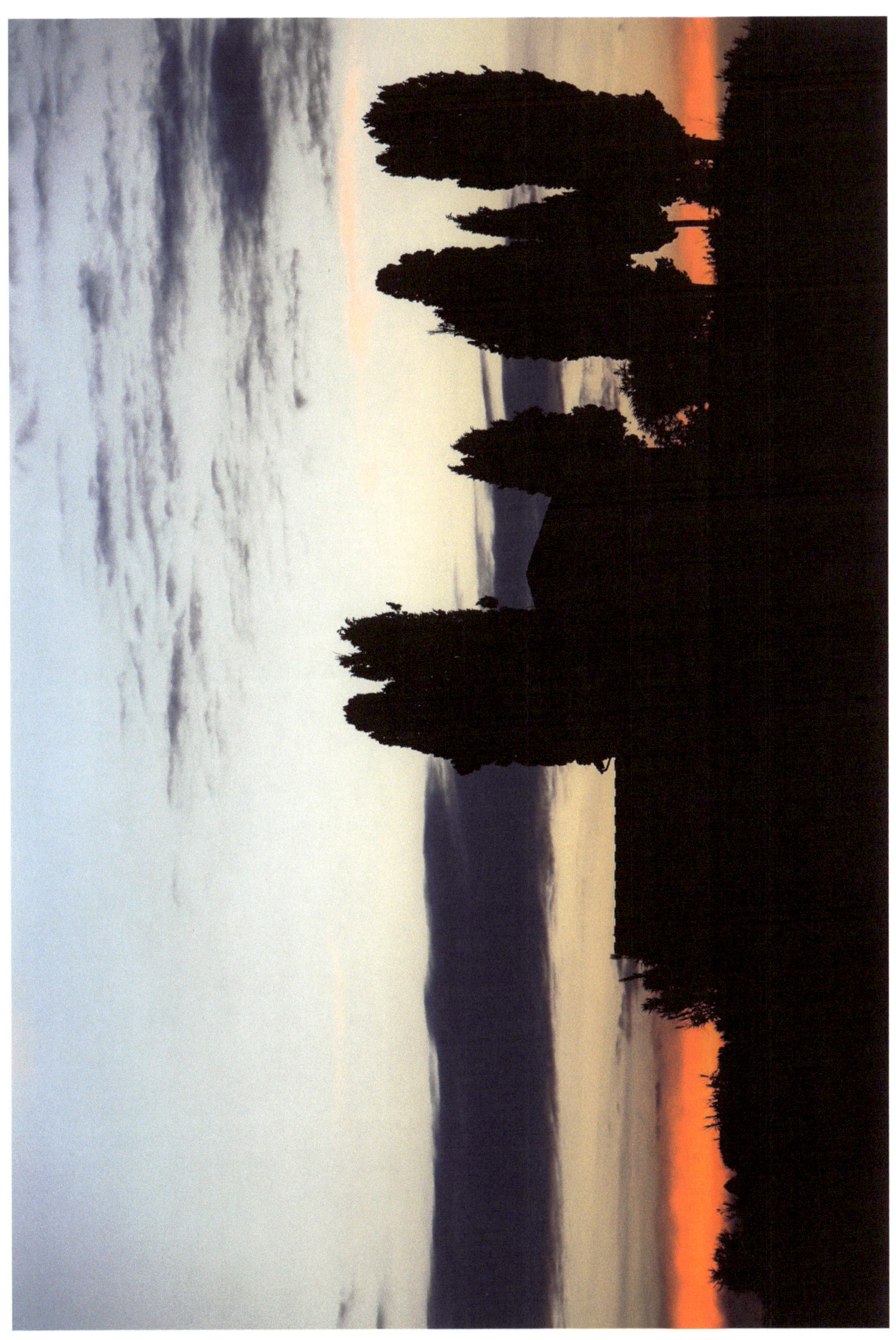

Silhouetted farmhouse and landmark Cypress pines just before sunrise.

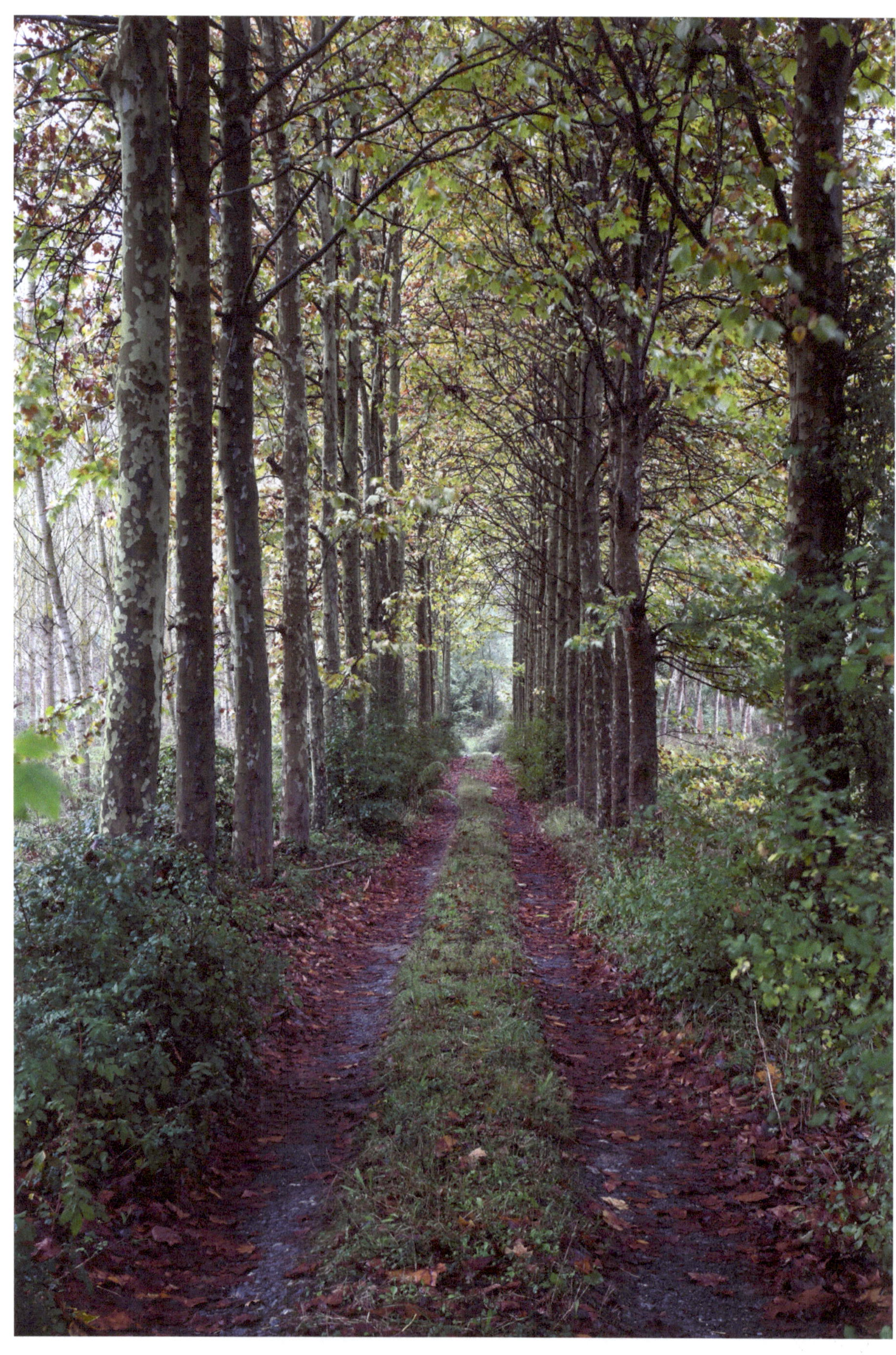

Autumnal colours between Peccioli and Castelfalfi.

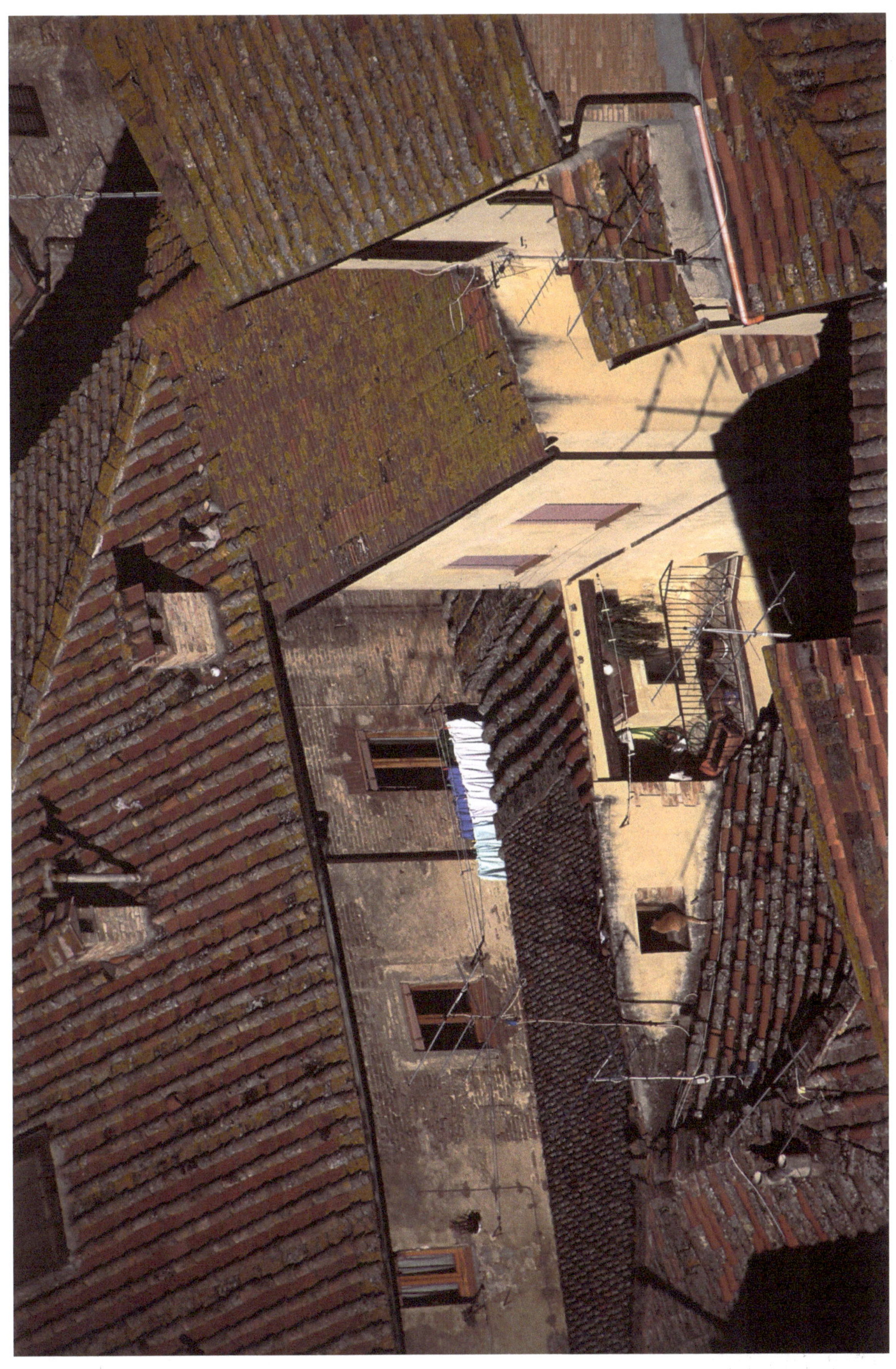

Rooftop view from the tower in San Gimignano – like the cat!

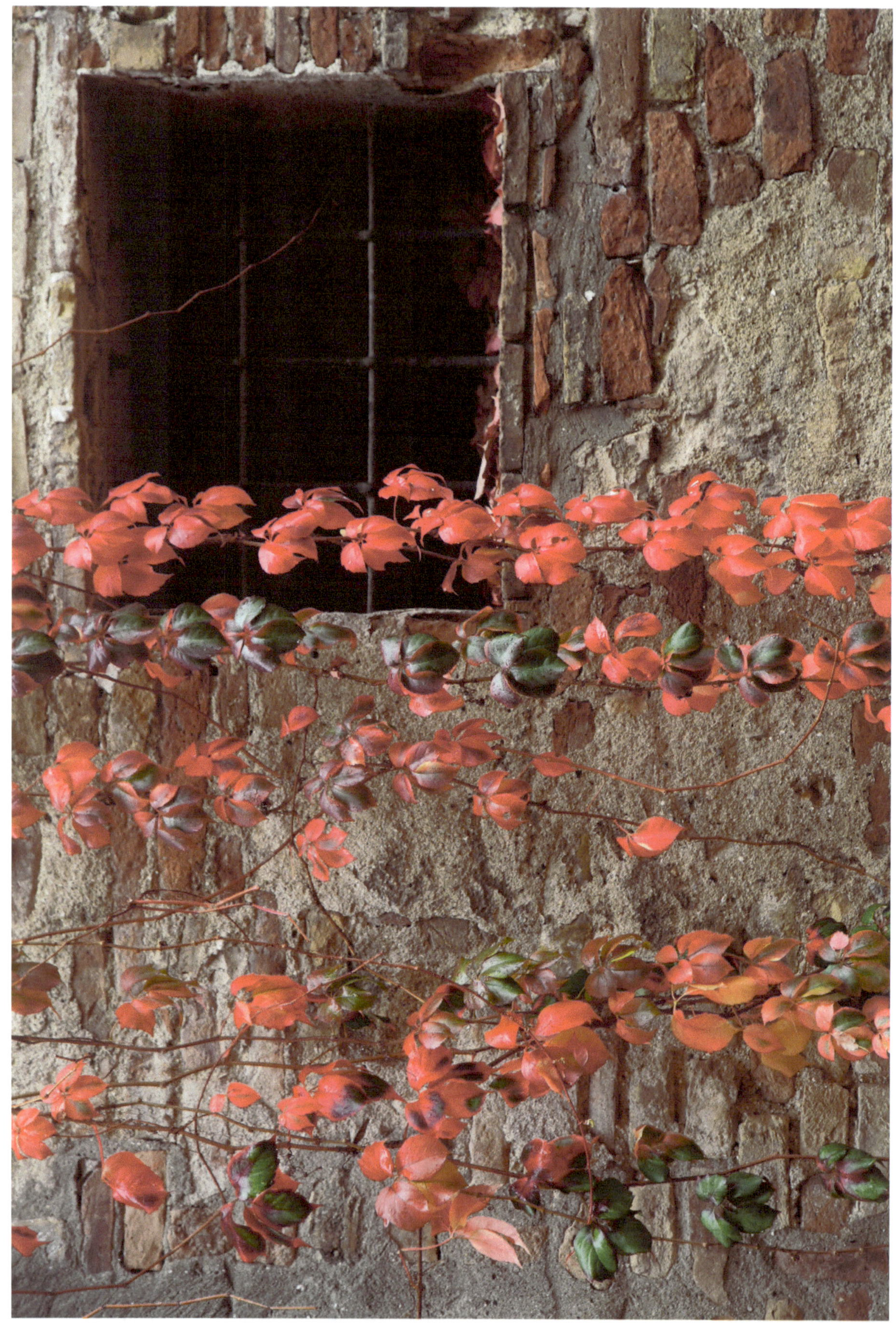

Rustic look down a side street in San Gimignano.

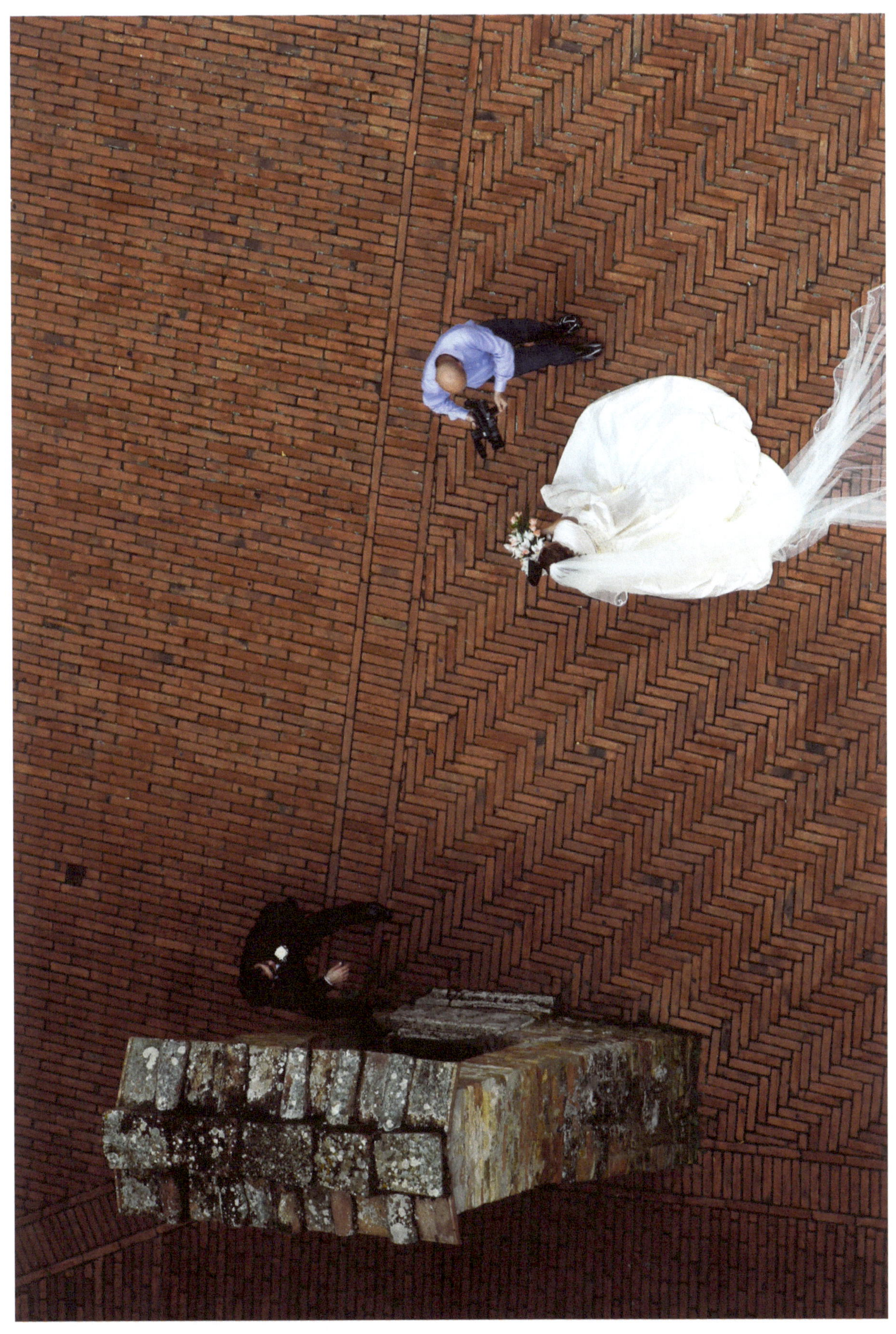

Amazing what you see from the San Gimignano tower, even this couple's special day.

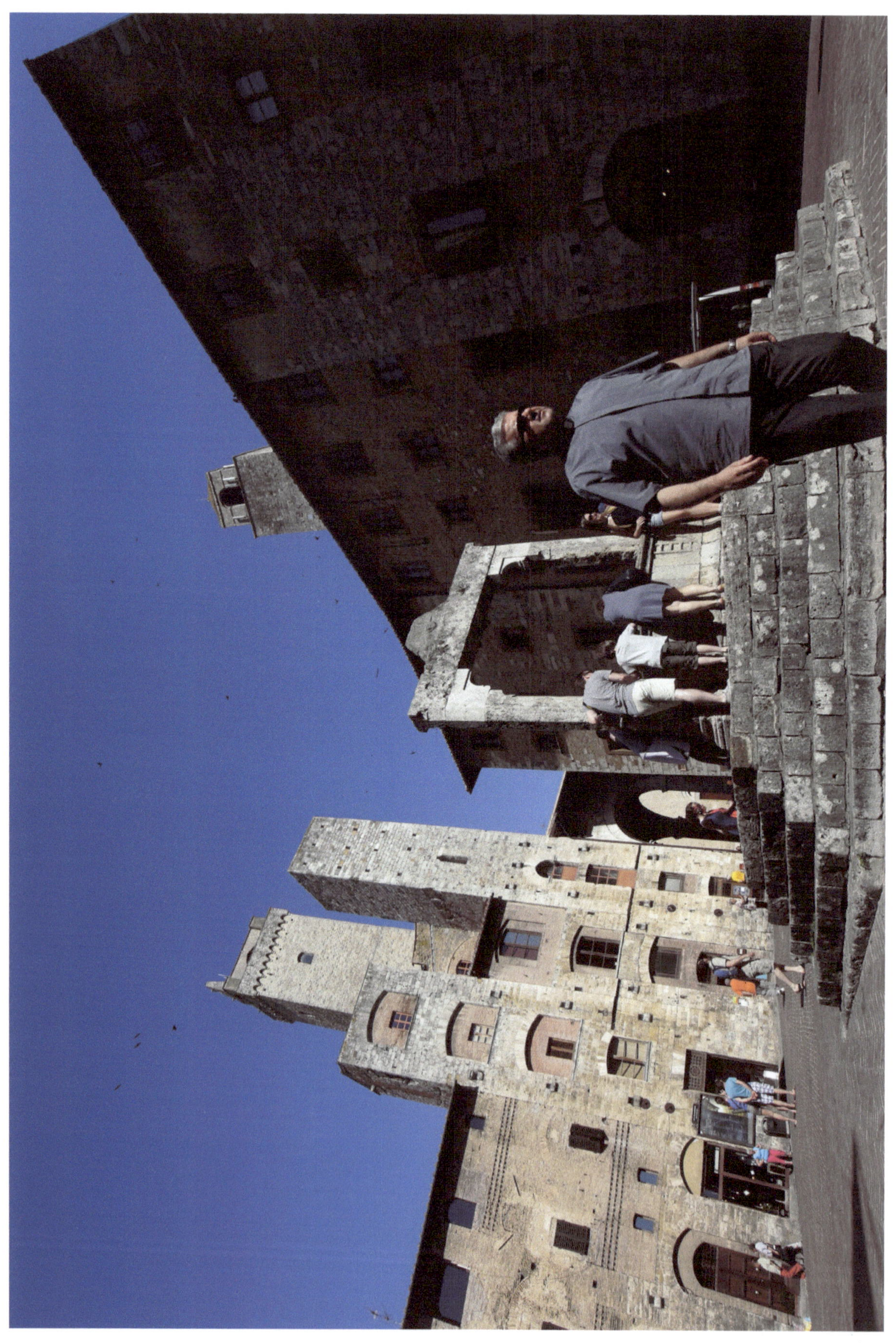

Low level view of the central Piazza in San Gimignano – liked the priest with his shades heading out of the shot.

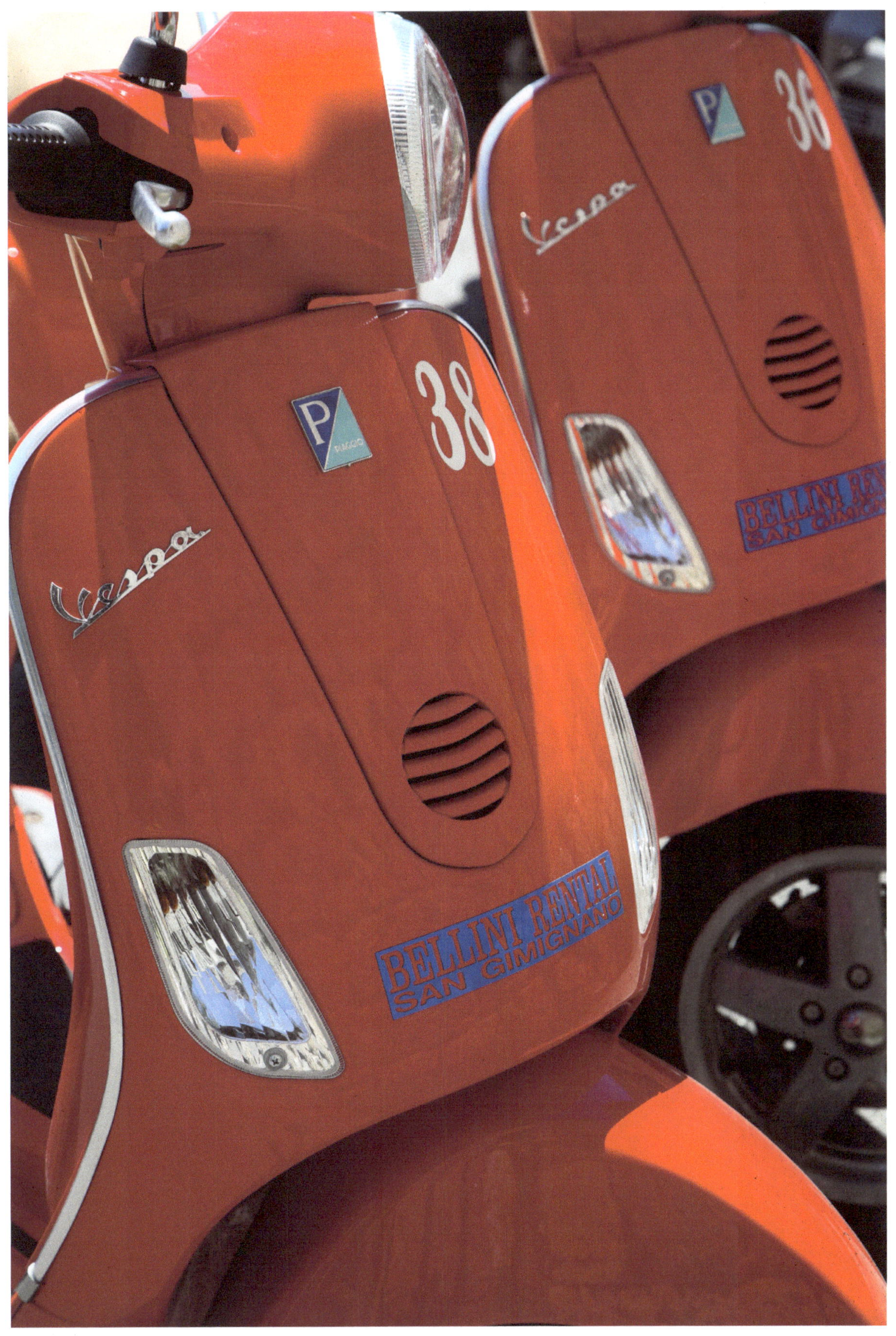

Colourful Vespas for hire just outside the city walls at San Gimignano.

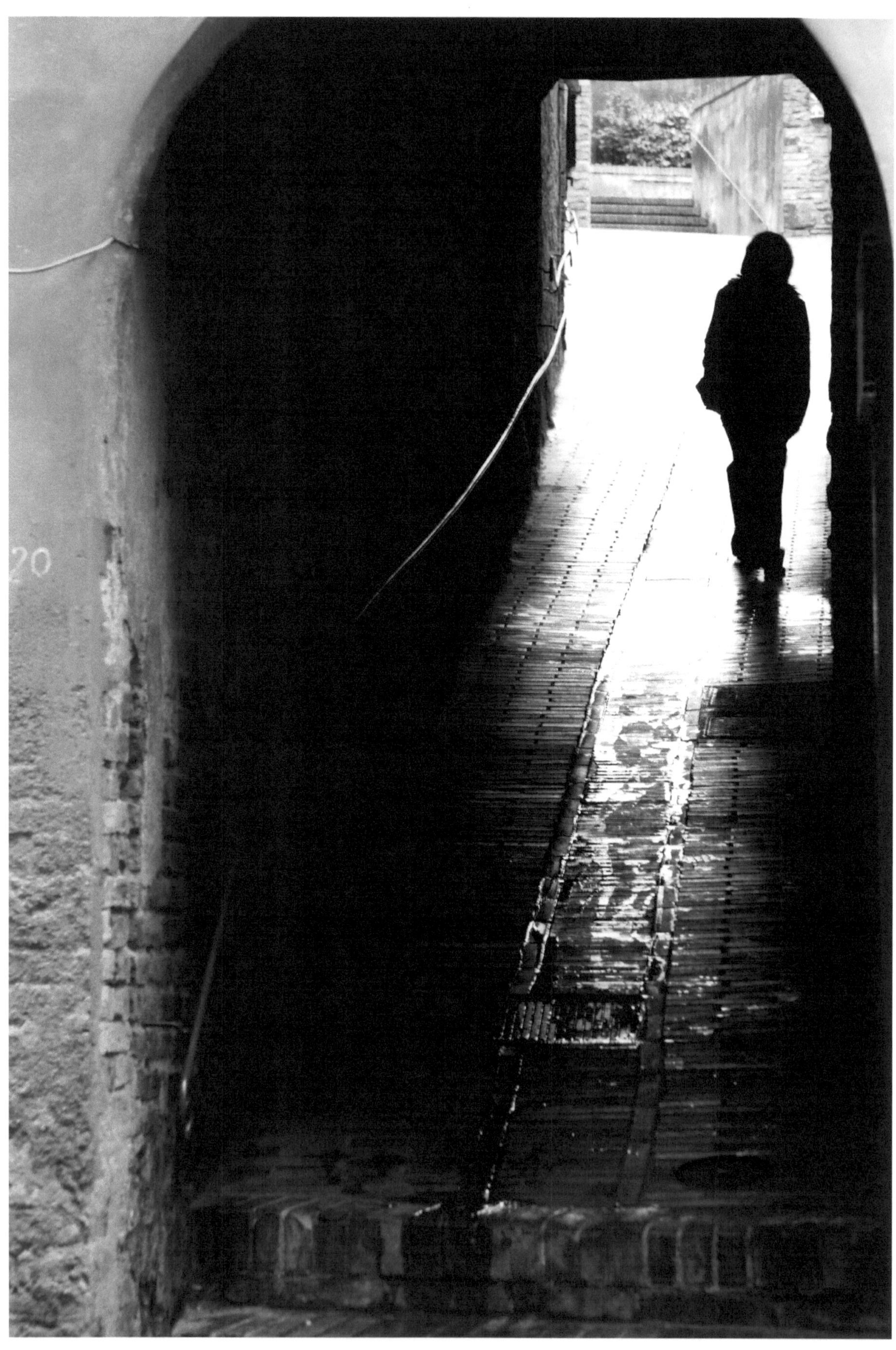

Black and white just works for this abstract shot up a passageway in San Gimignano.

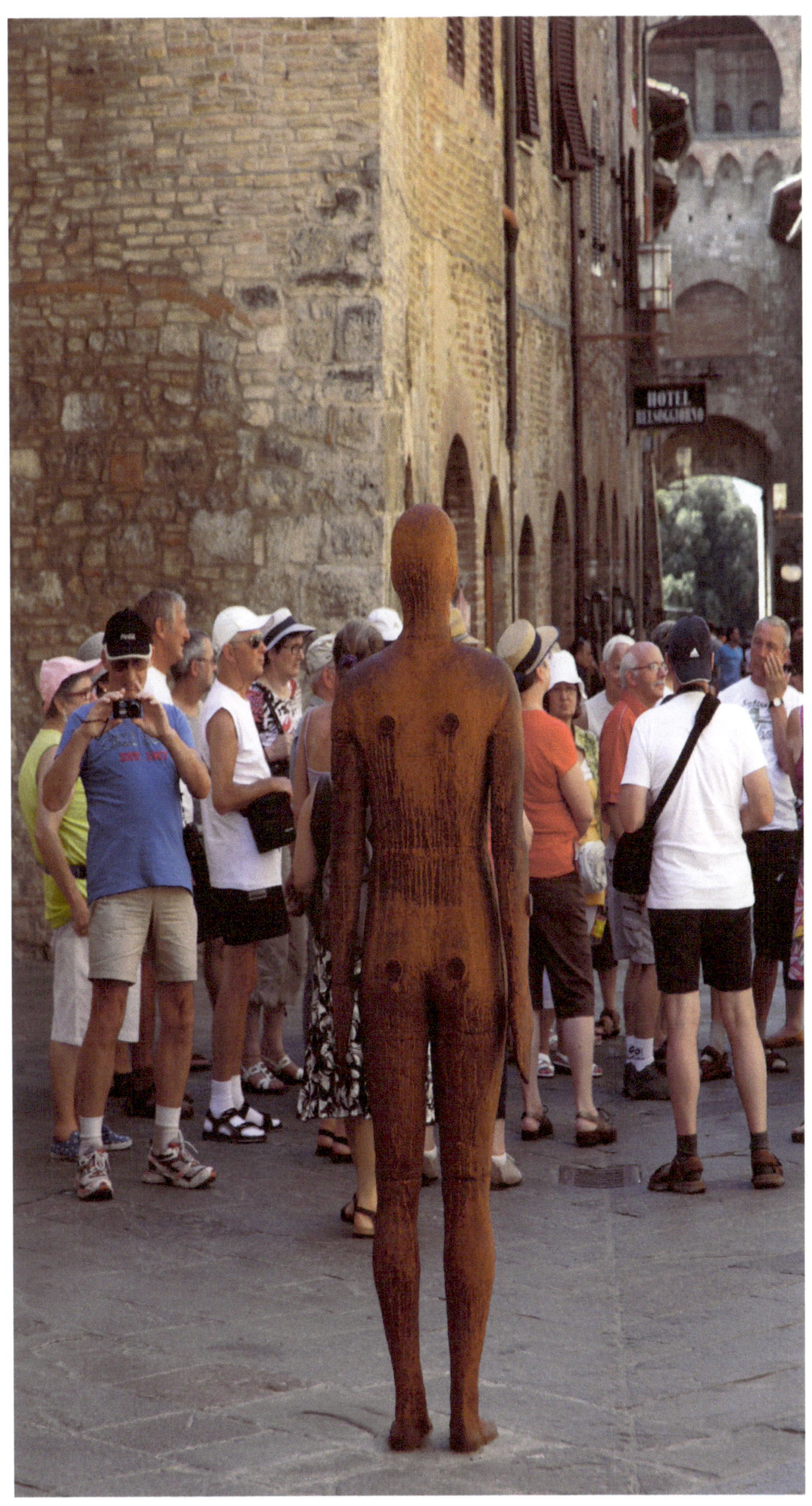

New tourist attraction in San Gimignano, summer 2012.

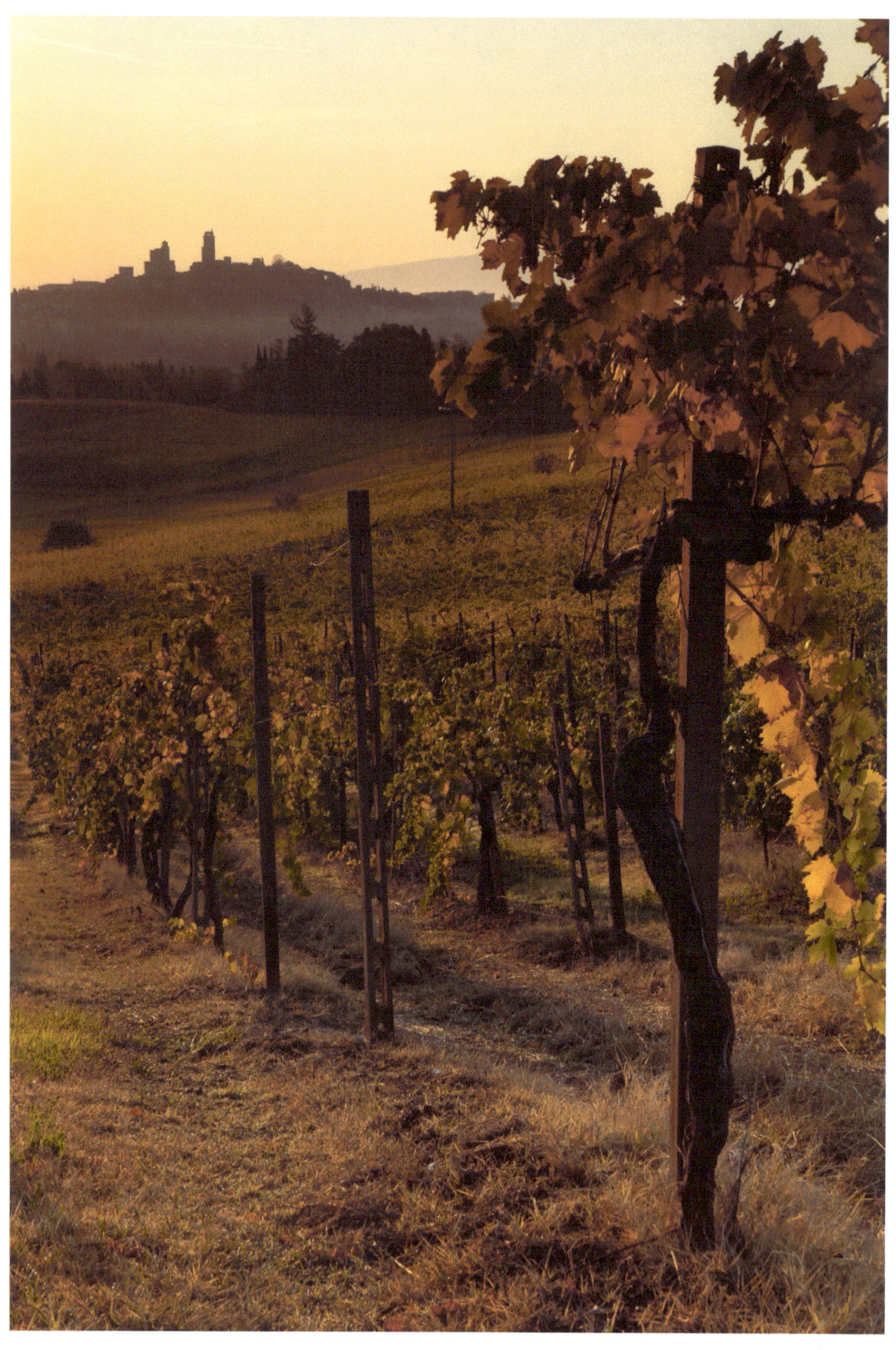

Soft, golden light in this early autumnal shot amongst the vines with the San Gimignano towers in the background.

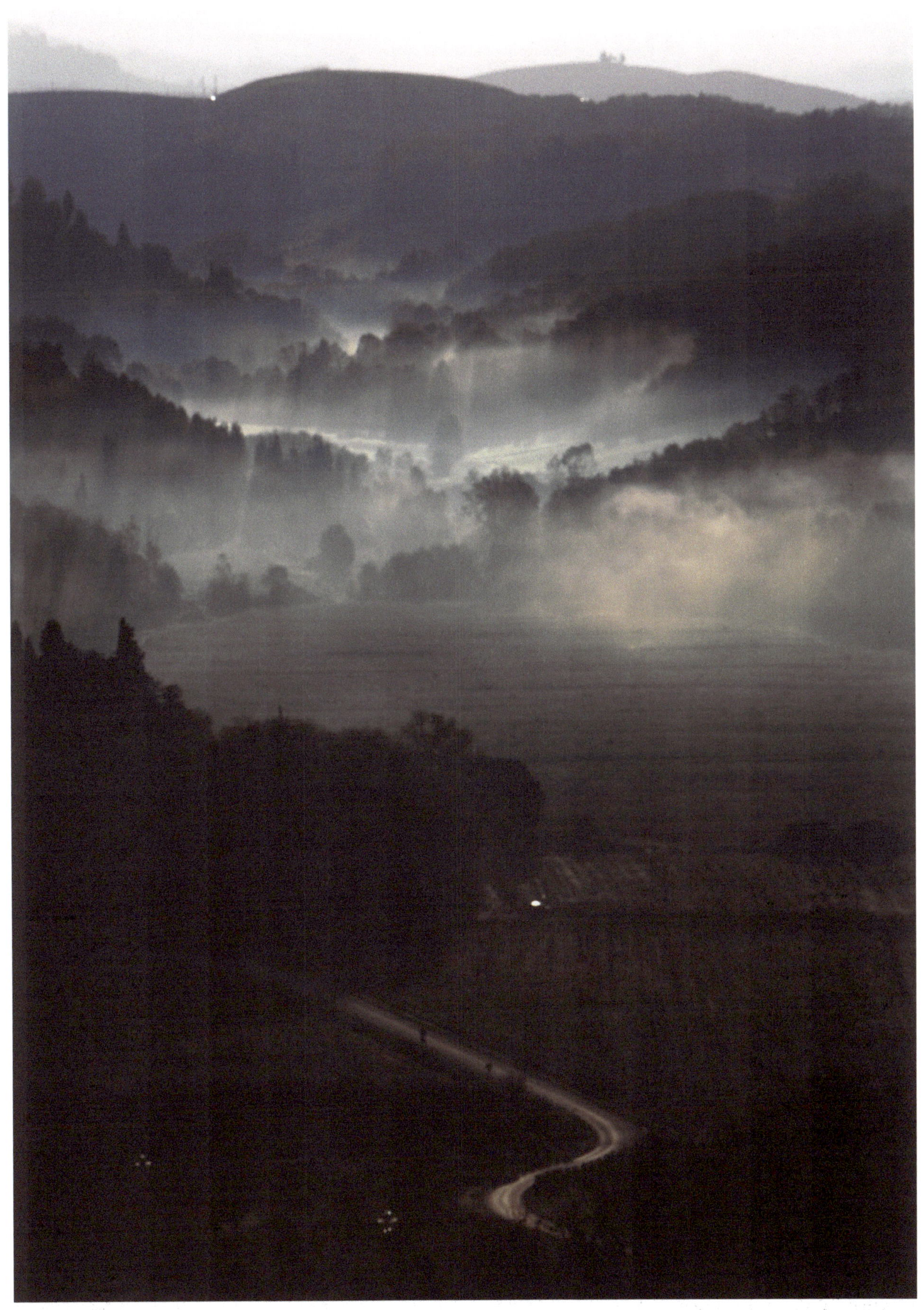

Autumnal sunrise view shot from the village of Montefoscoli.

Sunrise over San Miniato.

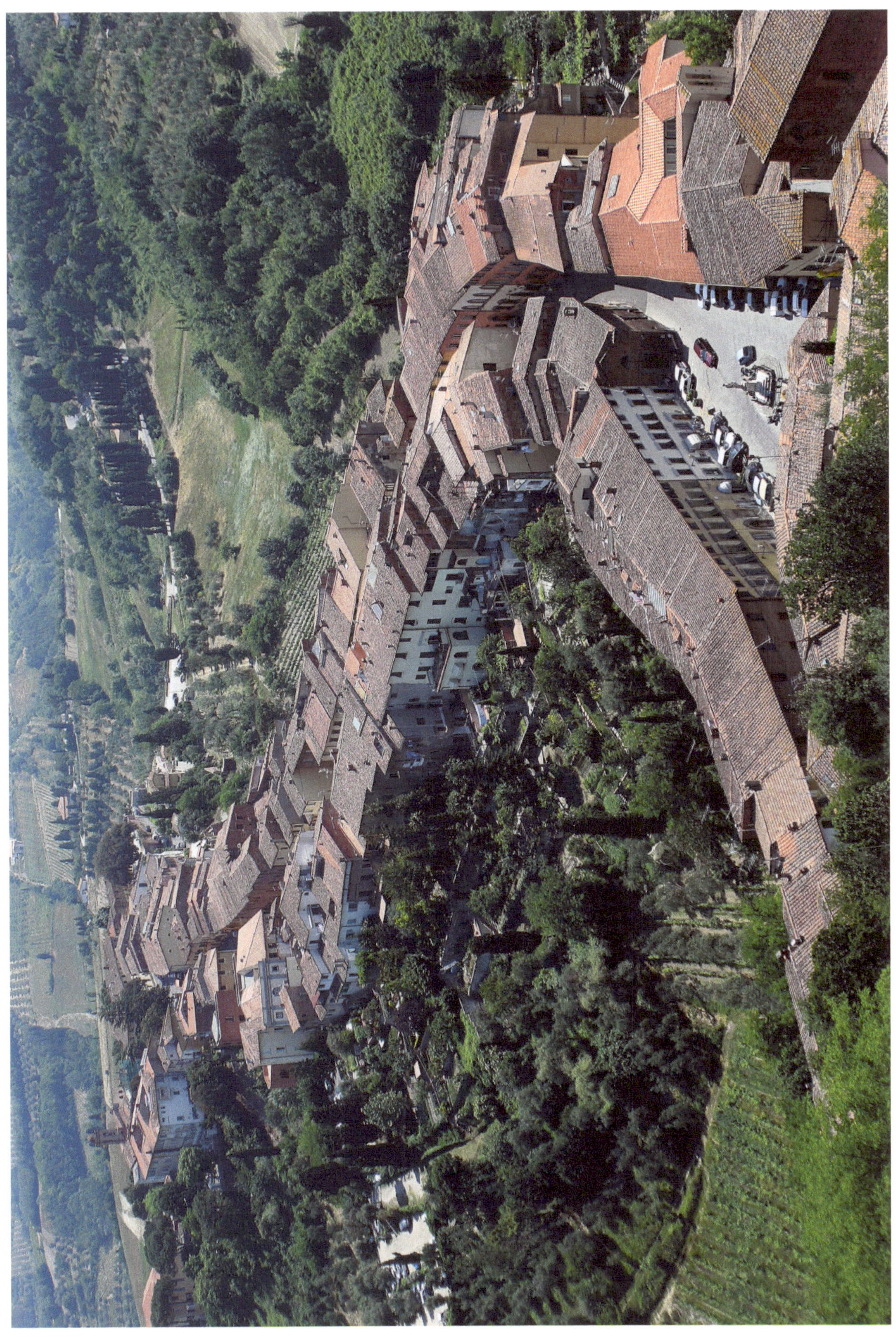

Looking down on San Miniato from the Frederico II tower.

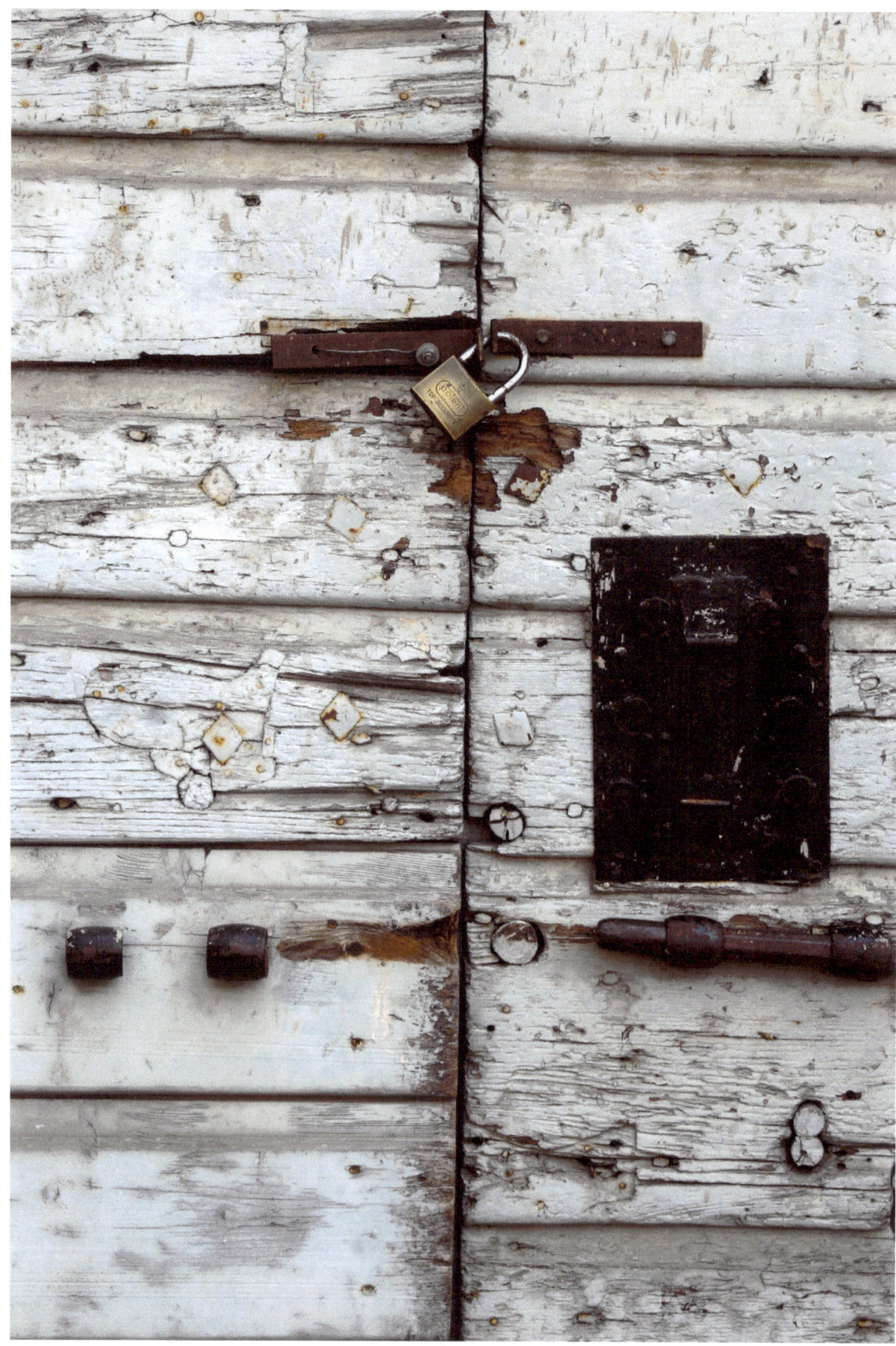

Liked the rustic look of these doors.

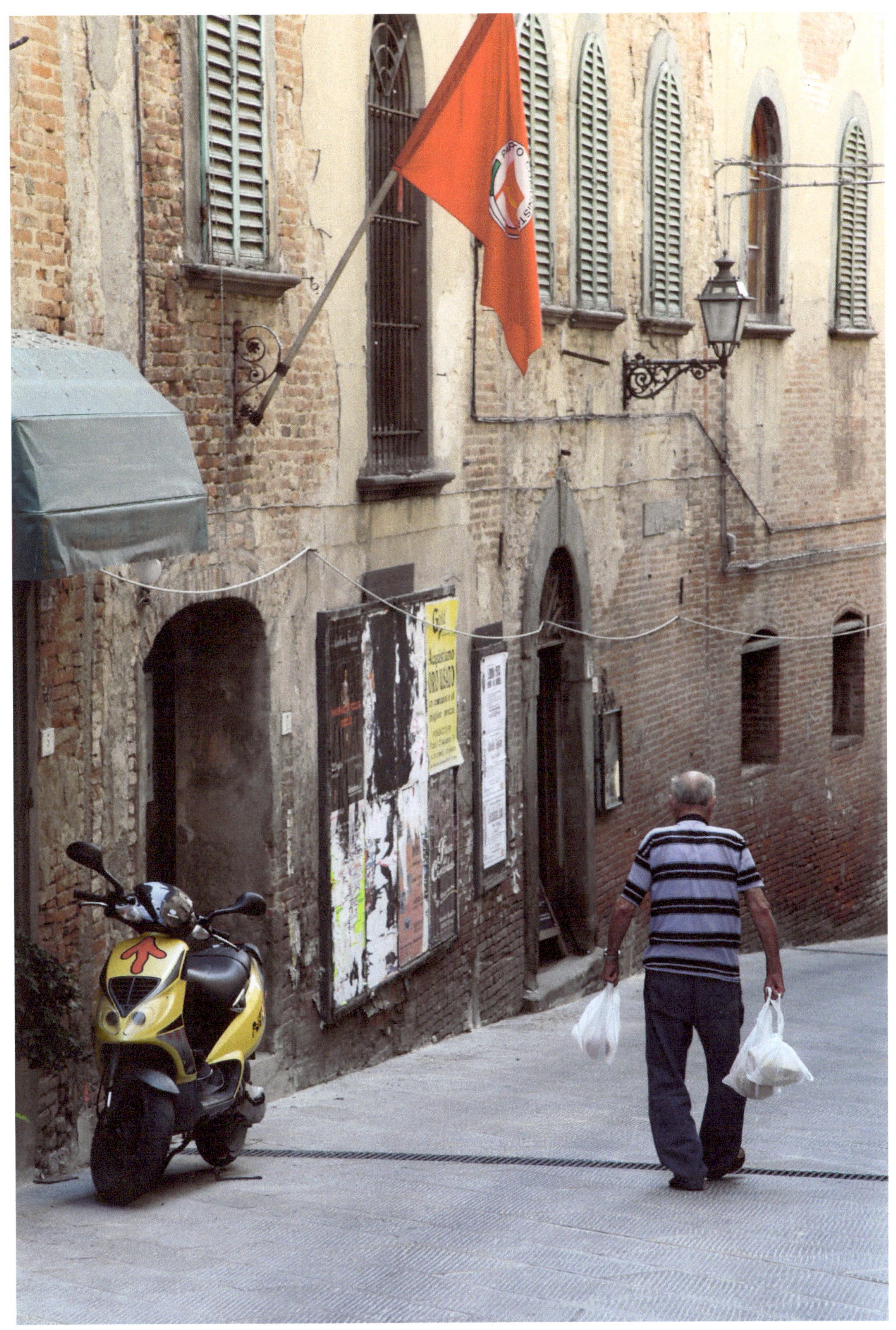

Leisurely stroll down a side street in Peccioli.

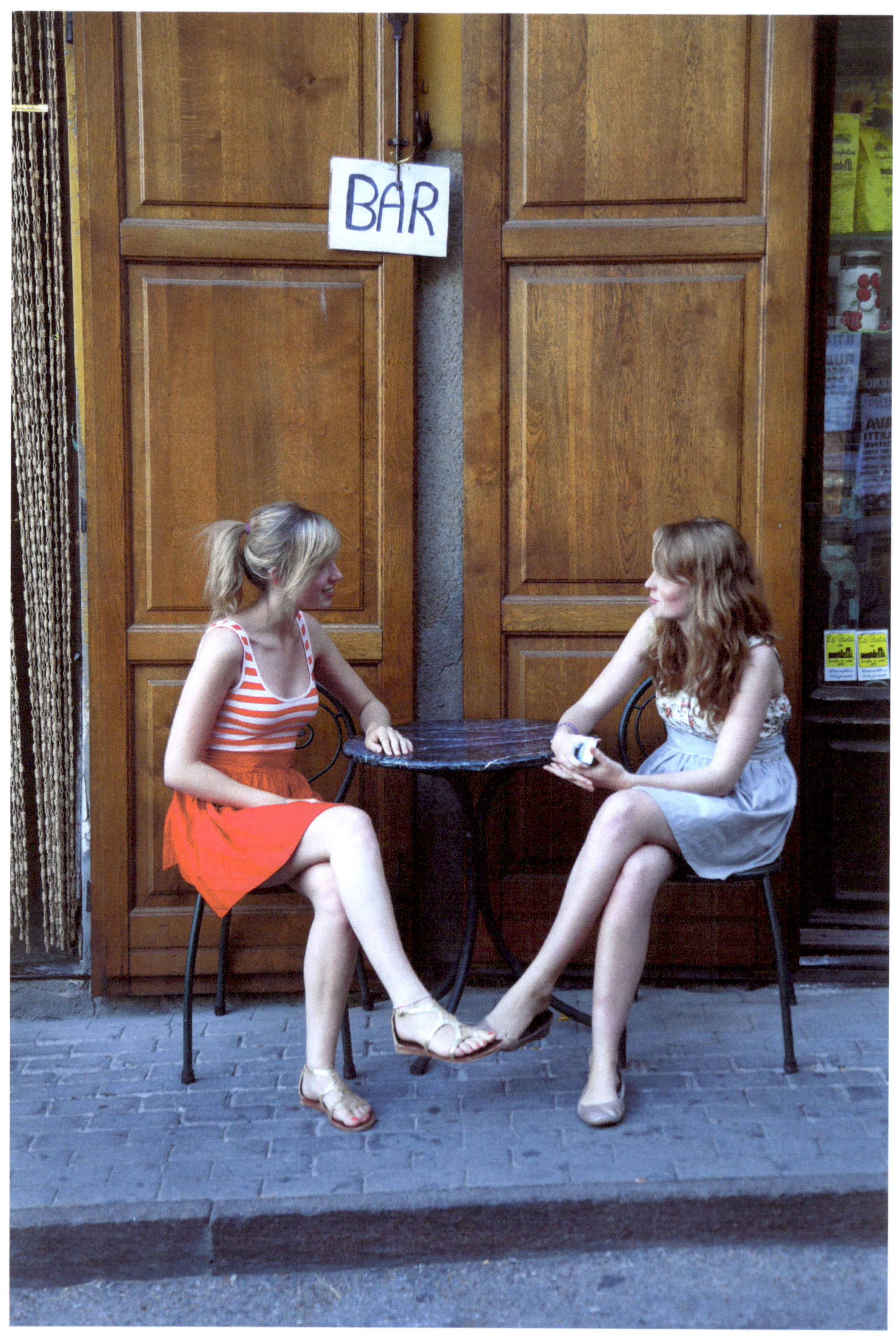

Social chat waiting for the coffee bar to open in Lari.

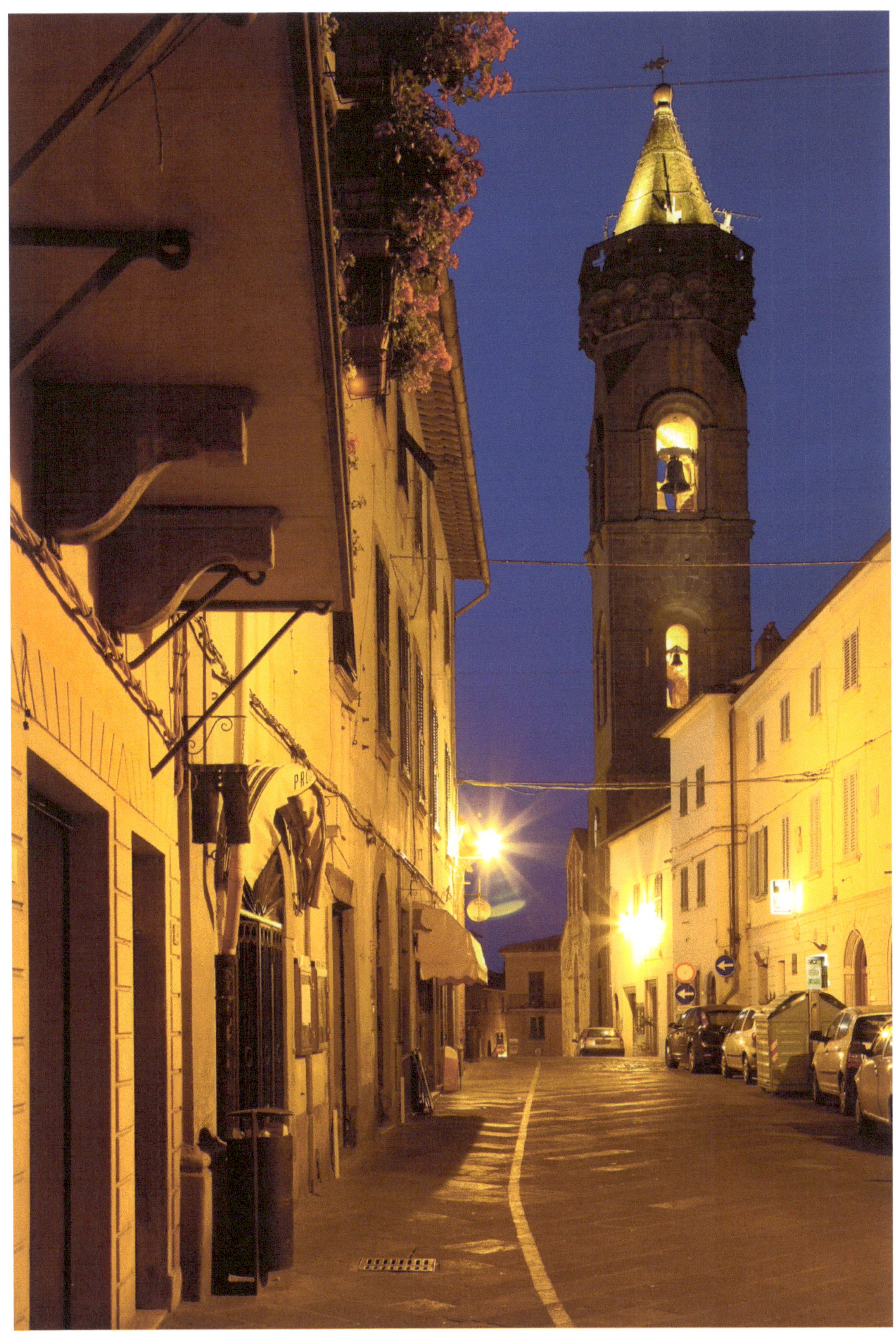

Pre-dawn street scene looking to the old bell-tower of Bellincioni in Peccioli.

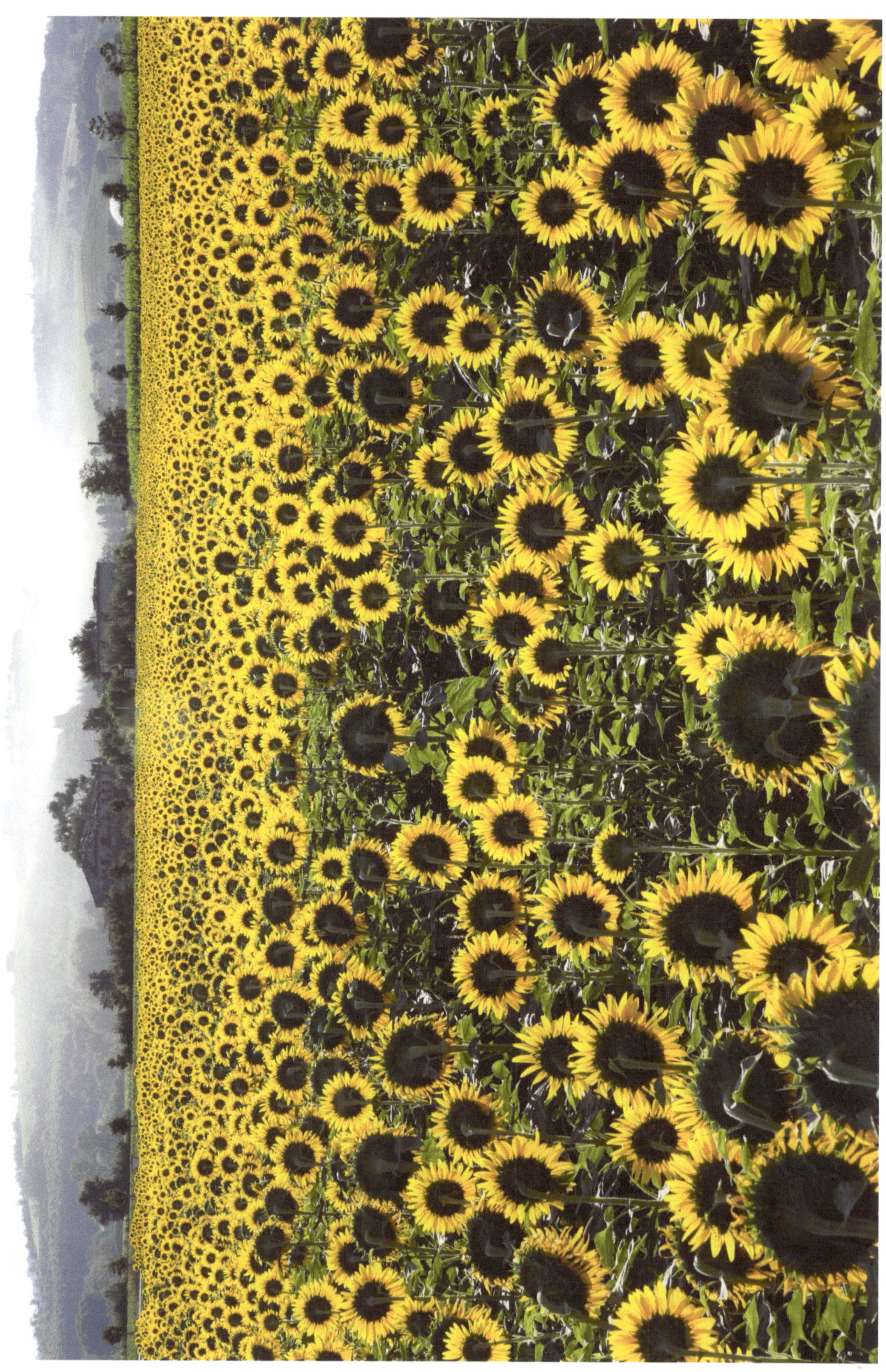

Early view over the sunflower fields near Peccioli.

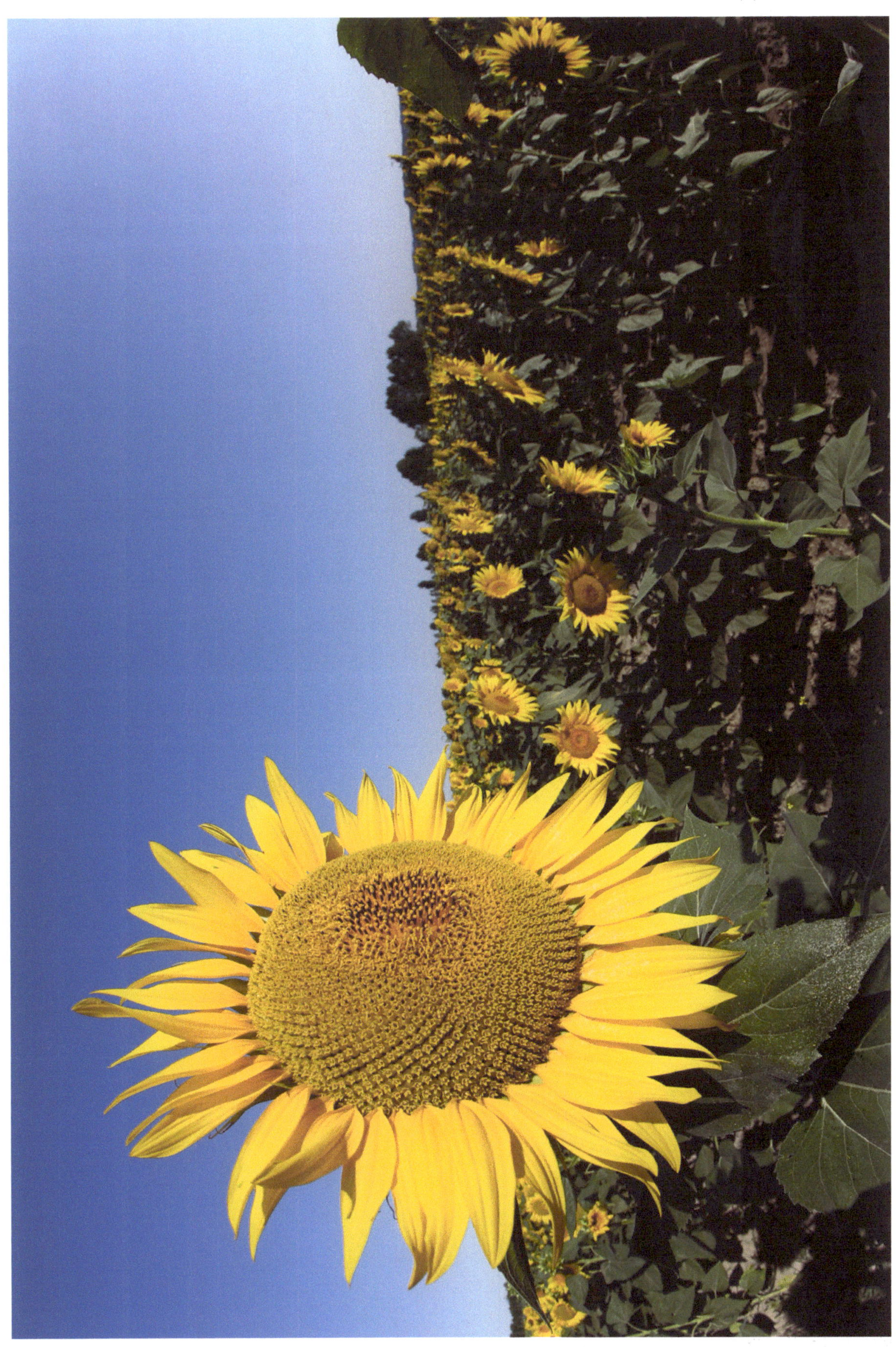

Like the contrast between bright yellow sunflower and the blue sky.

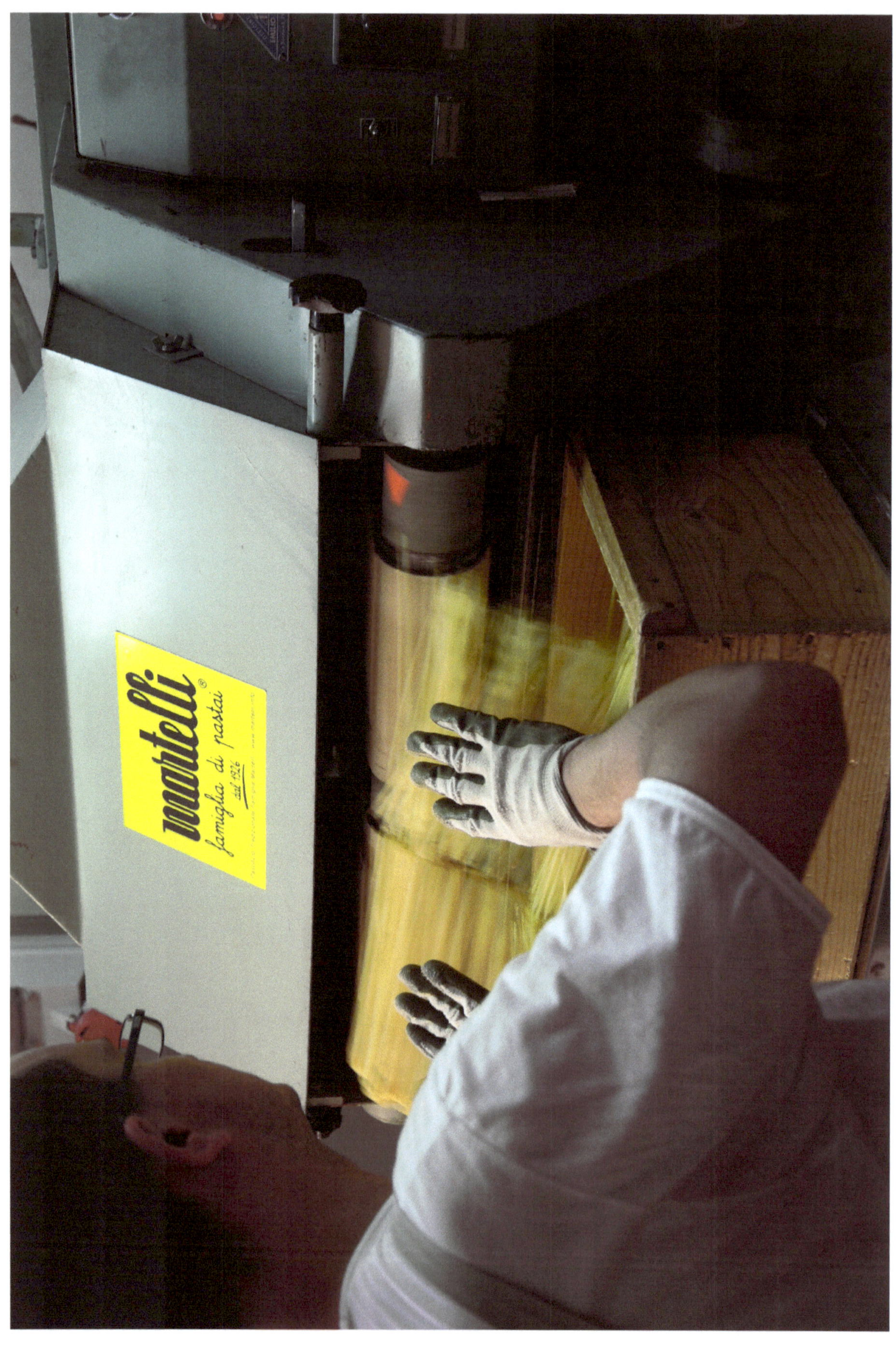

Inside the Martelli pasta factory in Lari.

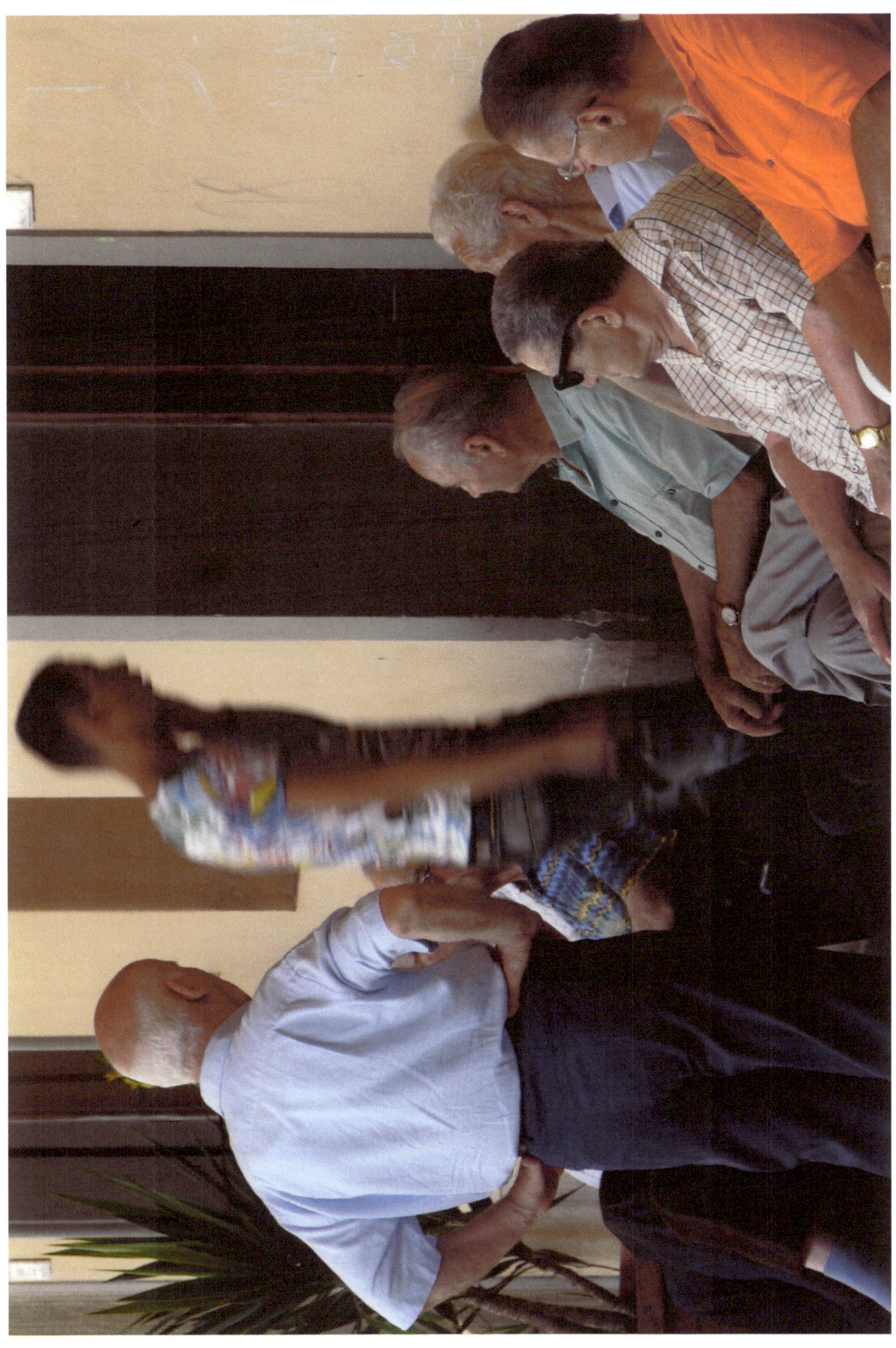

A unwelcome posture to the young arrival in this locals bar in Peccioli.

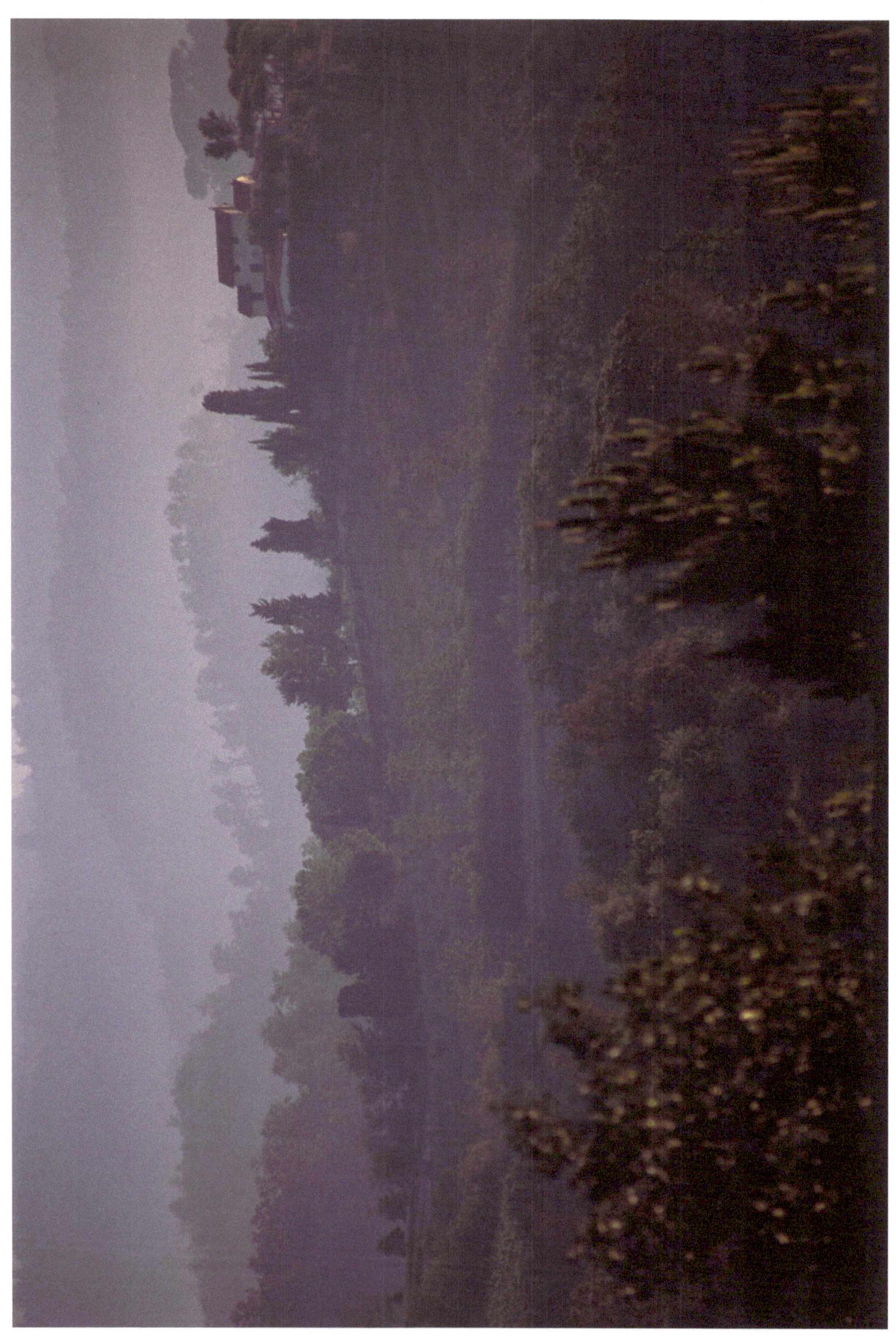

Early morning scenic view from just outside Palaia.

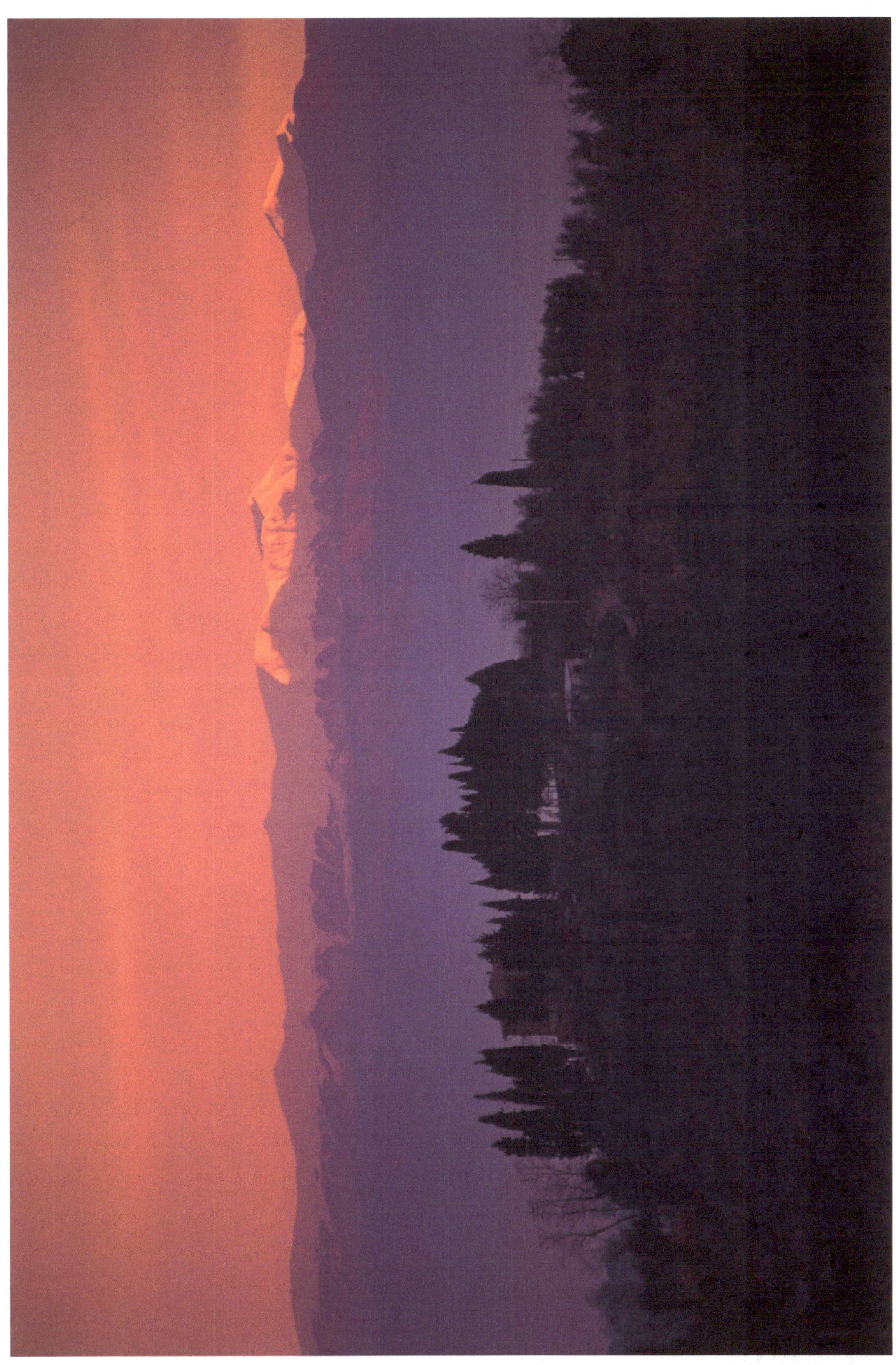

Using the rule of thirds on this view from the roadside between Colleoli and Palaia.

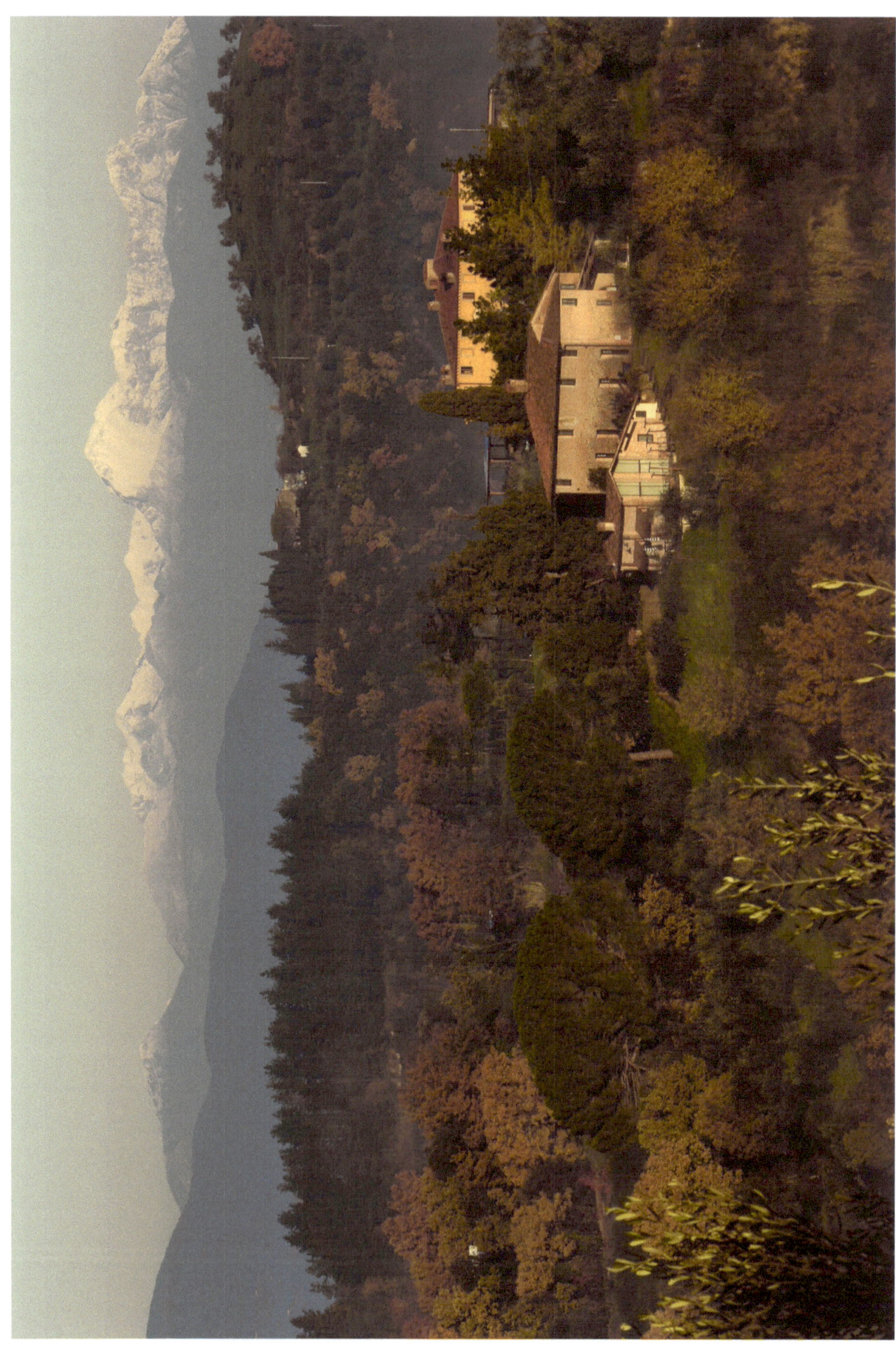

Soft colours in this early morning autumnal country view from Colleoli.

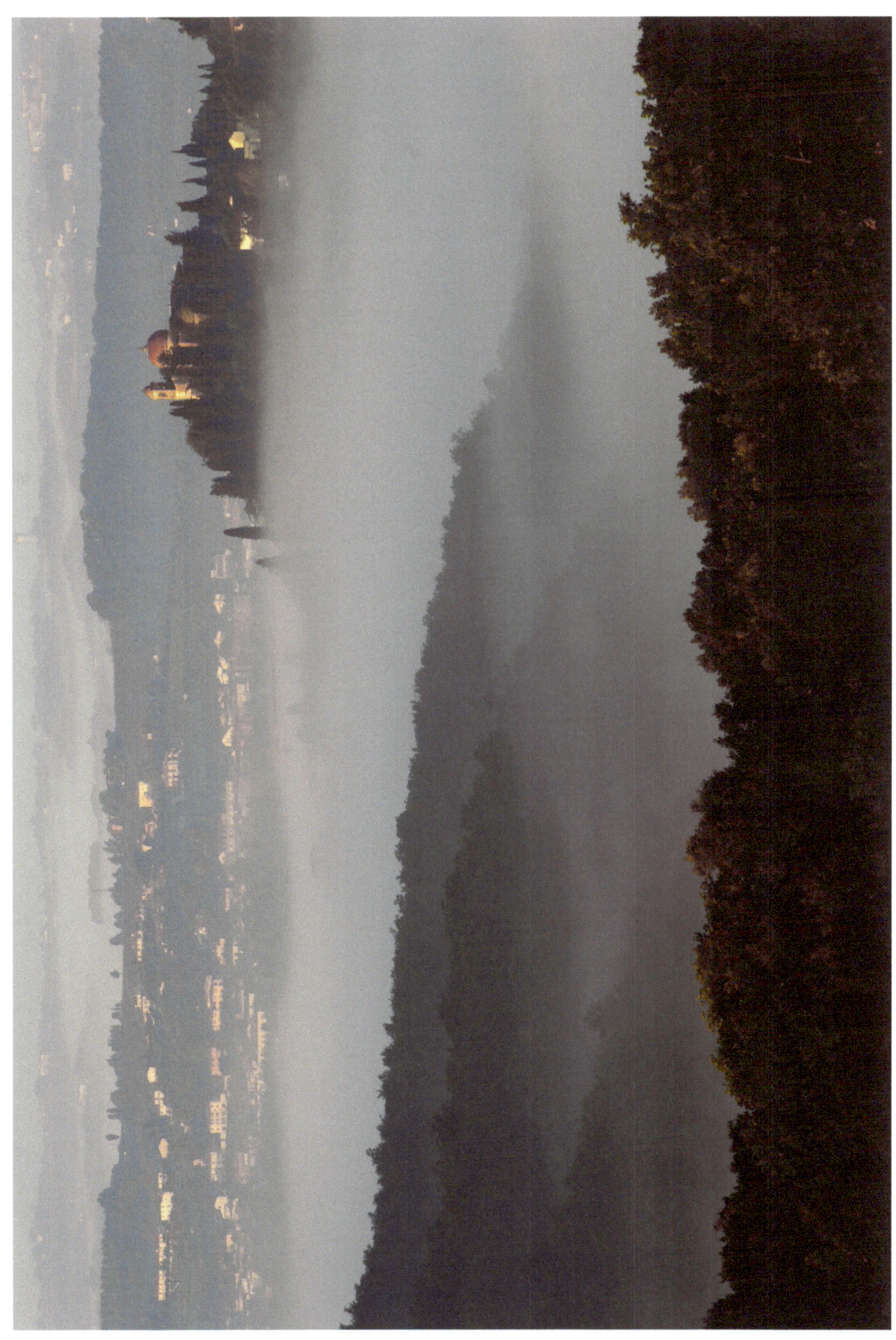

Mist-covered valleys from the road between Colleoli and San Gervasio.

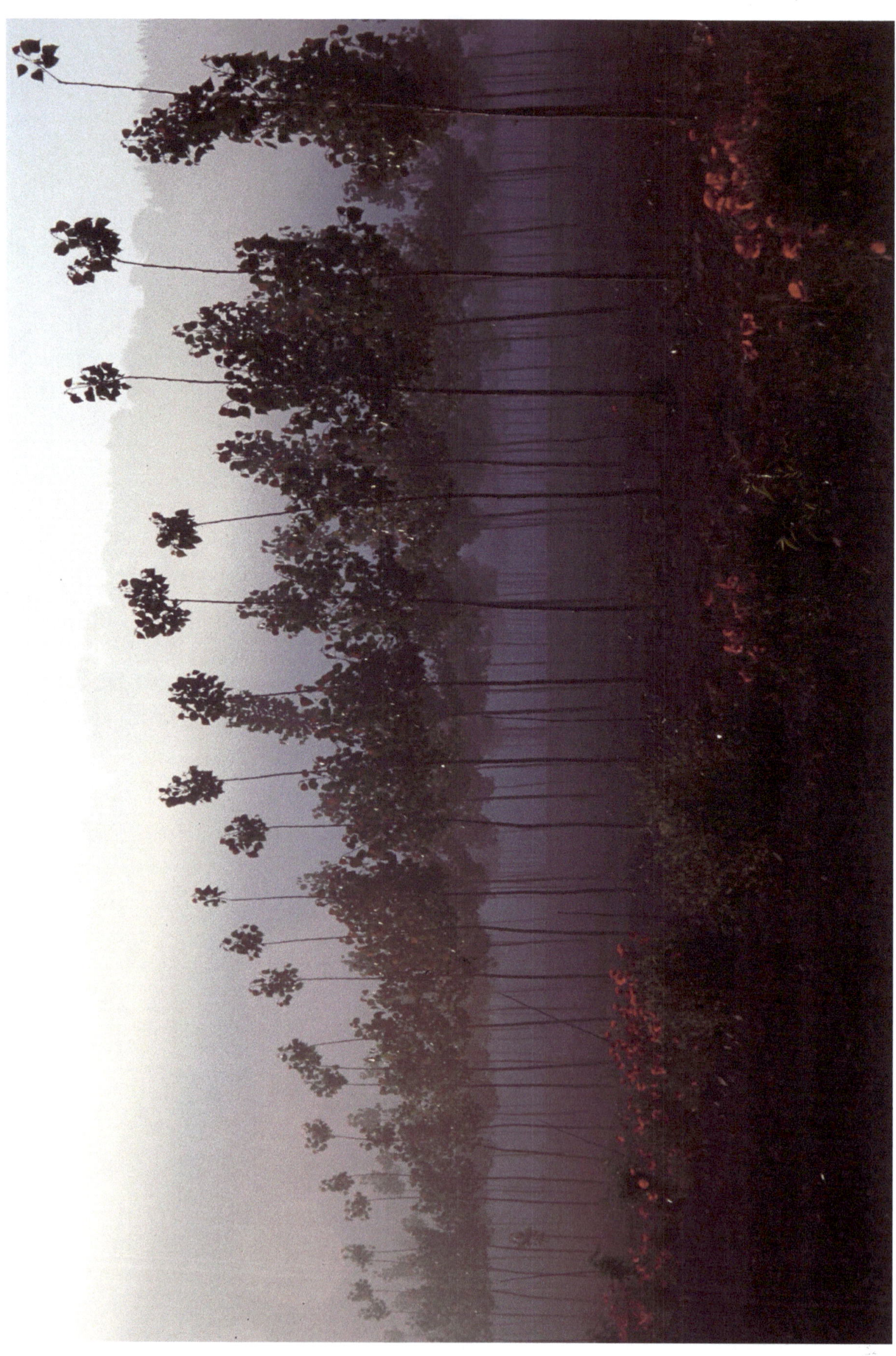

Early mist and the red poppies make this shot at Chiecinella.

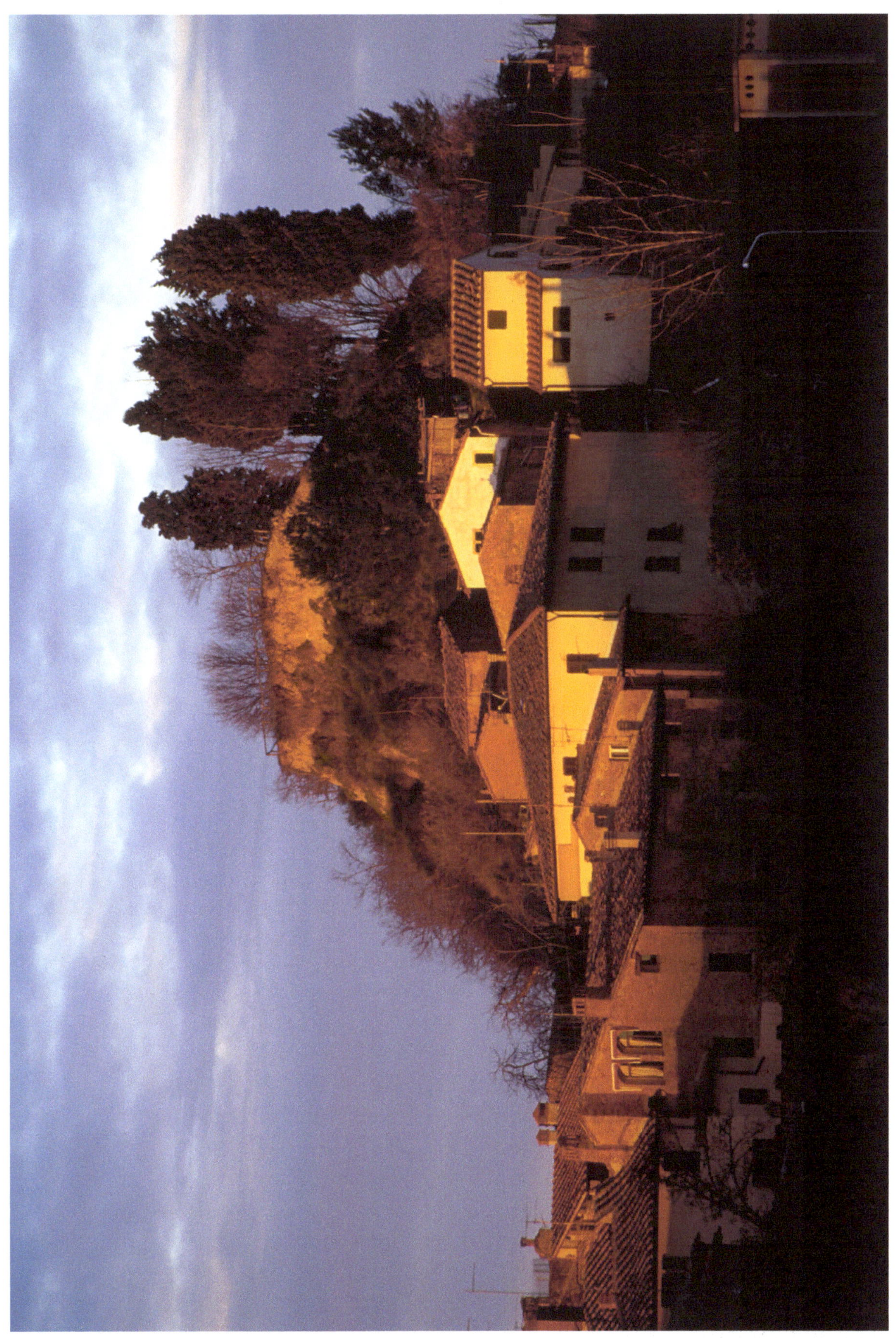

Bright early morning colours of Palaia.

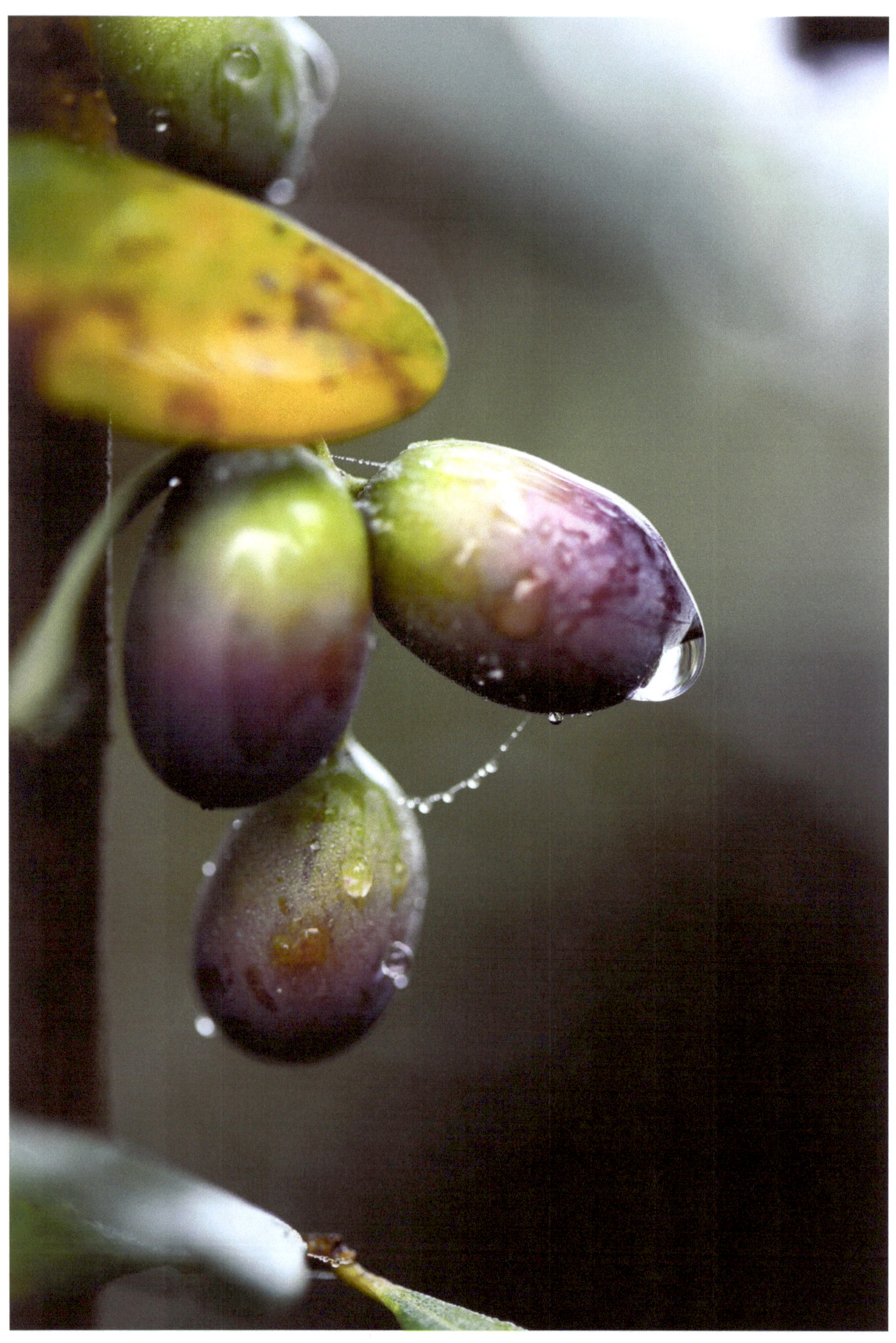

Macro lens shot of one of many olive trees near Montefoscoli.

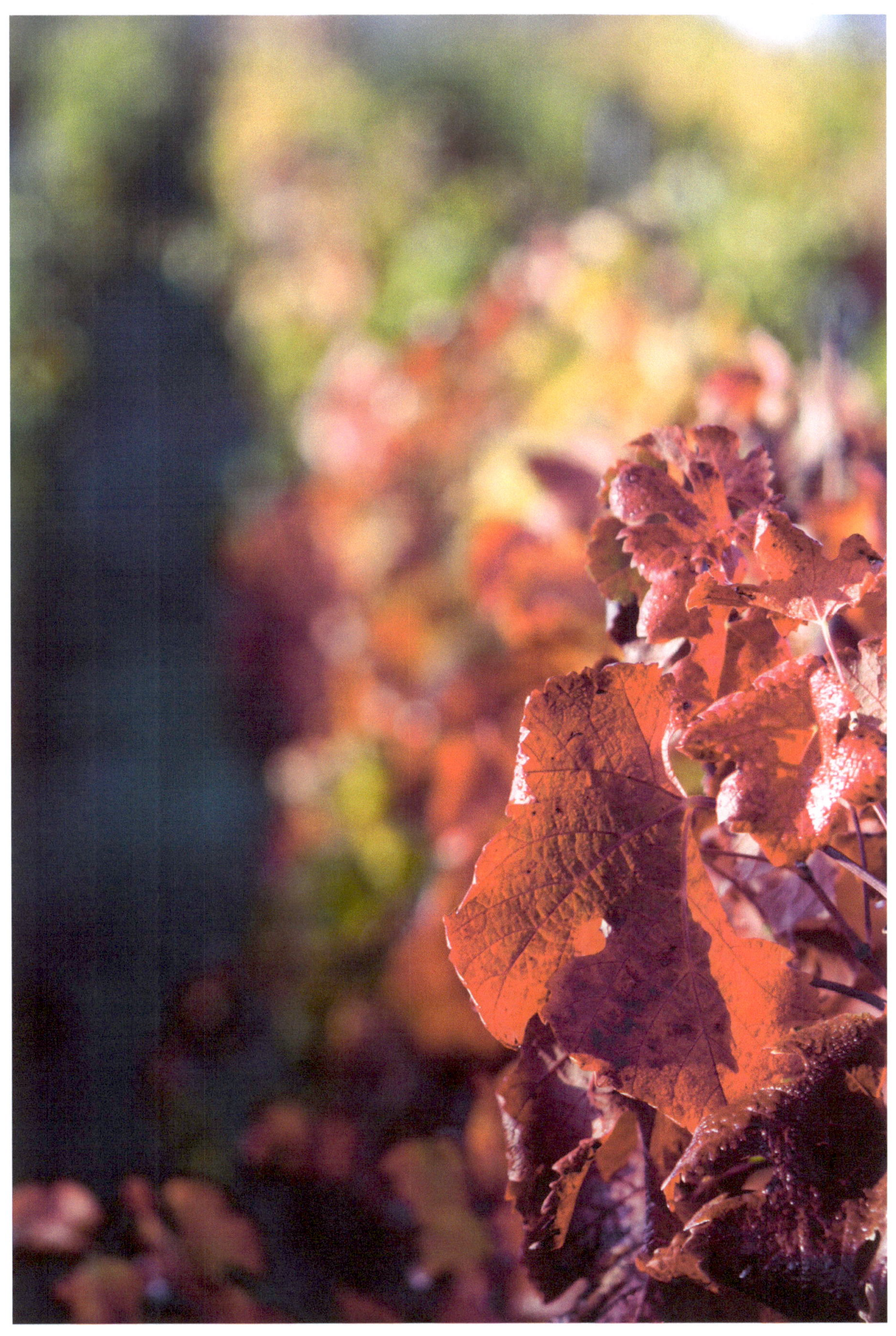

Shallow depth of field and autumnal colours in this vineyard in Colleoli.

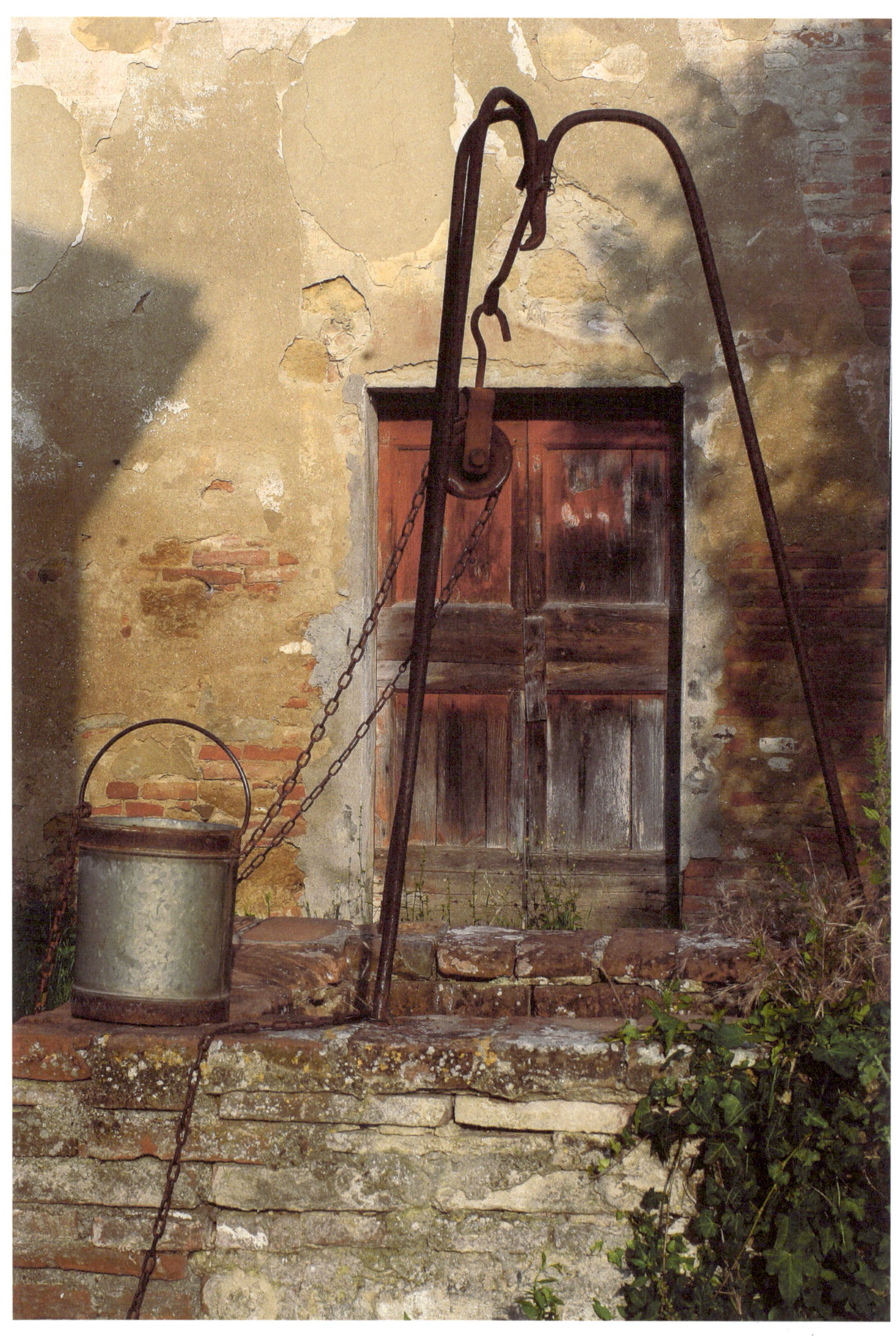

Came across this rustic scene walking down a pathway in Colleoli.

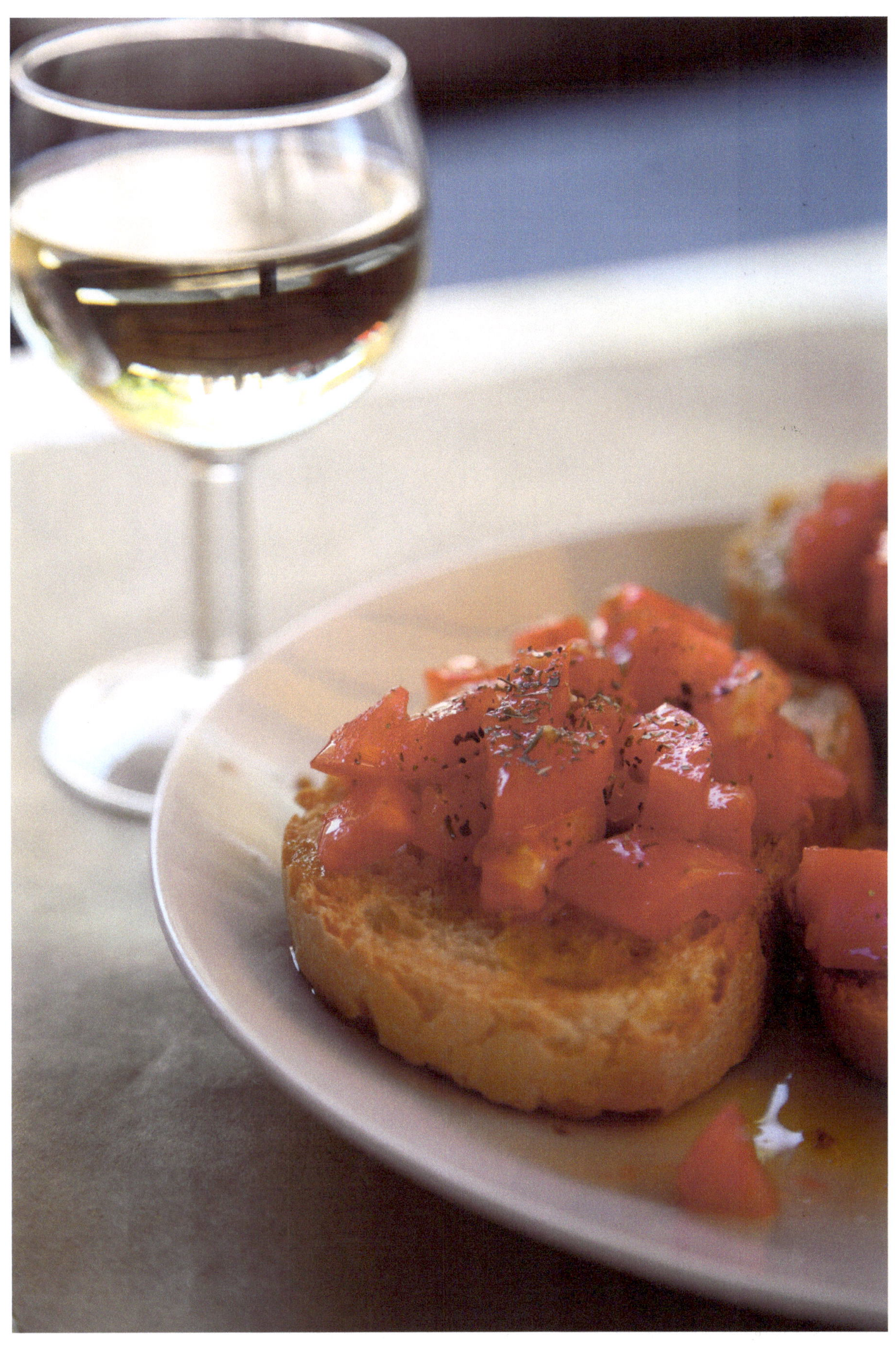

Very tasty bruscetta and a glass of vino blanco at the Peggio Palaia Pub.

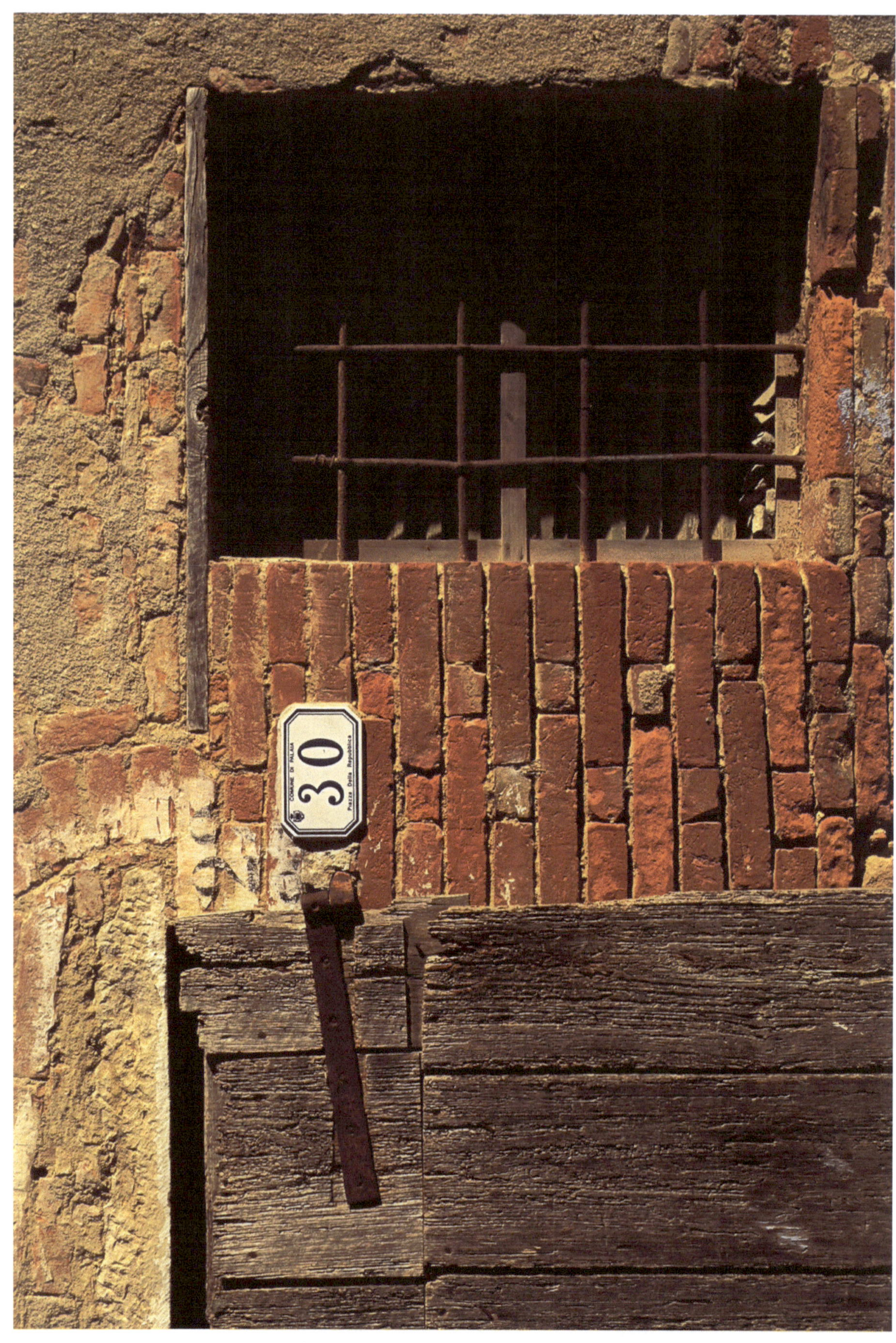

Quaintly dilapidated frontage down a side street in Palaia.

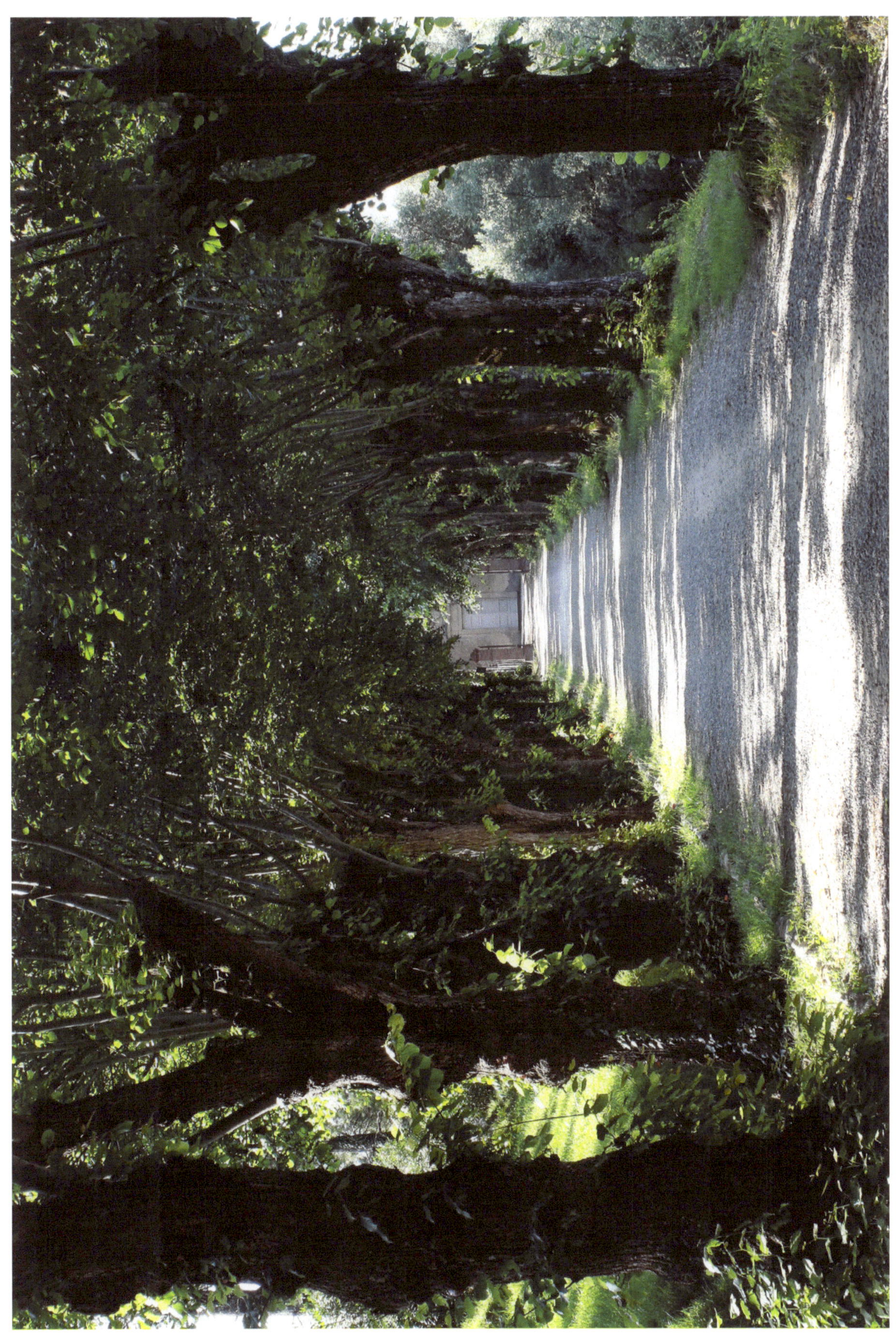

Picturesque avenue of trees at the Borgo di Colleoli.

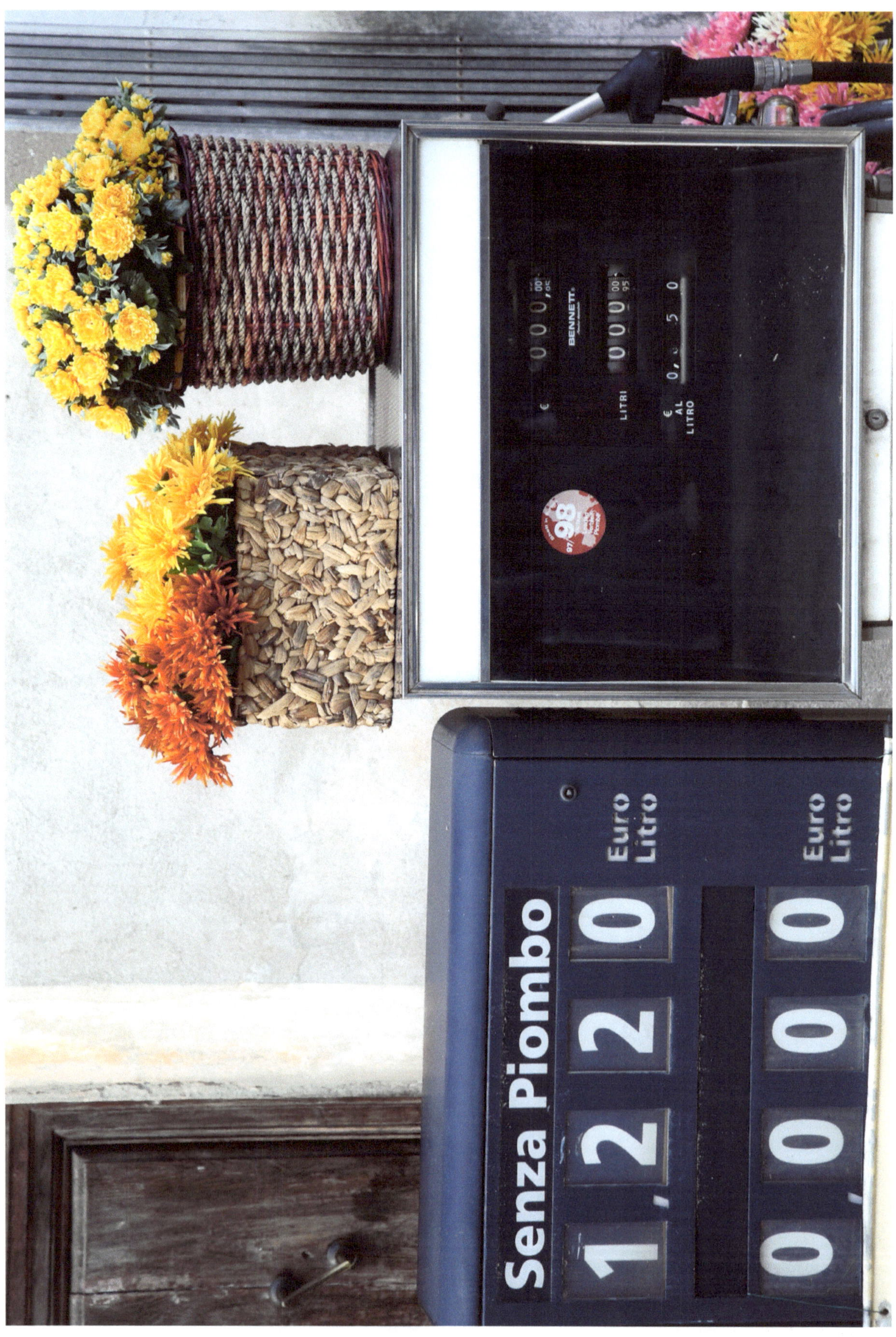

Improving the look at this ‘downtown’ petrol station in Palaia.

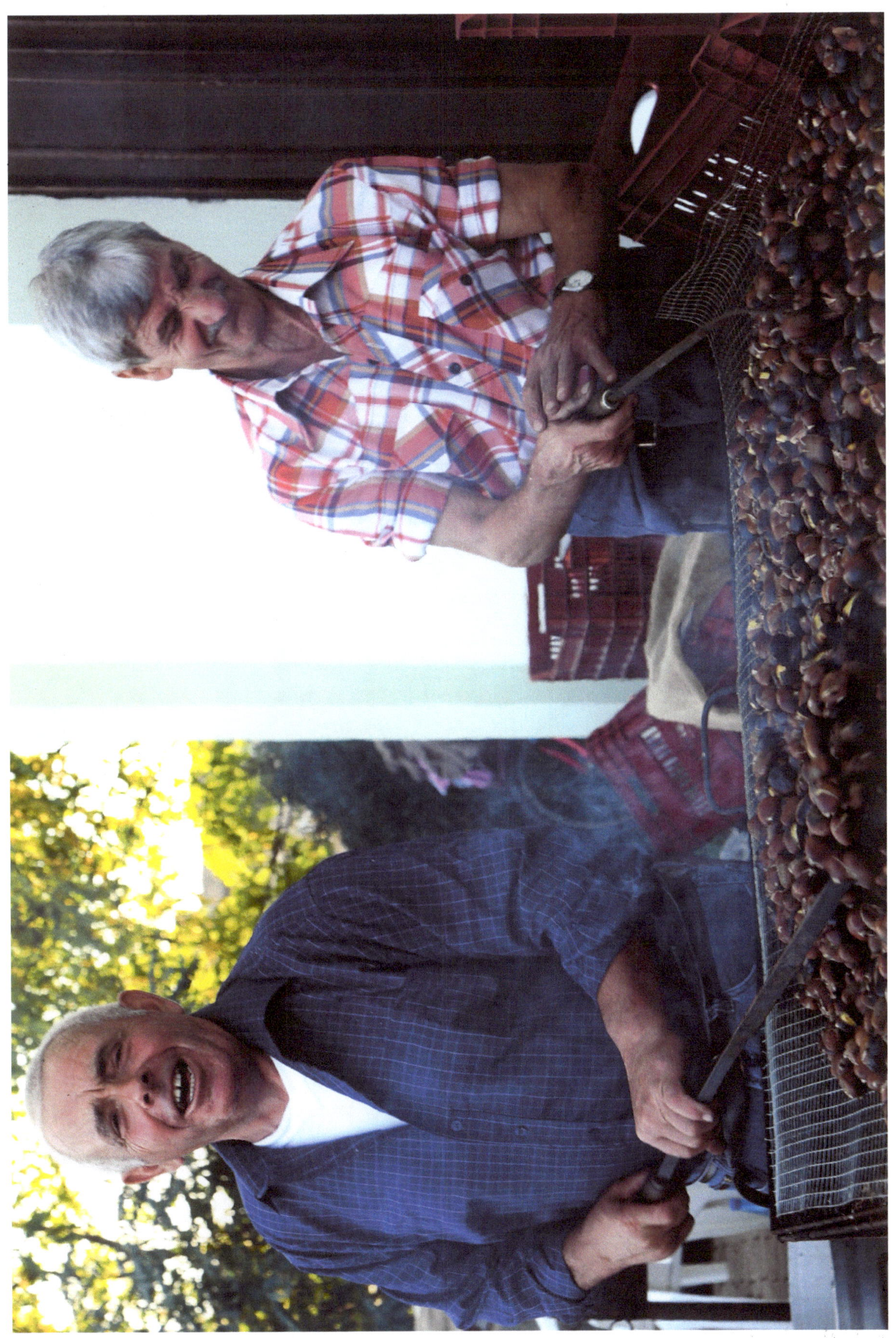

Lively couple of chefs at the annual chestnut and truffle festival in Palaia.

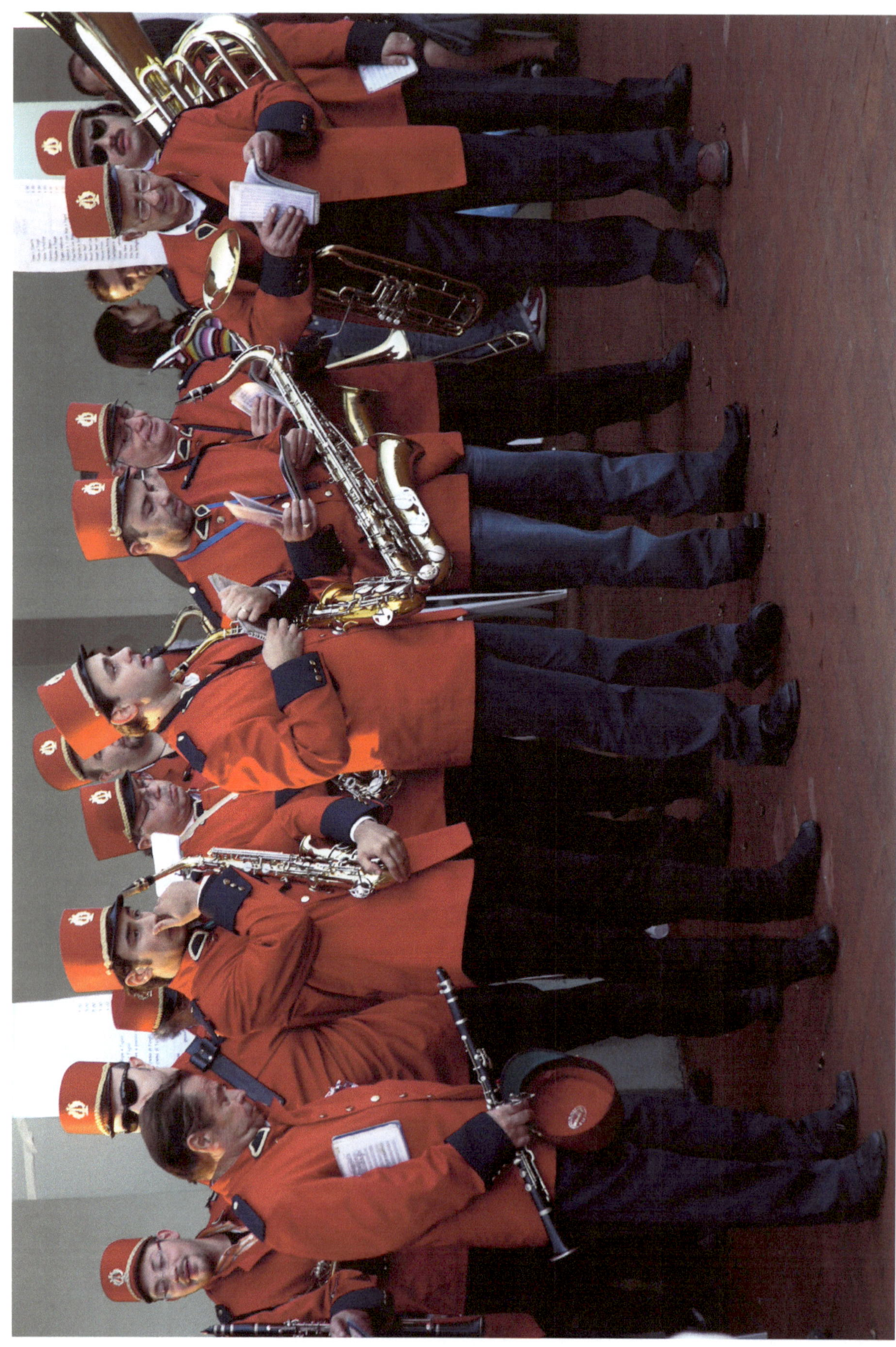

The band take a breather at the chestnut & truffle festival in Palaia.

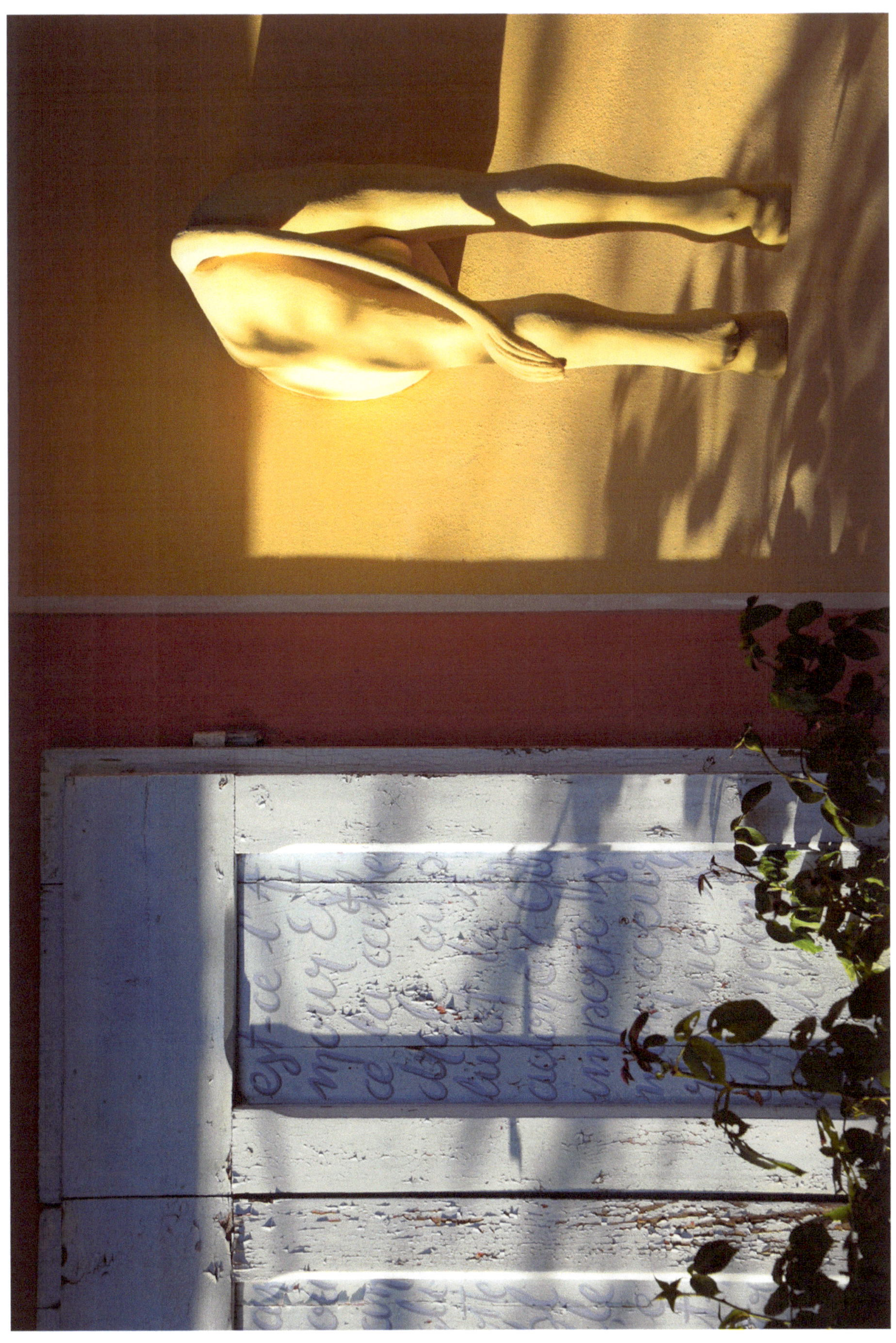

Abstract artwork outside the Fattoria Santa Lucia near Pontedera.

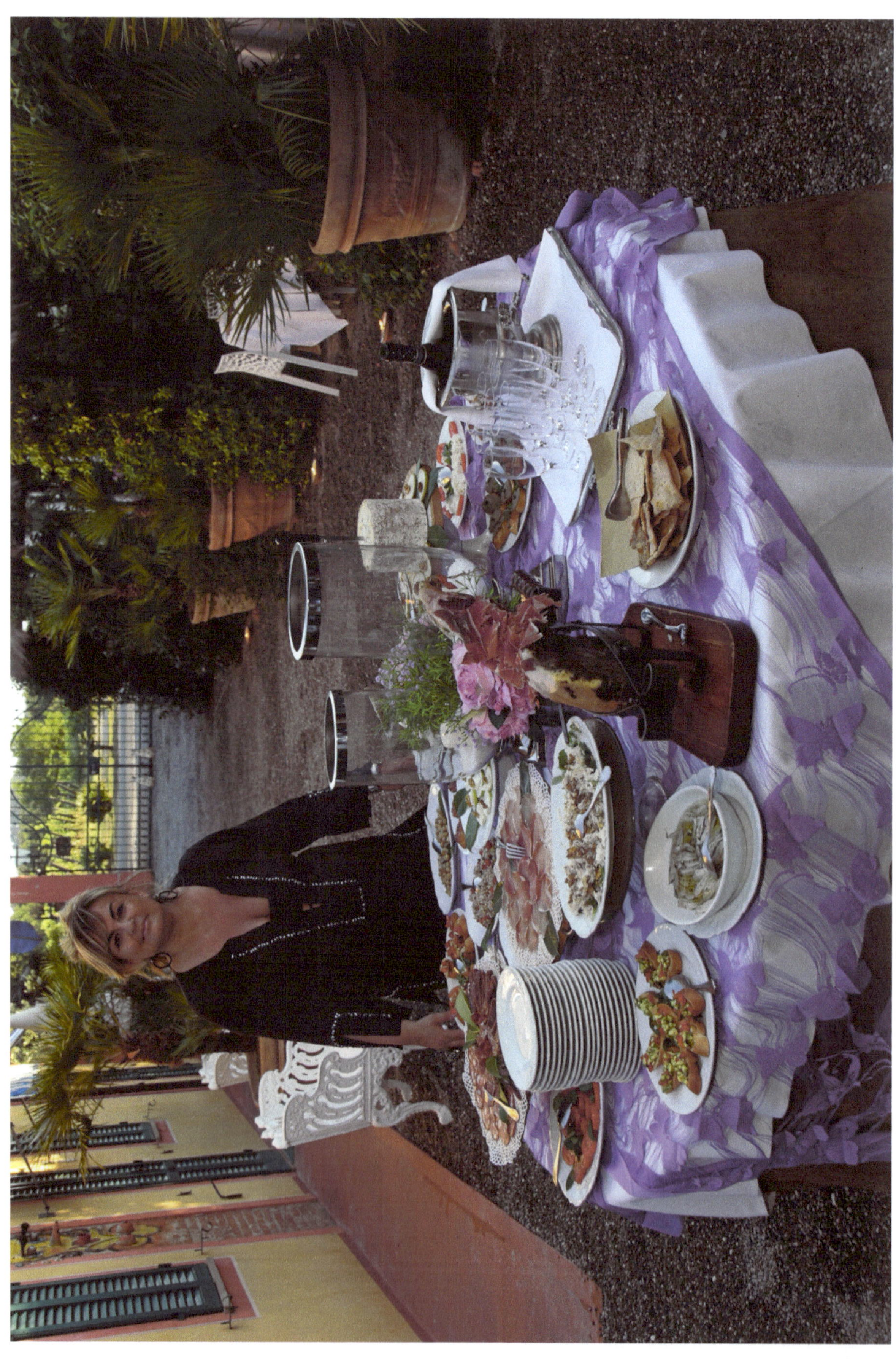

Extrovert owner of the Fattoria Santa Lucia and the way she reels of the varied menu is worth a visit itself, never mind the fabulous food!

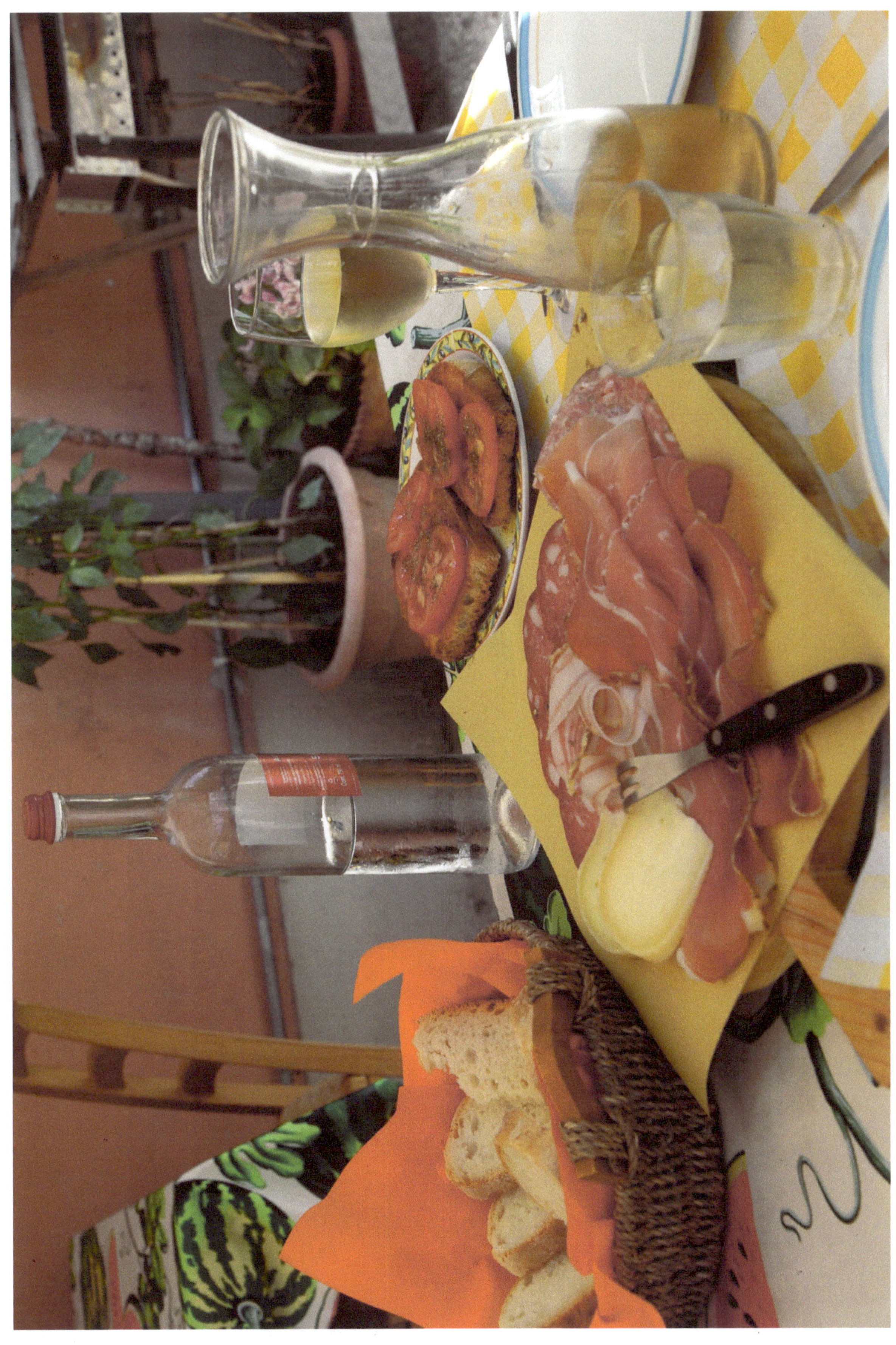

Roadside lunch stop between Palaia and San Miniato – well worth it.

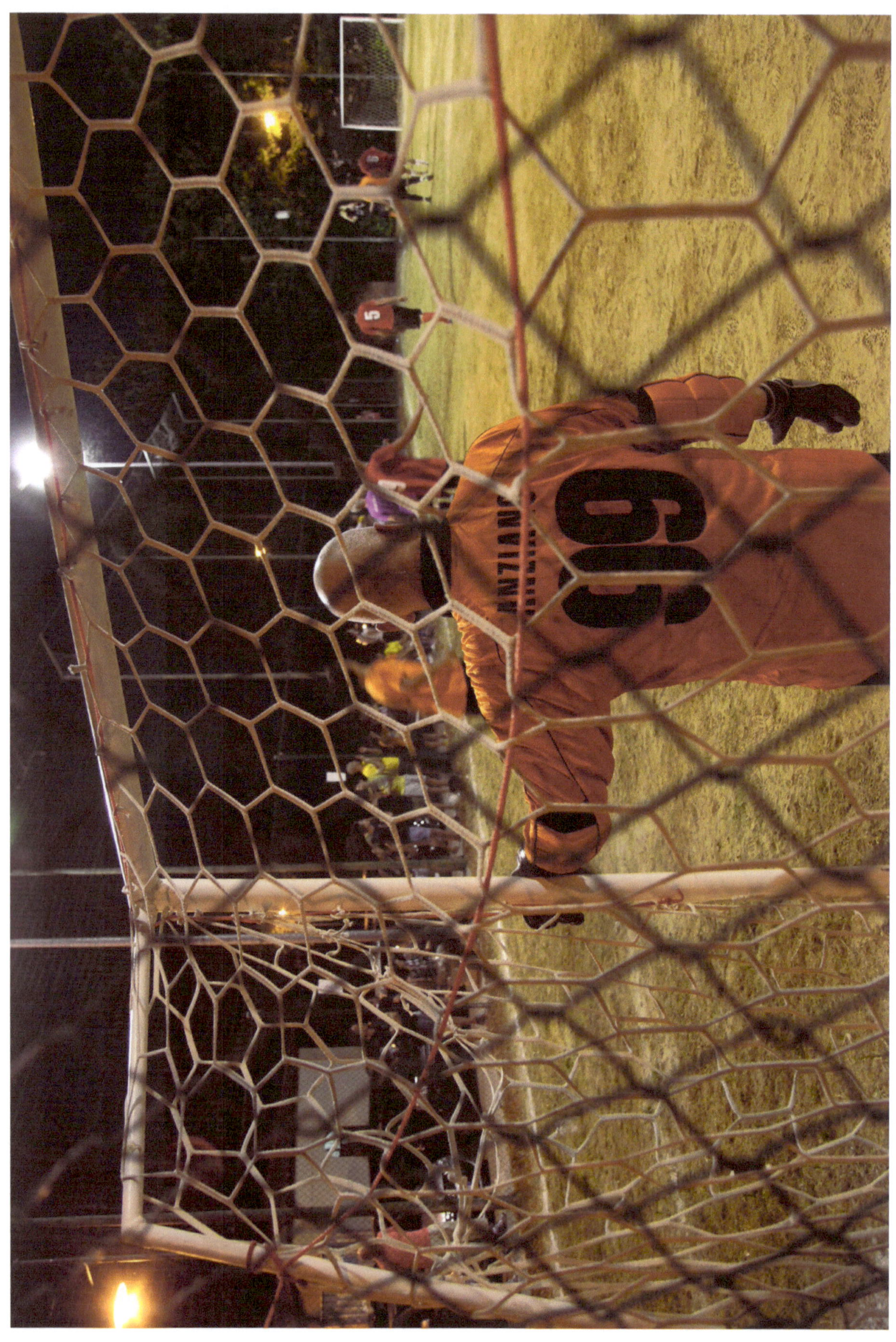

Night-time football in Palaia attracts some local interest.

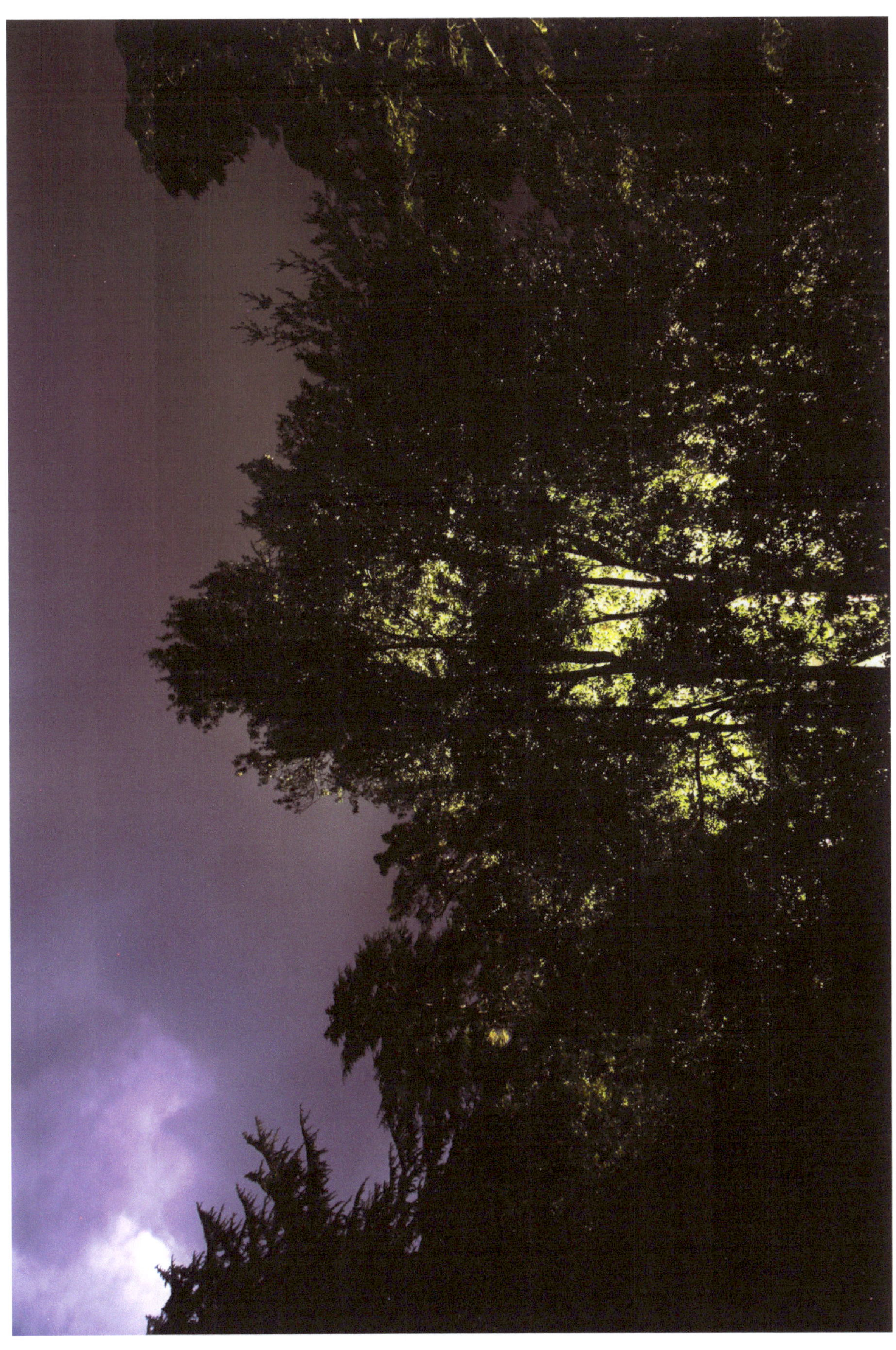

Strange mix of electric light and storm clouds make for quite a dramatic sight.

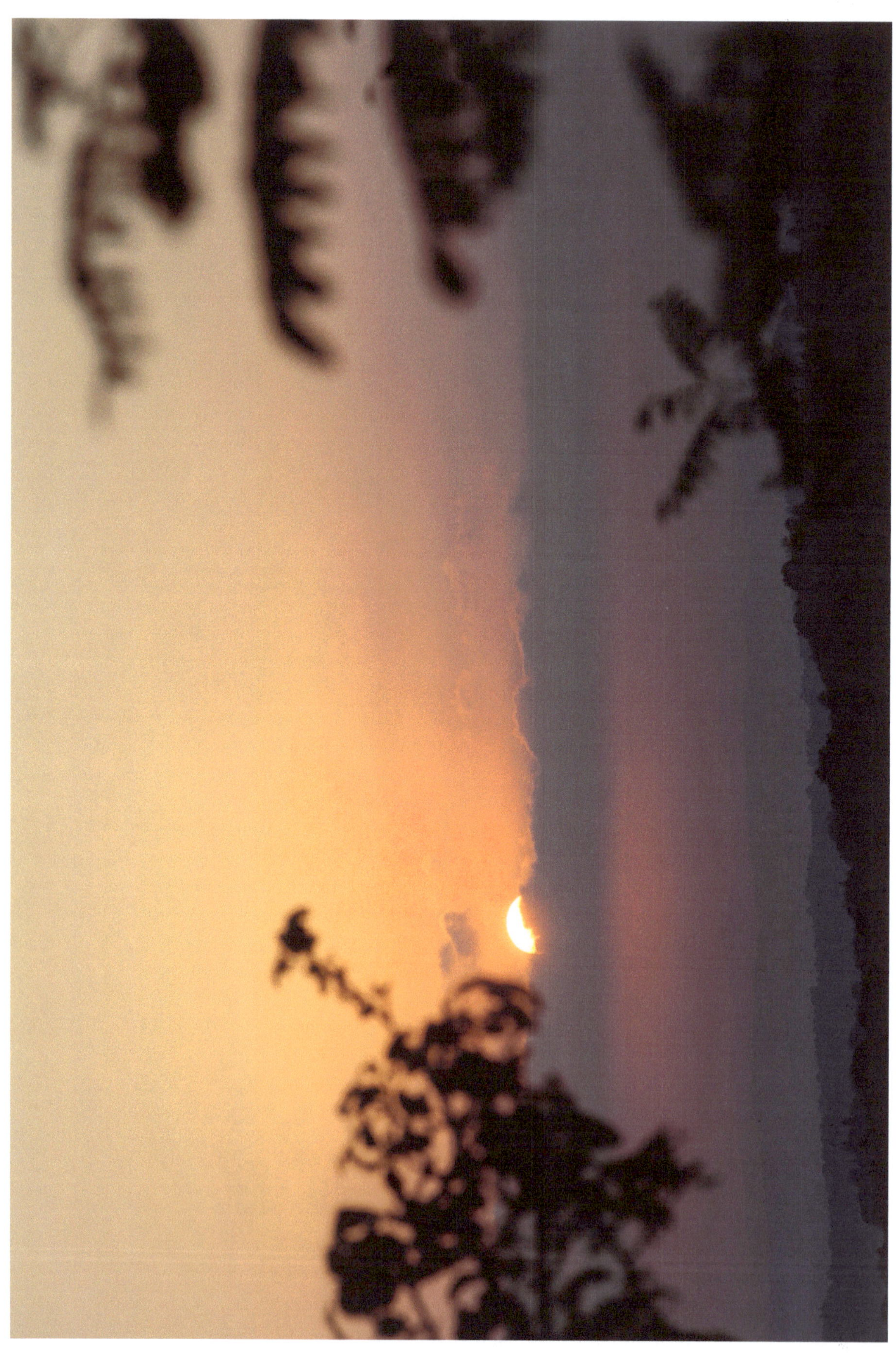

Sunset view taken in the Colleoli/Palaia area.

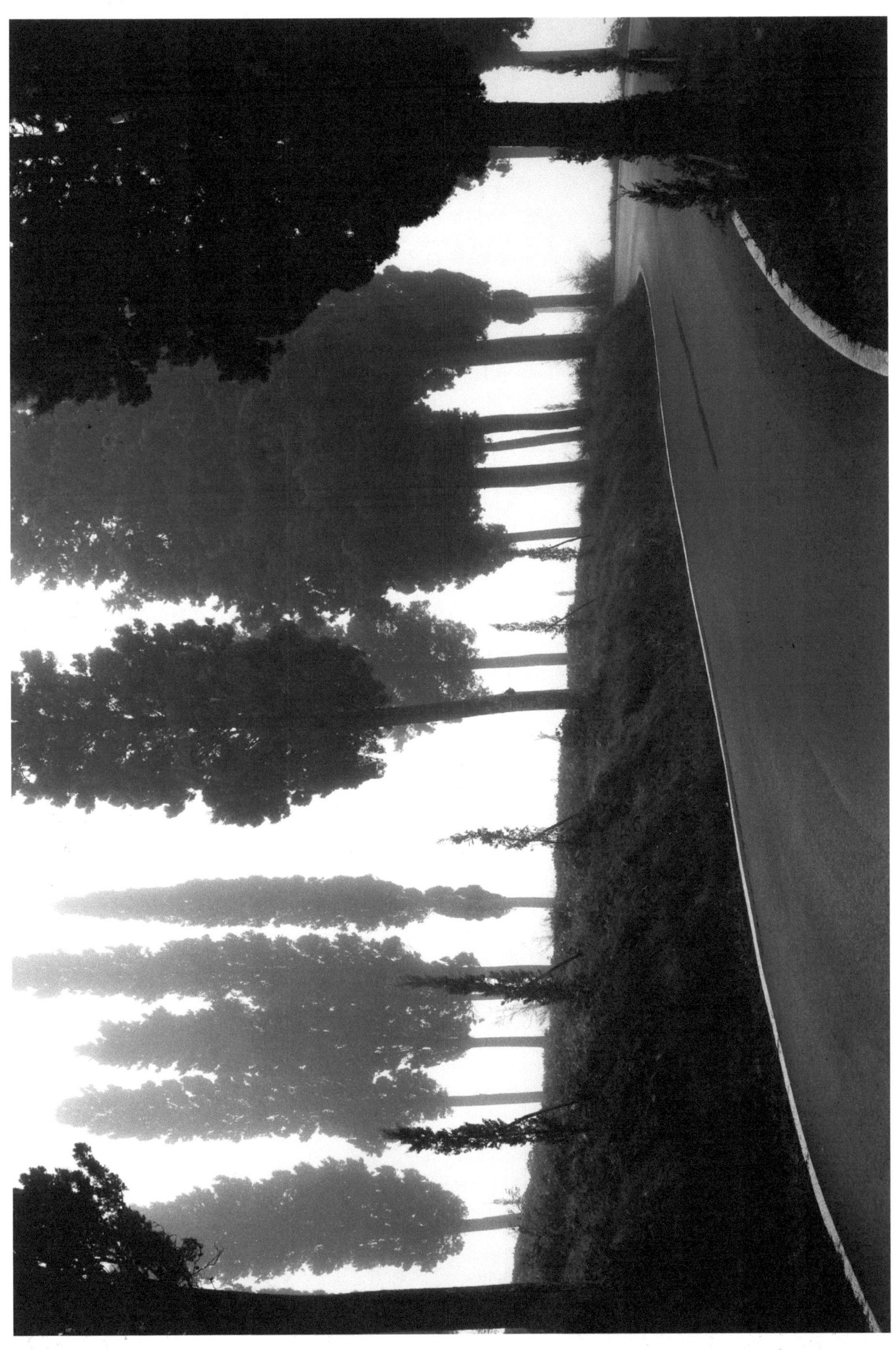

One of those occasions when black and white has more impact on this twisty tree-lined road near Montefoscoli.

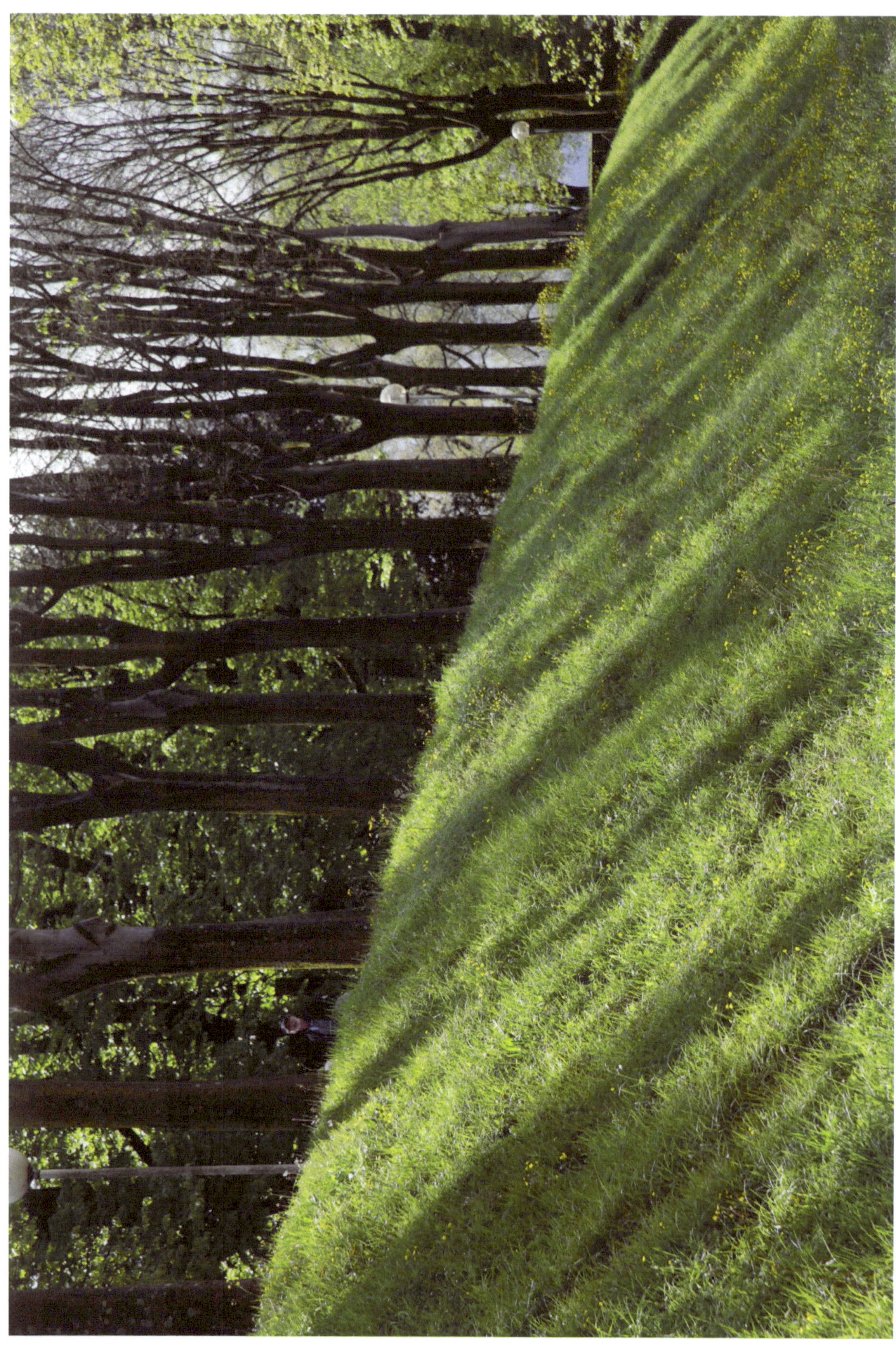

Vibrant colours just inside the city wall in Lucca.

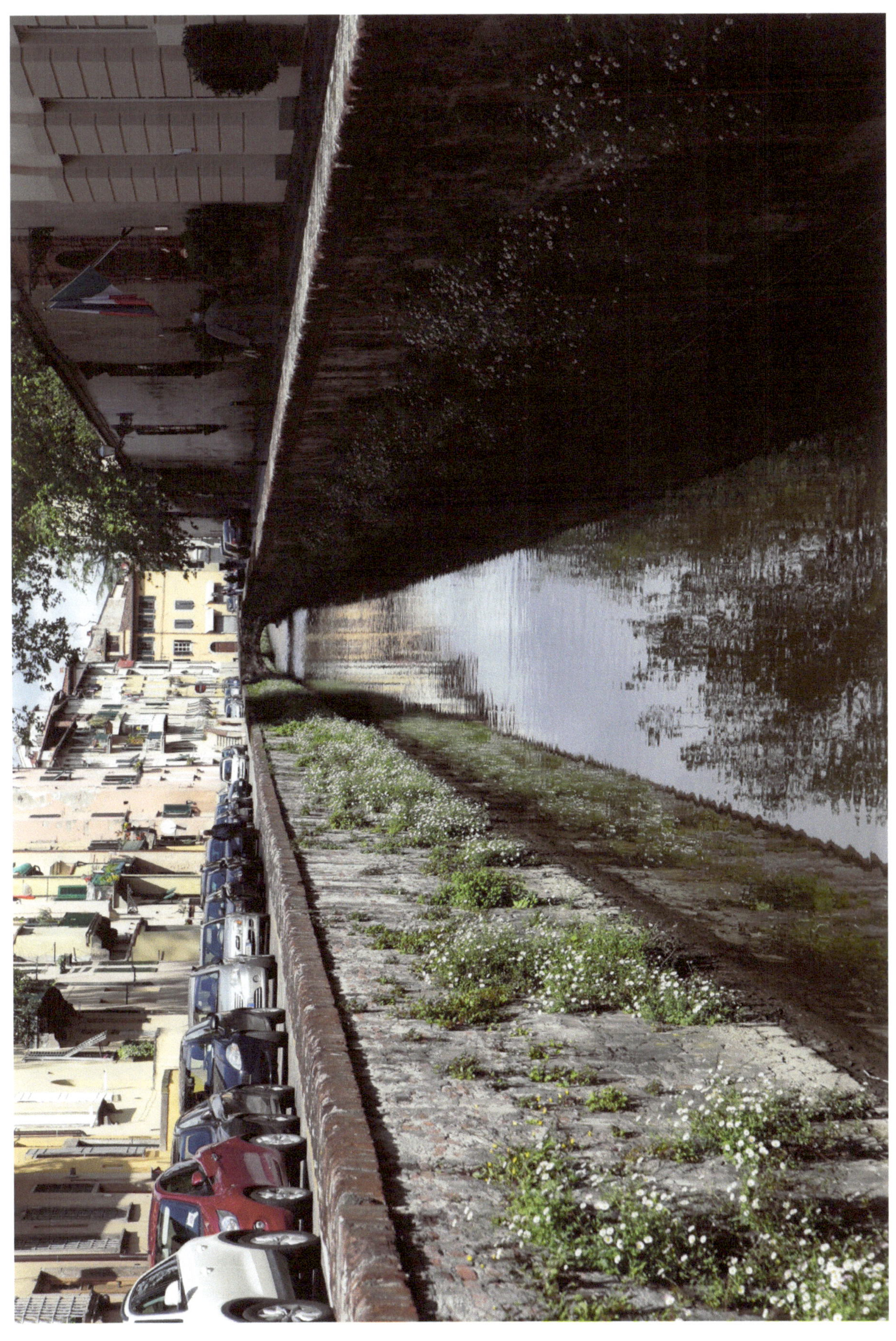

View along the moat that used to be the boundary of the ancient city of Lucca.

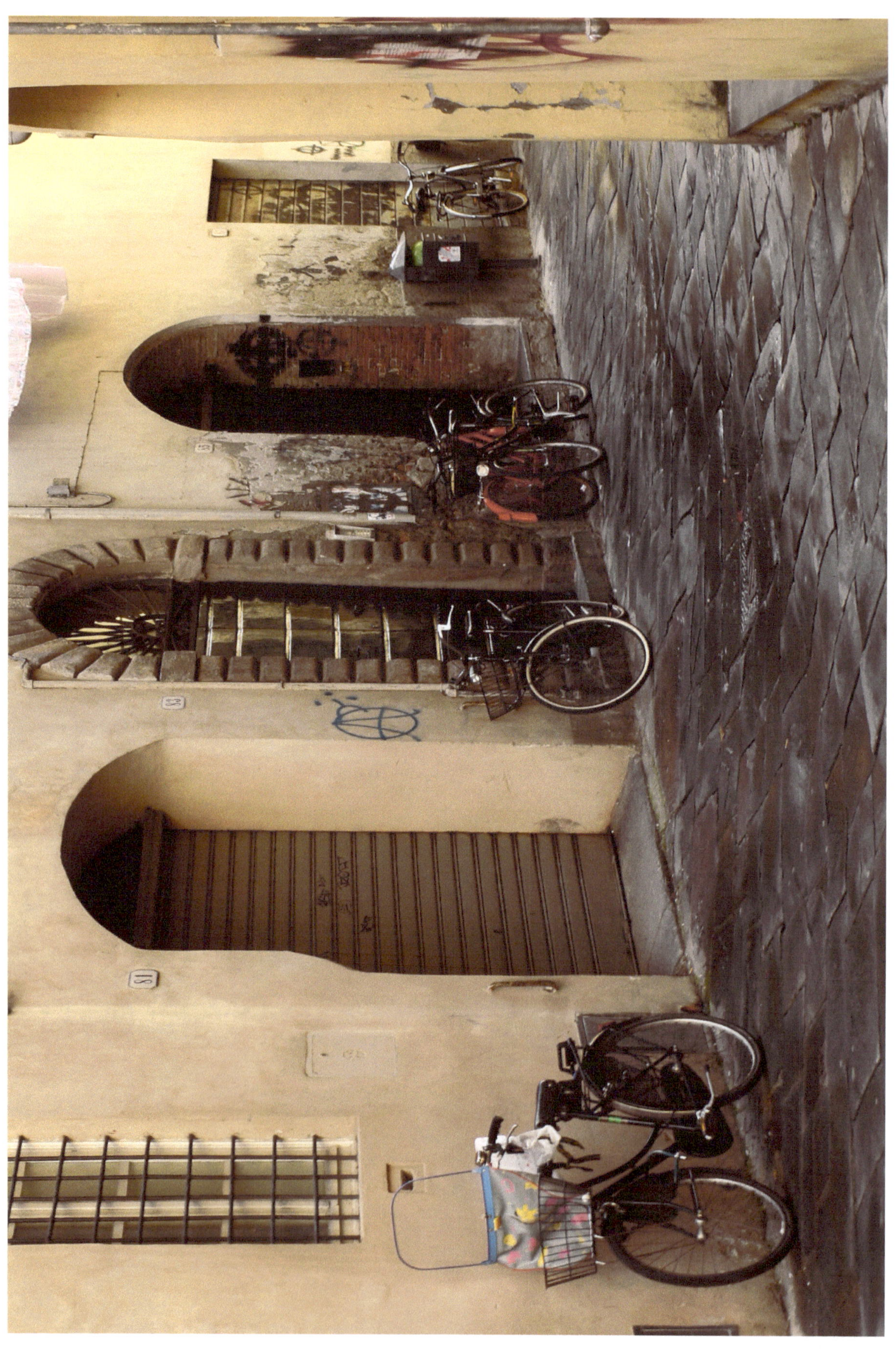

Bicycles, cobblestone streets, window grills – all part of the charm of the wonderful old town that is Lucca.

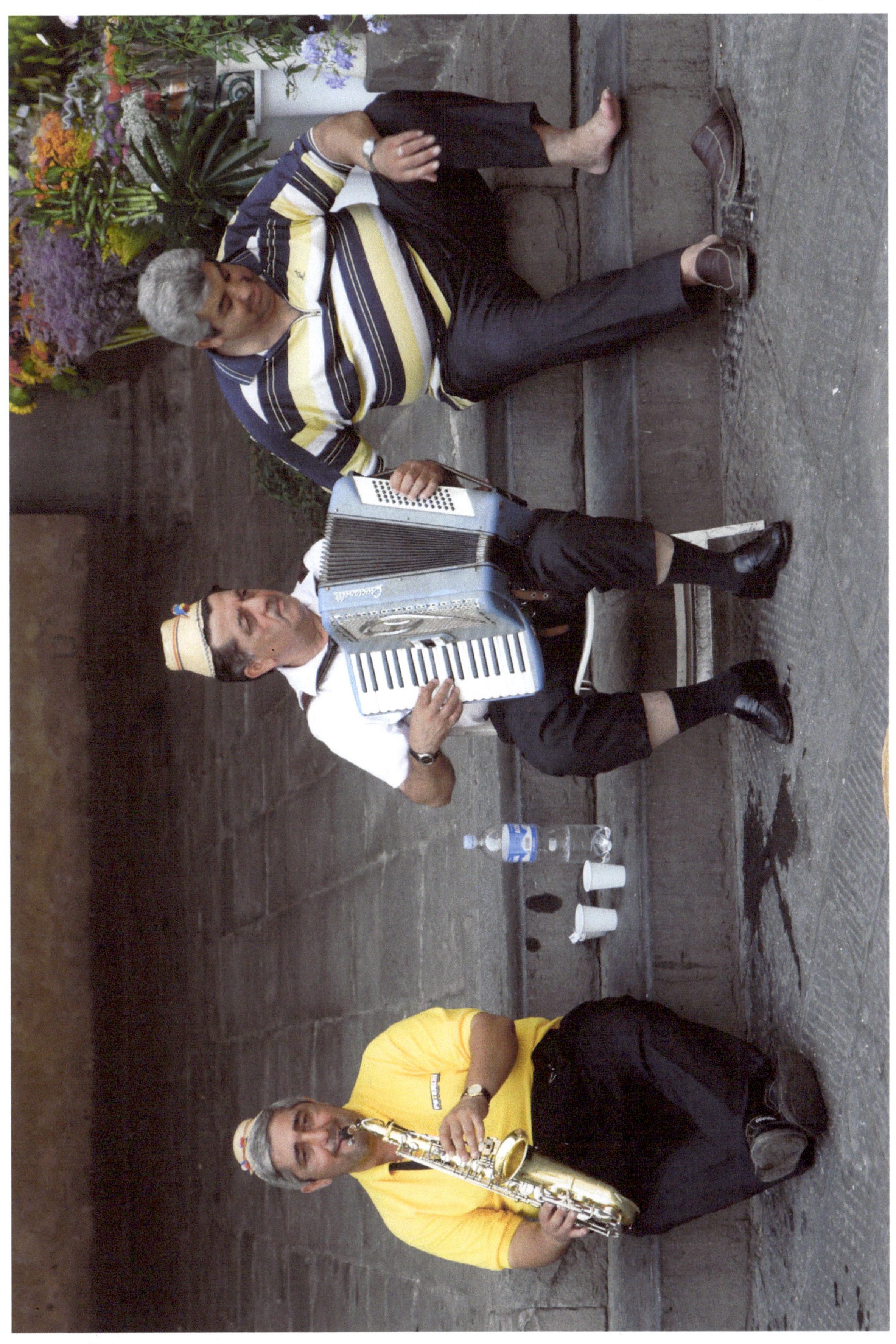

I just liked the way each of these guys look so different.

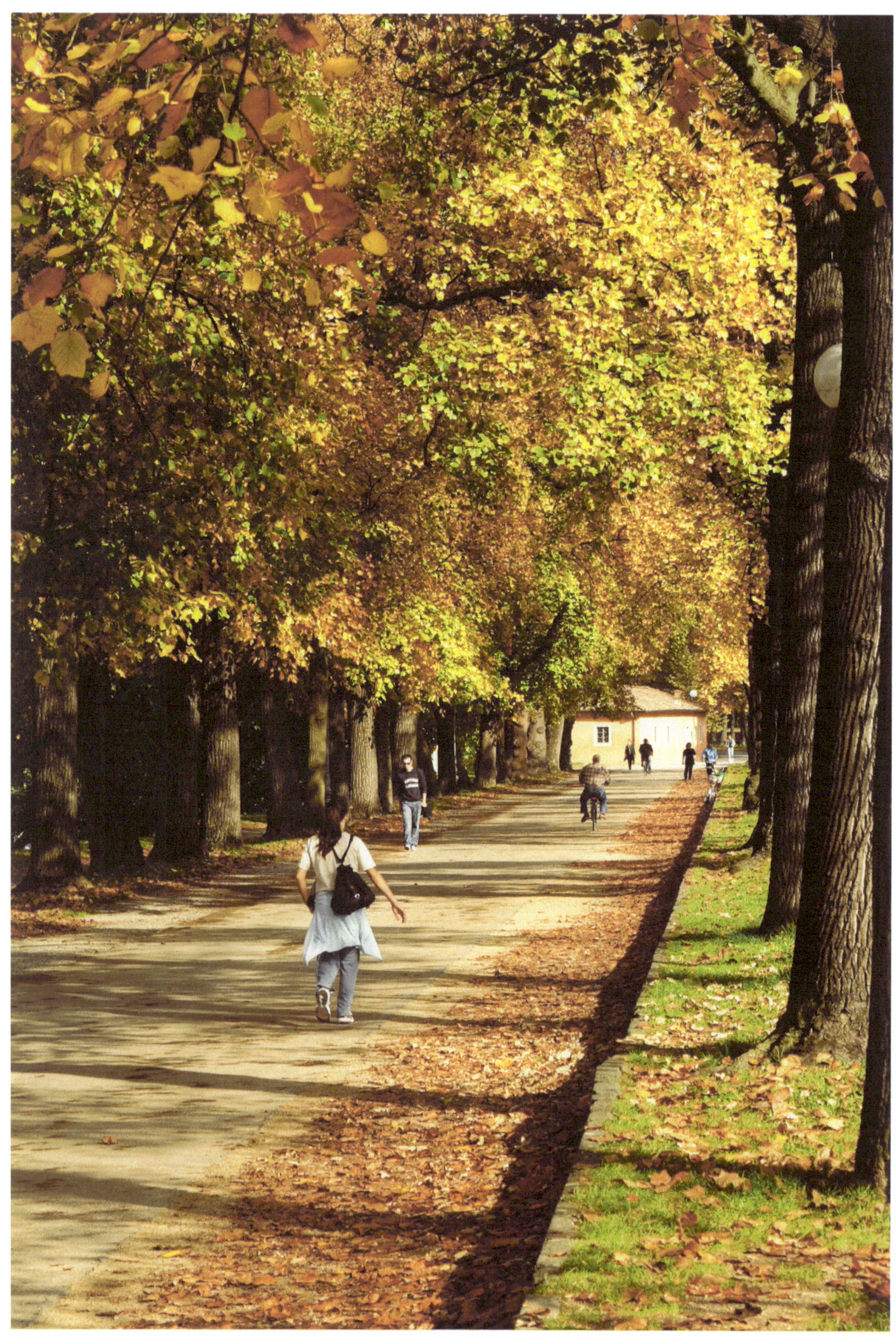

Autumnal colours on the city wall path that goes round Lucca.

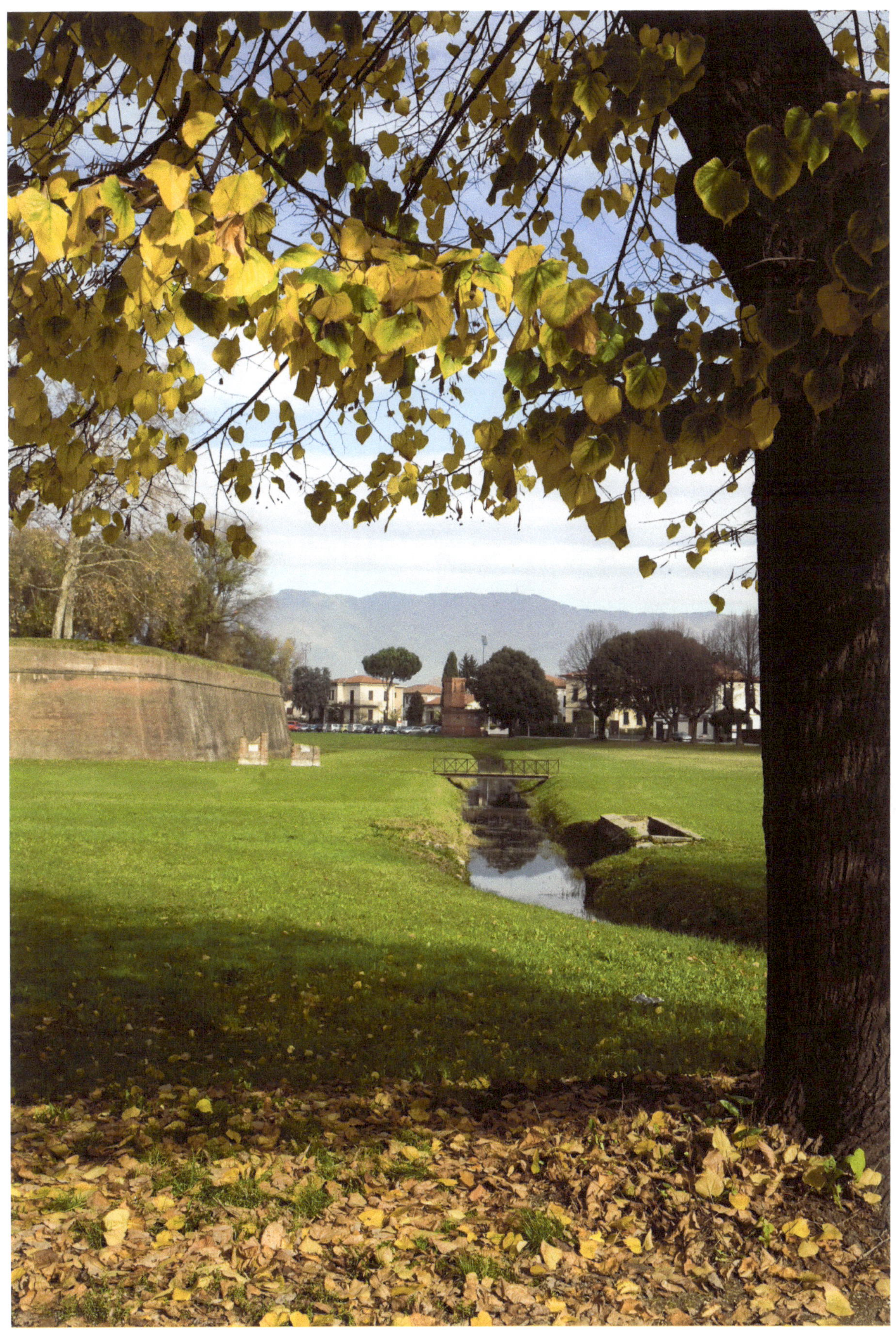

Soft, warm autumnal colours outside the wall of Lucca.

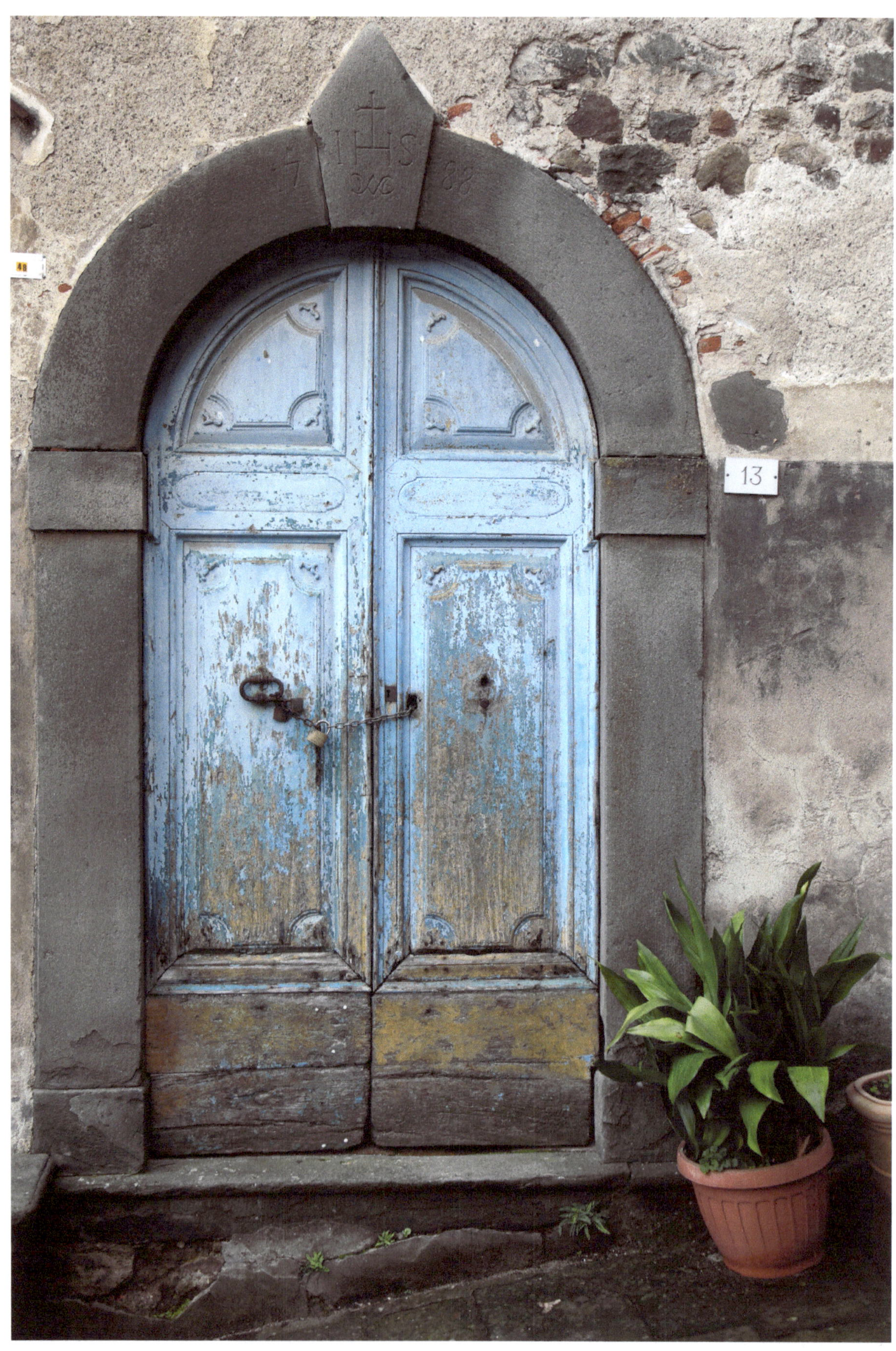

One of those doorways that just had to be photographed.

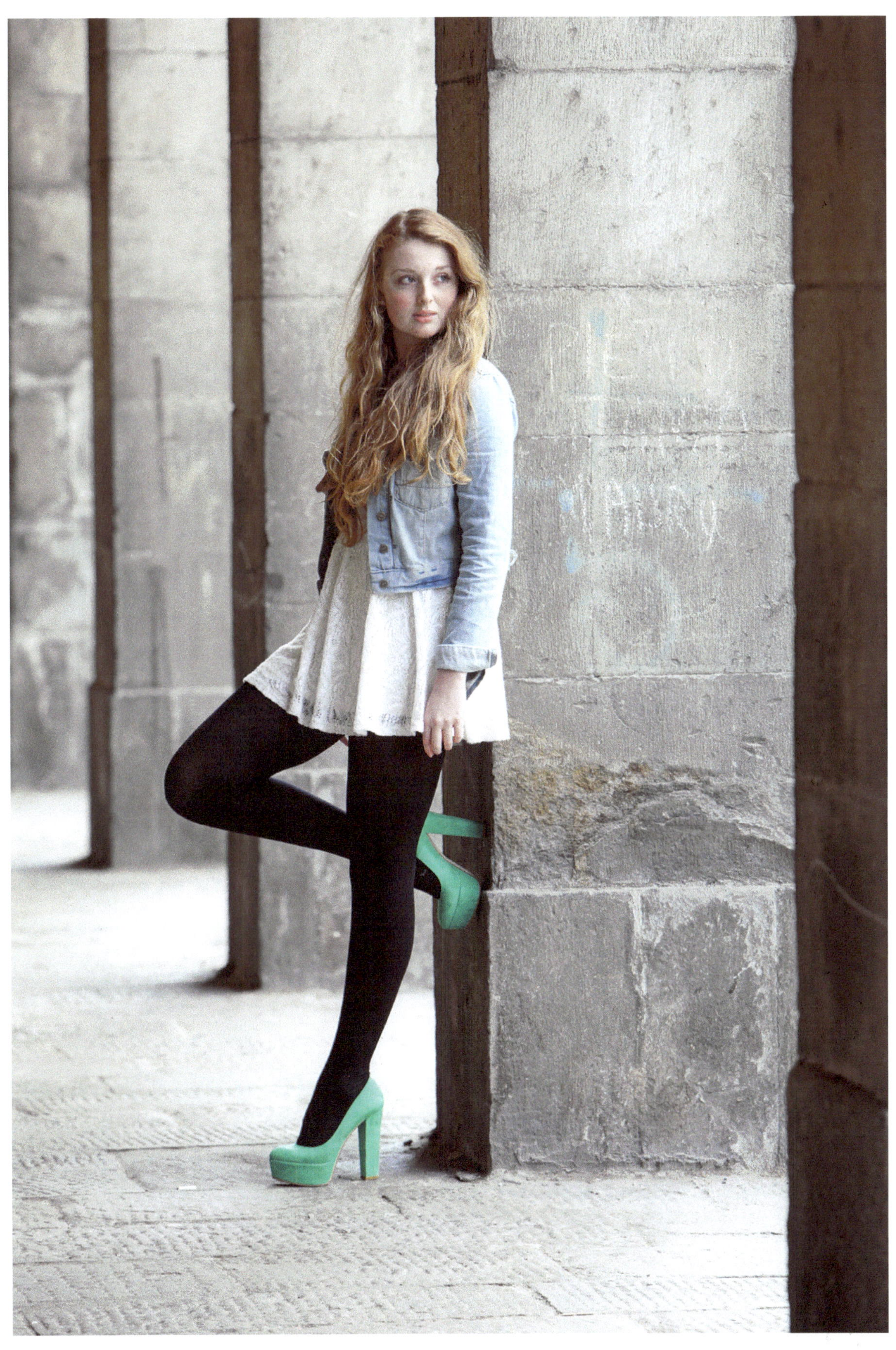

A spot of impromptu modelling under the arches in Lucca.

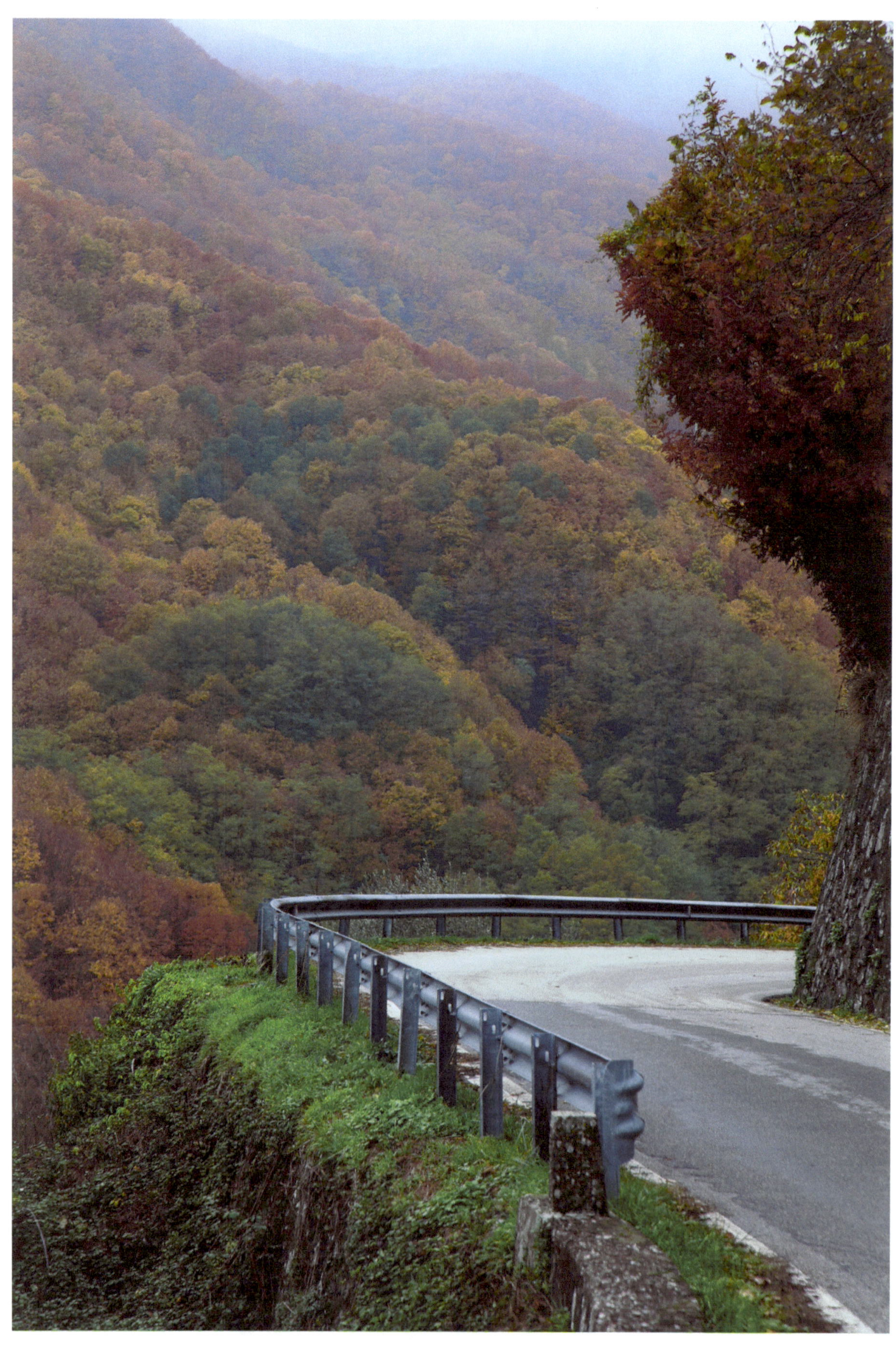

Colourful landscape from the road between Lucca and Borgo a Mozzano.

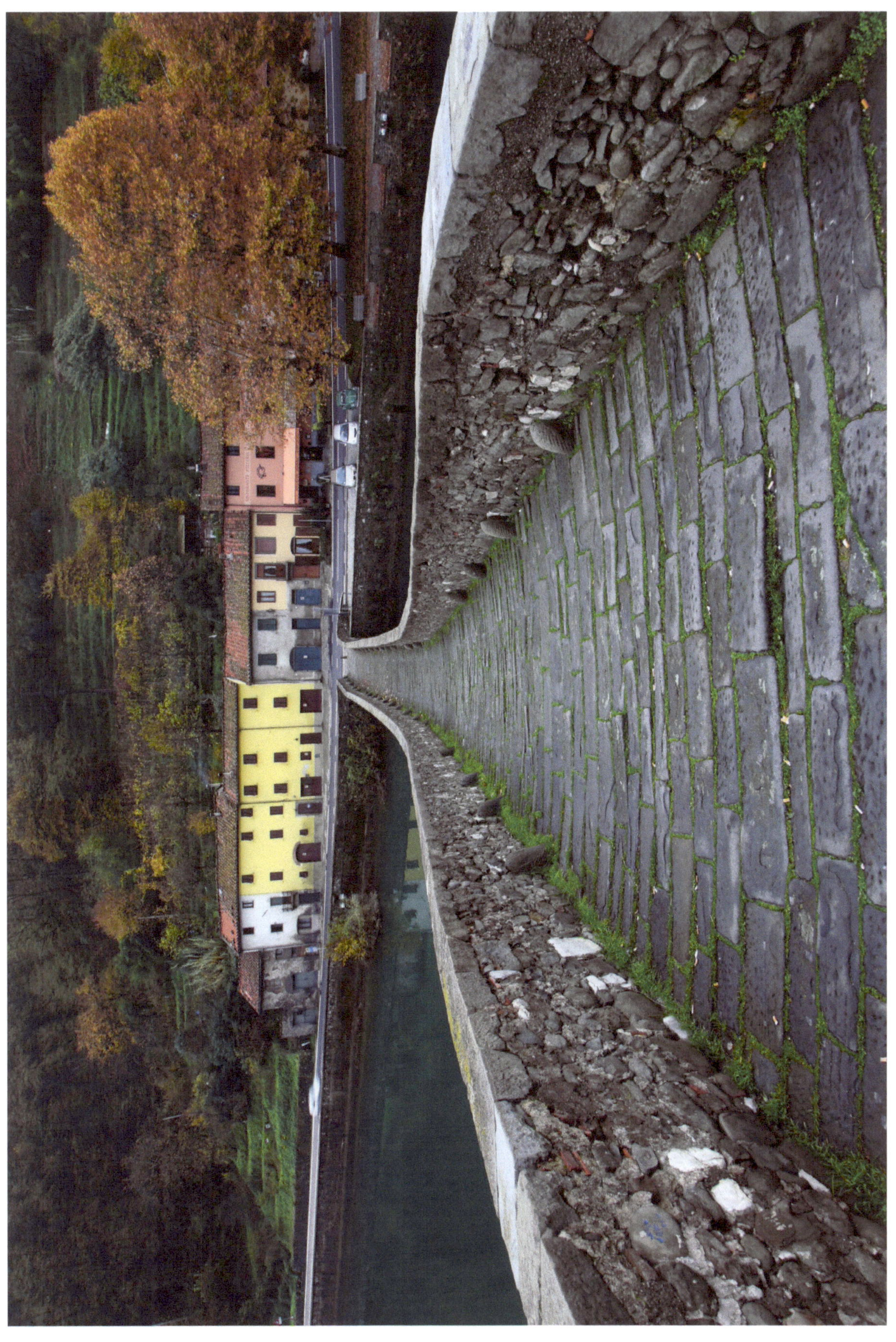

Looking down ‘Devil’s Bridge’ (also known as Maddalenas Bridge) near Borgo a Mozzano.

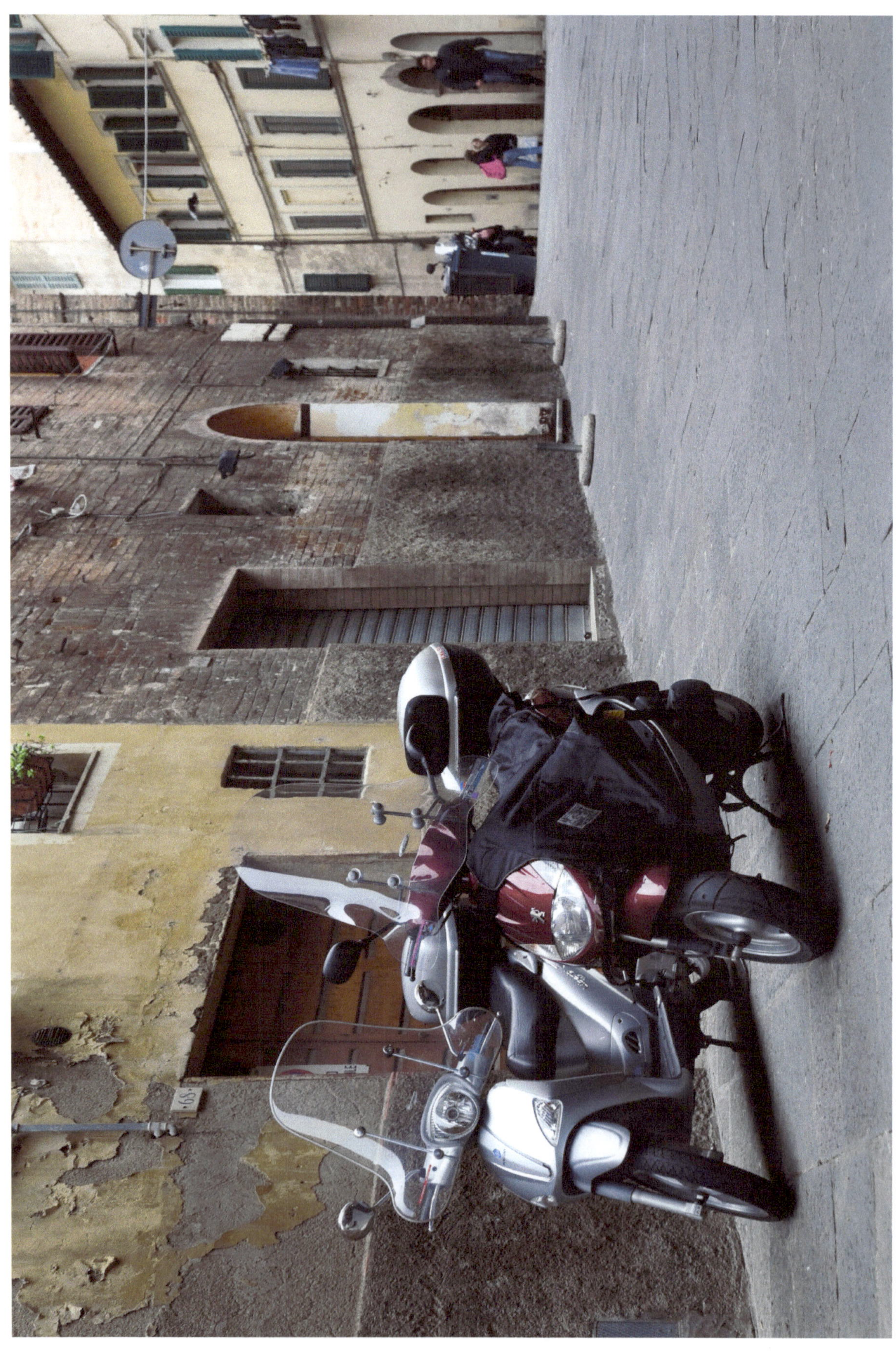

Typical Italian city street scene, this time in Siena.

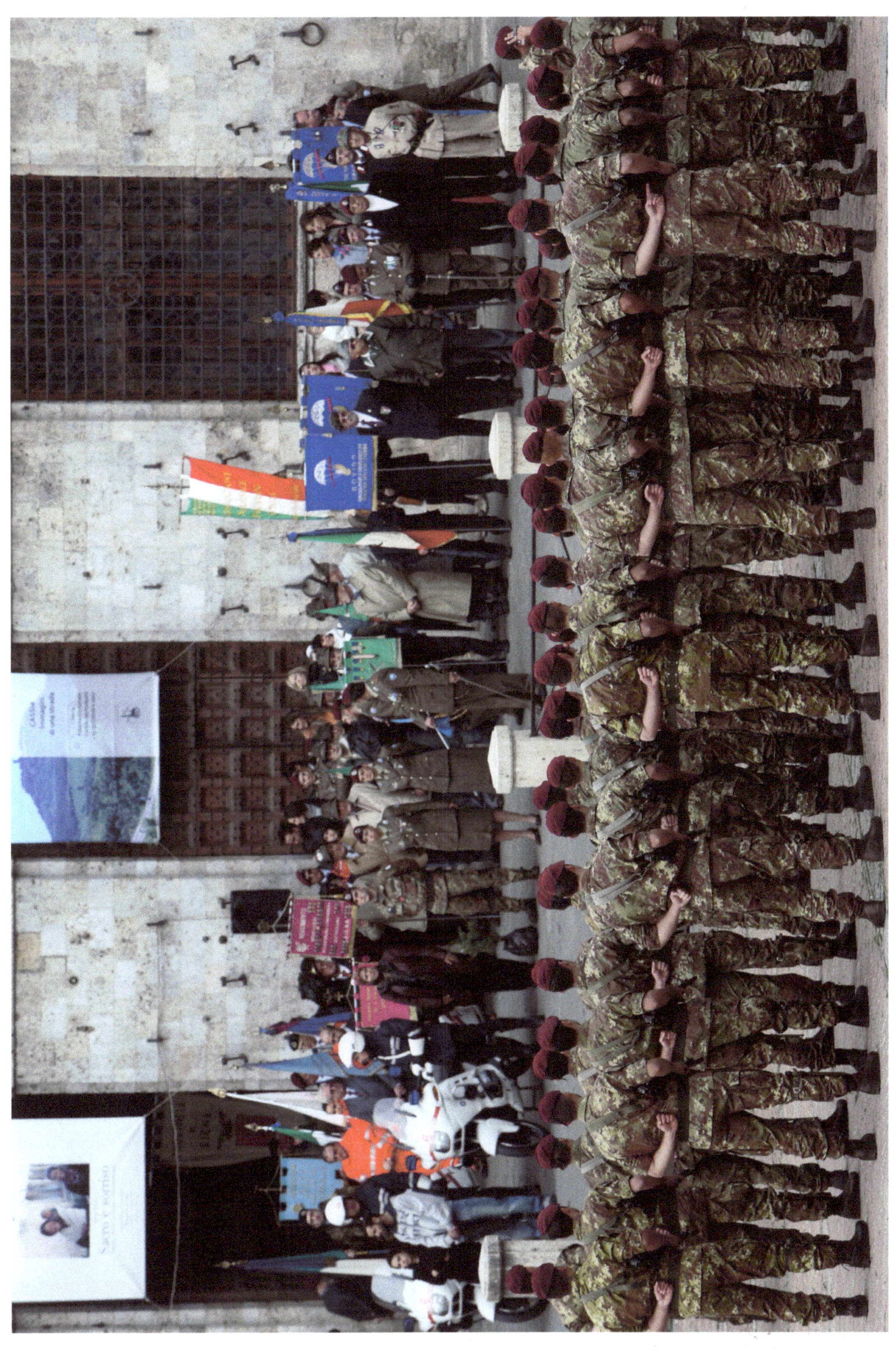

Military celebration in Piazza del Campo, Siena after NATO activities, wonder what the soldier back right is pointing at?

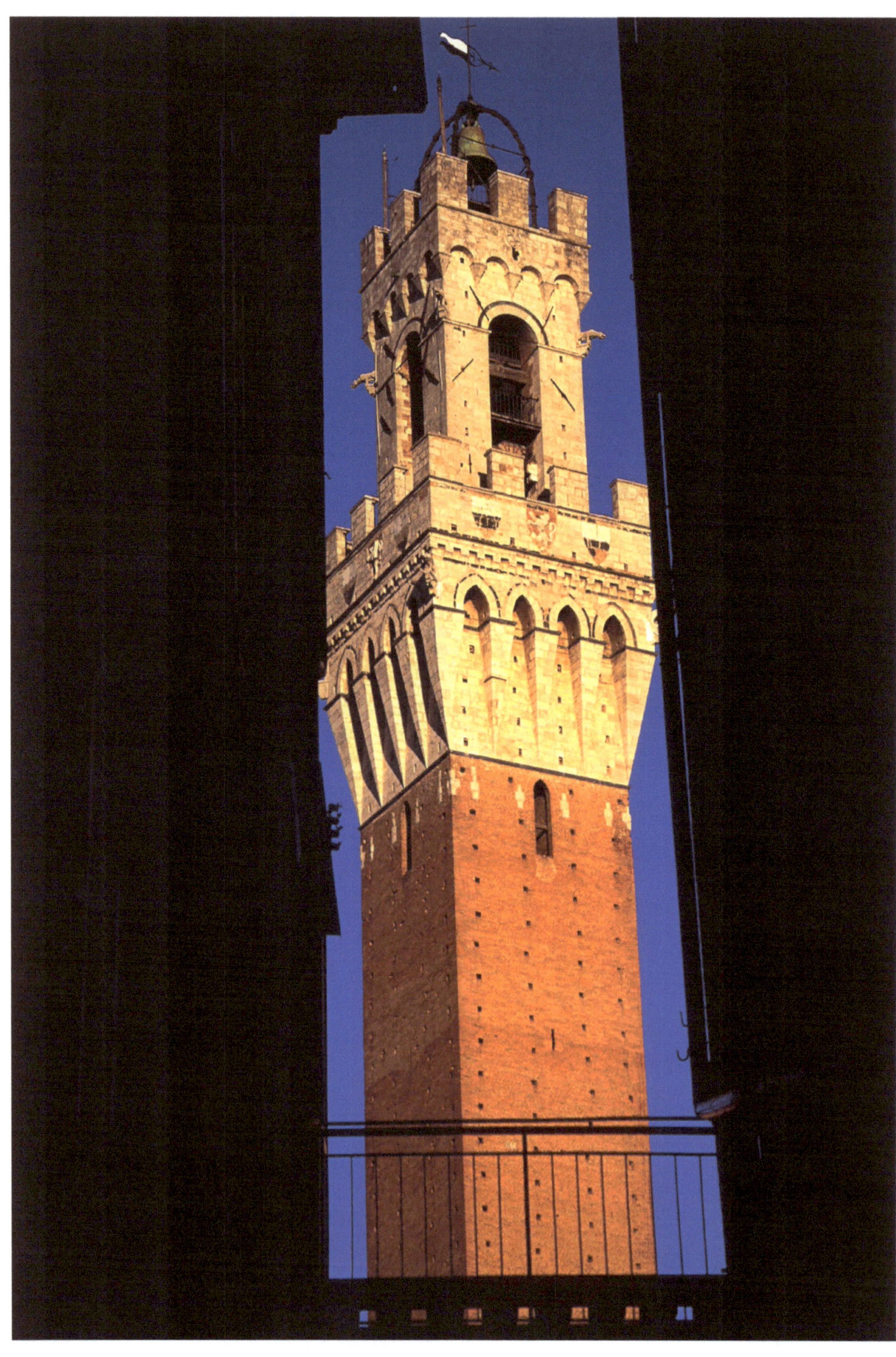

Torre del Mangia, Siena.

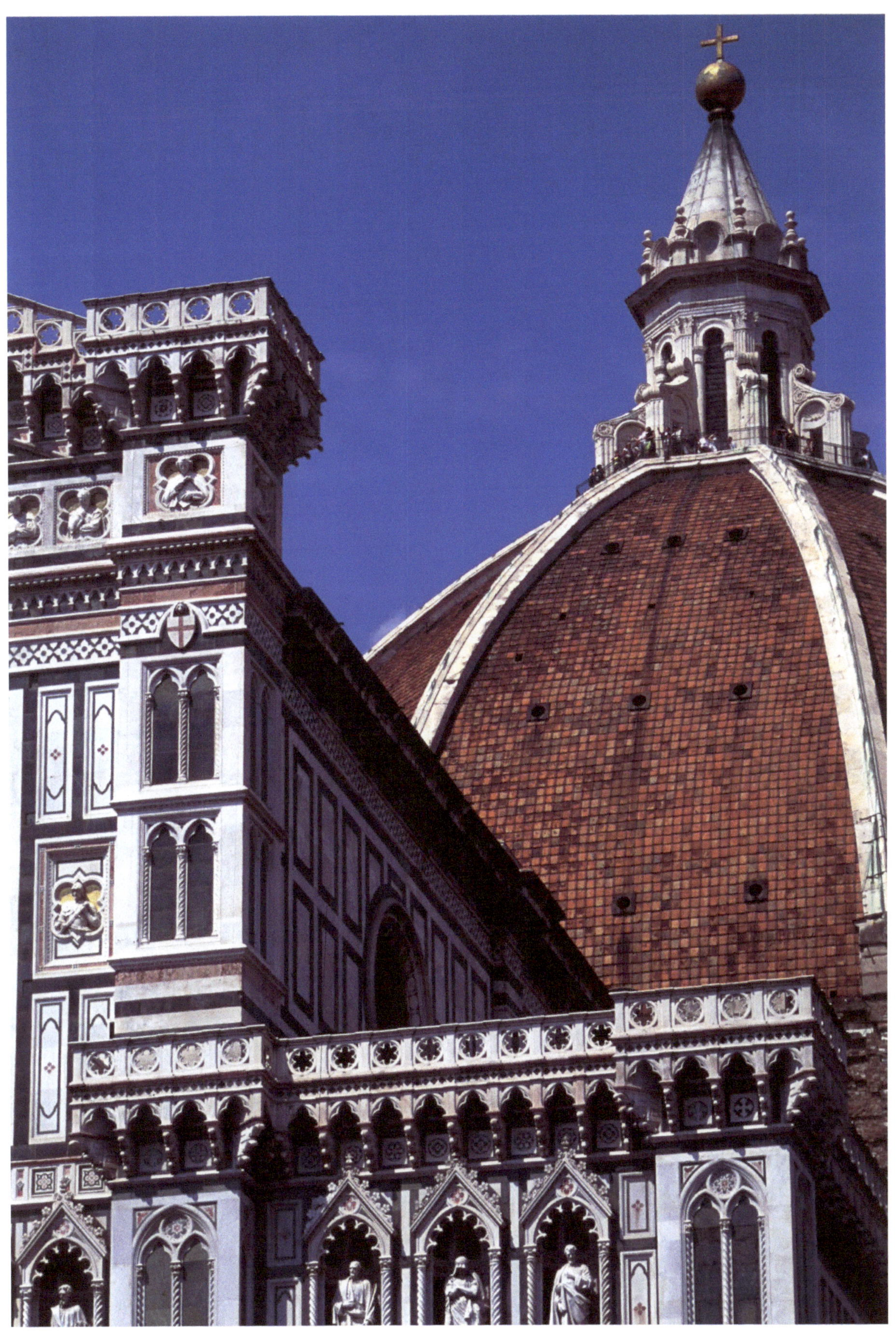

The very impressive El Duomo in Siena.

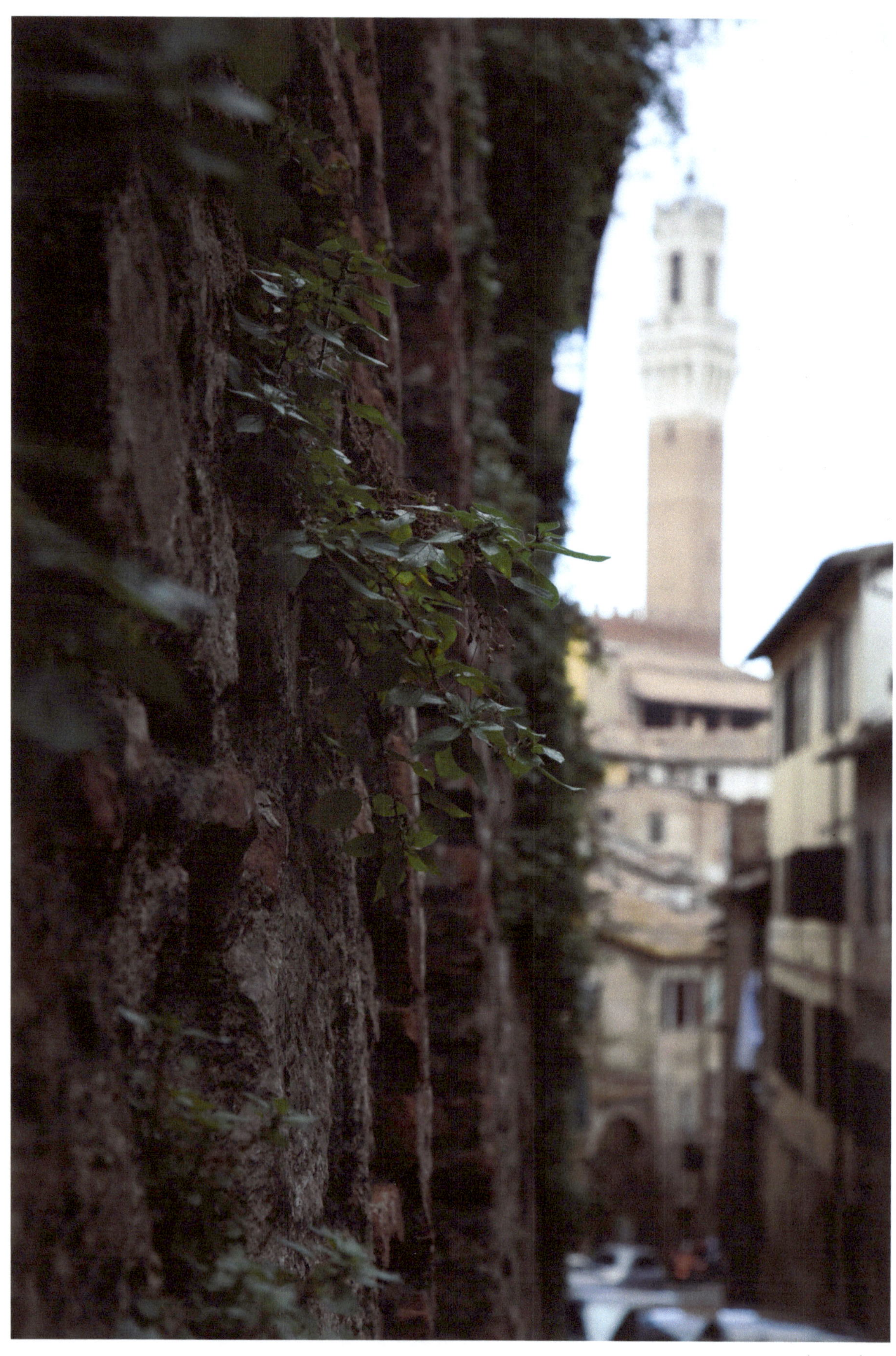

Slightly different approach to photographing the Mangia Tower in Siena.

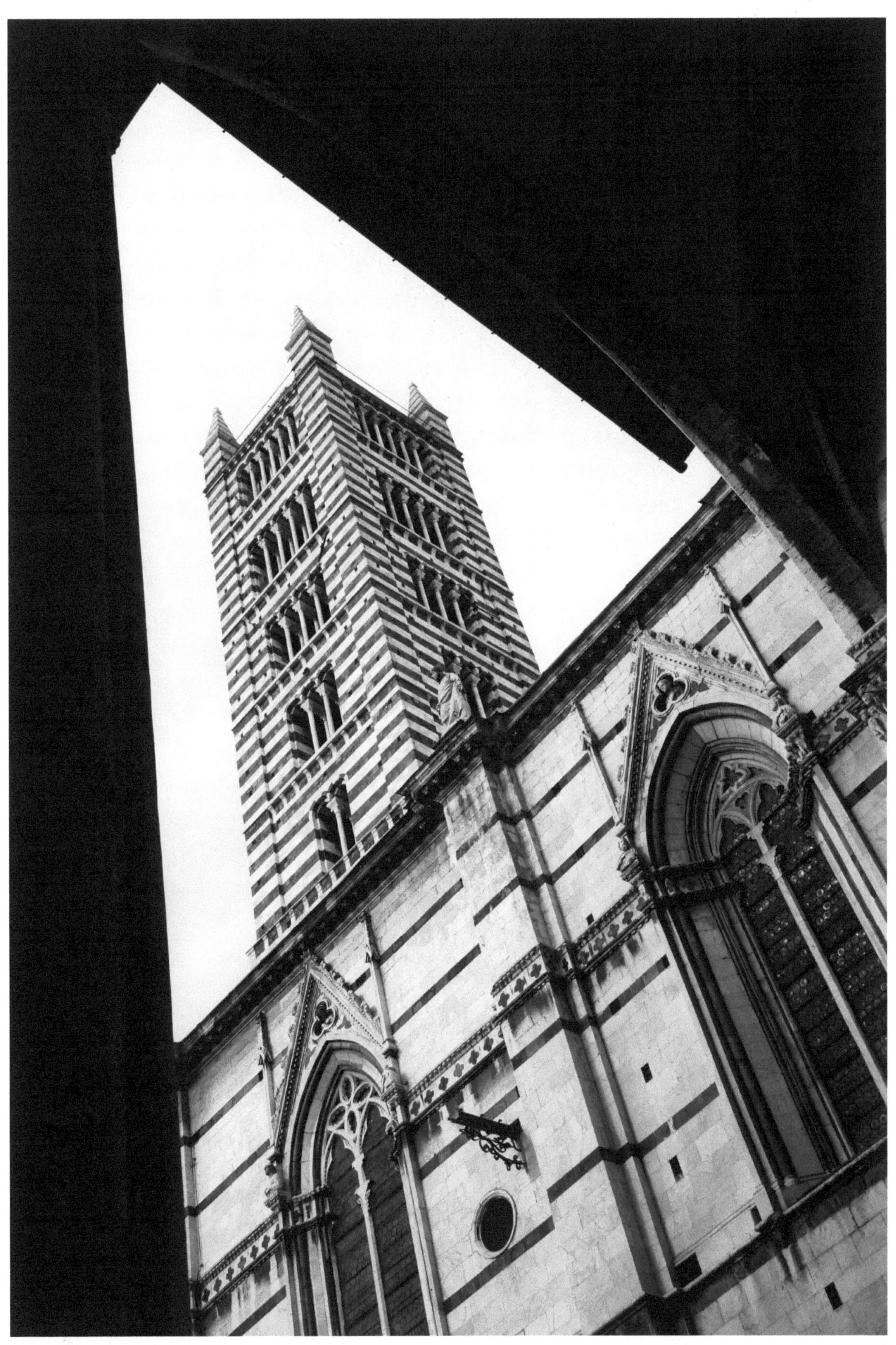

Using buildings to frame the bell tower of El Duomo in Siena,
and as it was a grey day black and white seemed a better option.

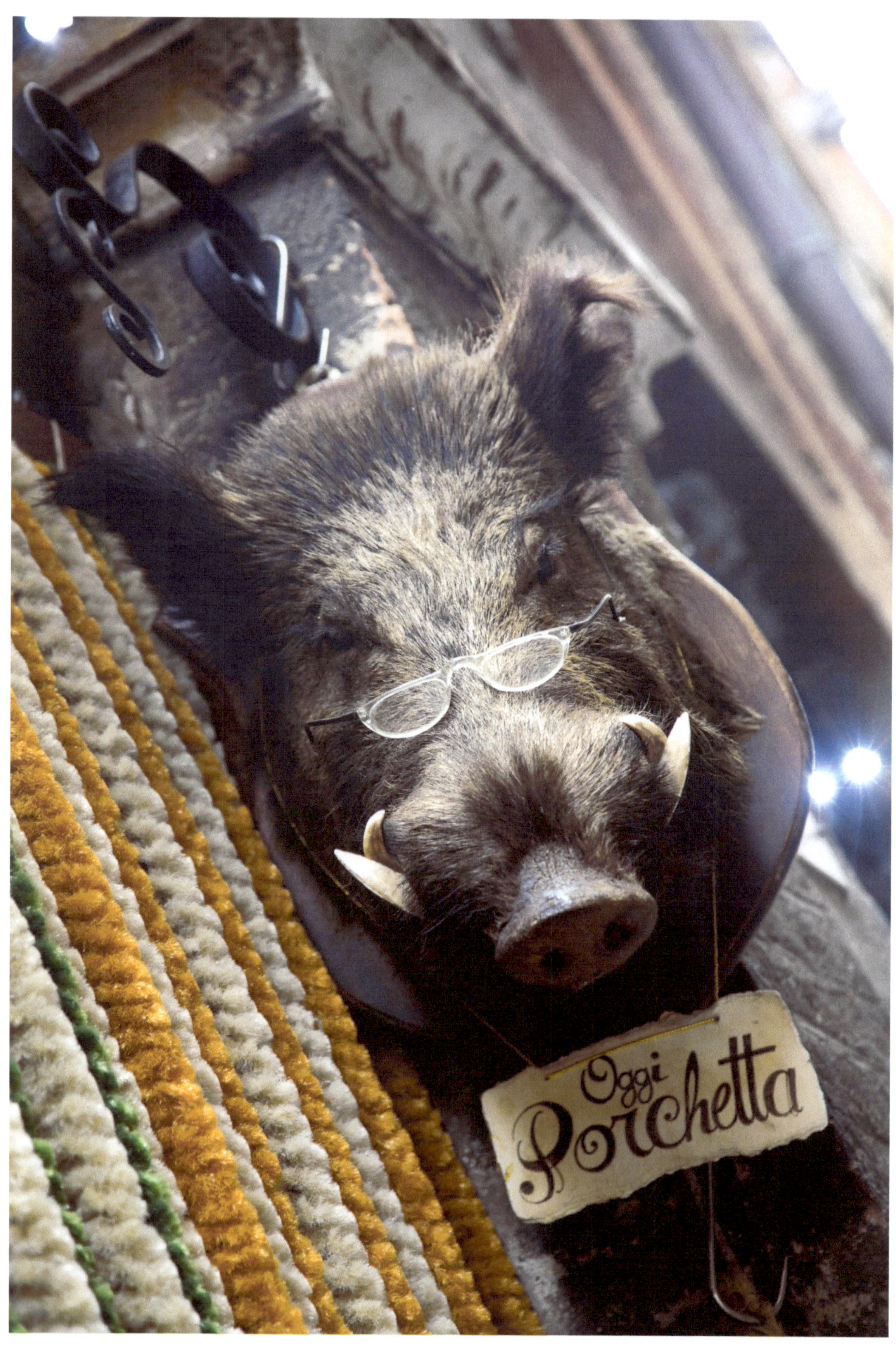

Unusual way of advertising what's on the menu today, Siena.

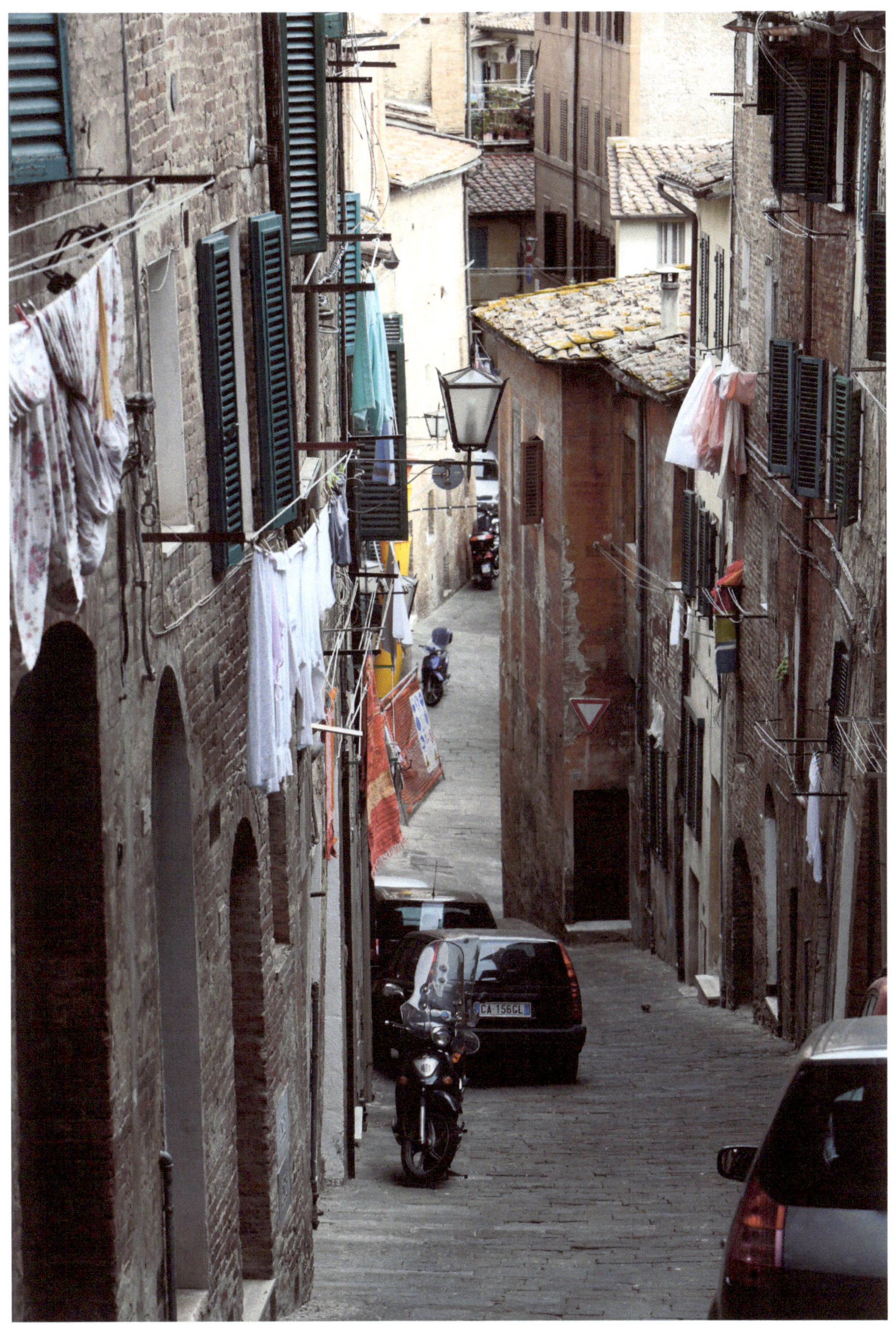

Quiet, peaceful side street scene in Siena.

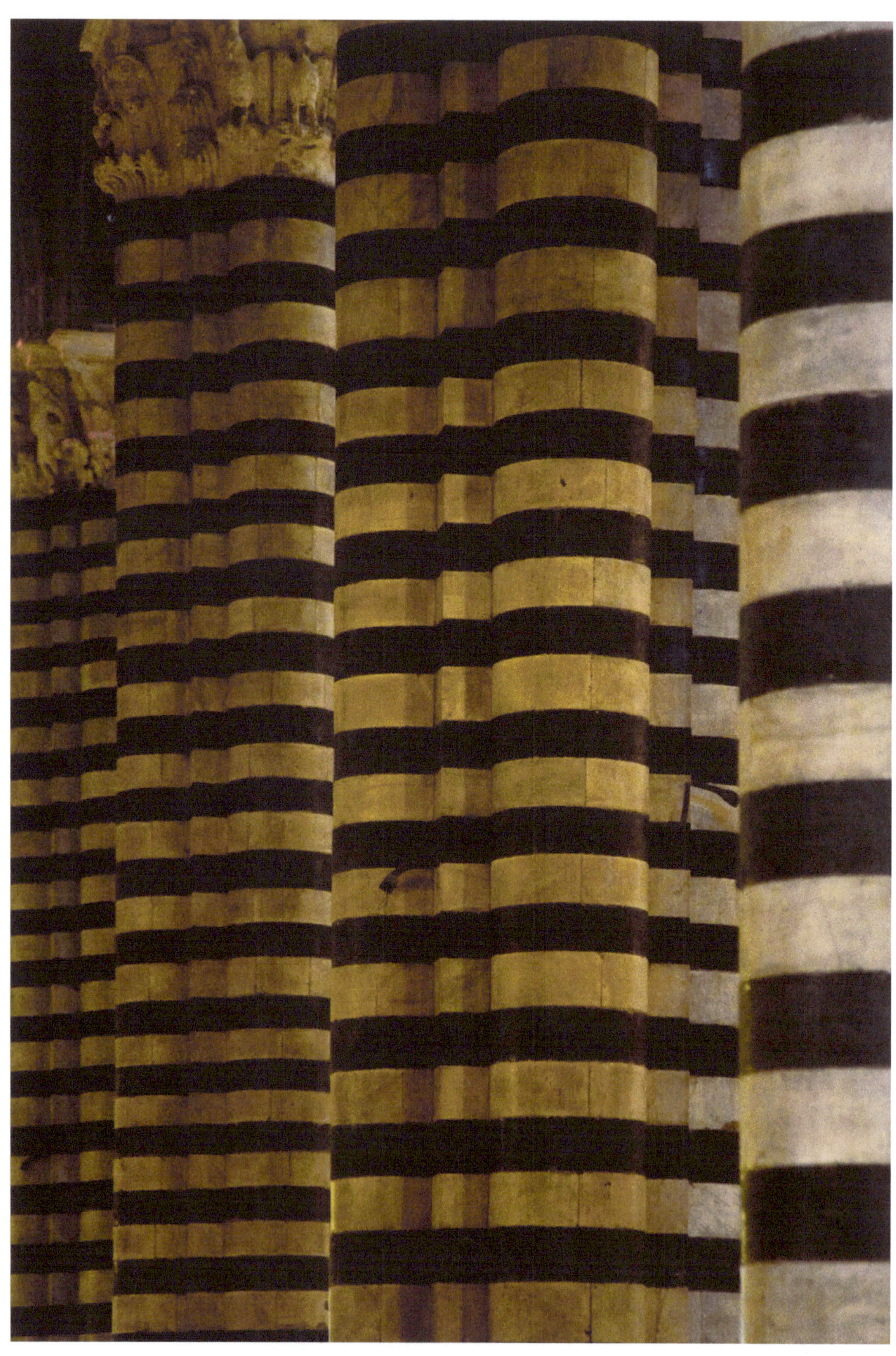

Abstract-style shot of the columns inside El Duomo in Siena.

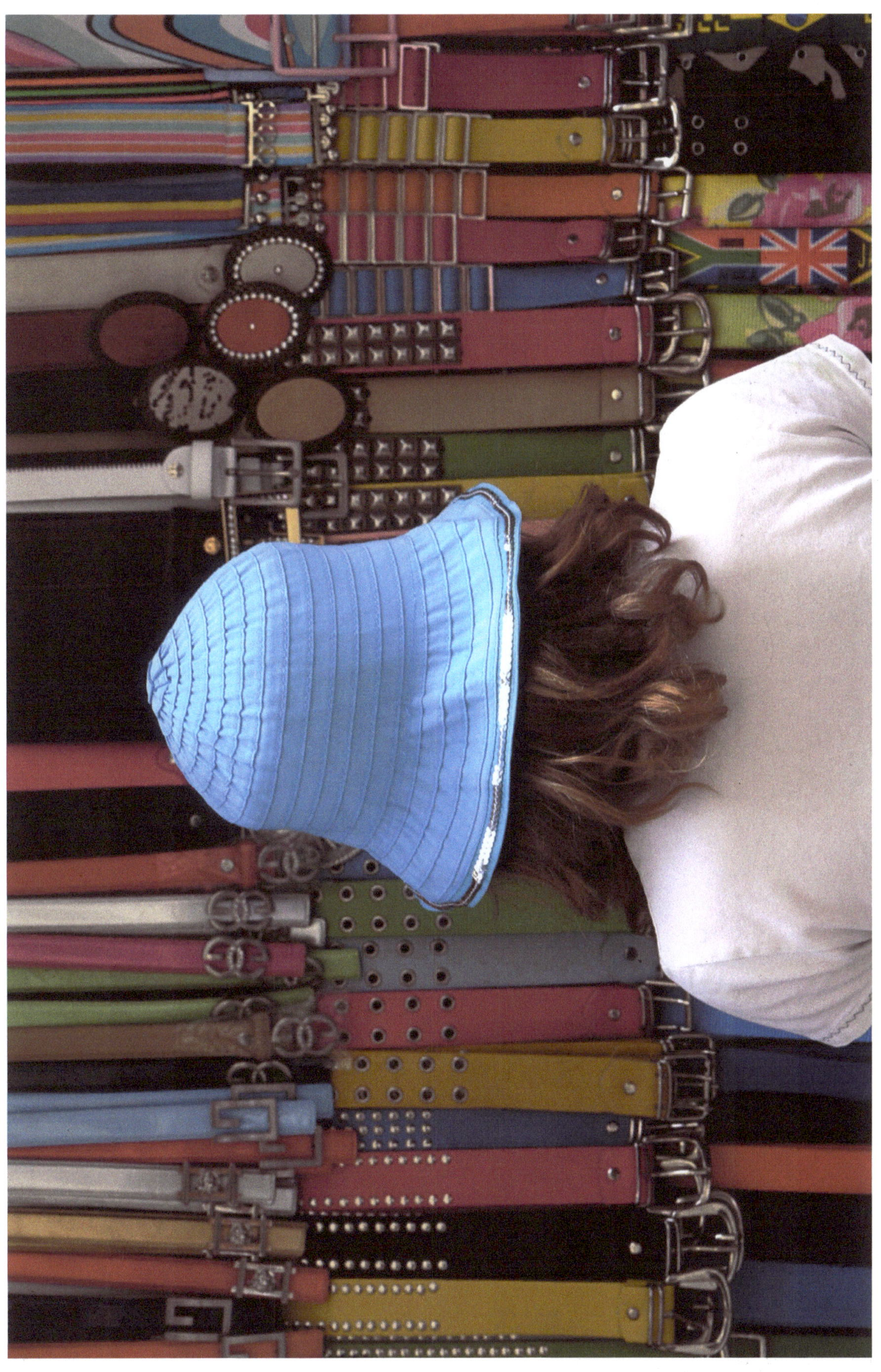

Young tourist contemplating what to buy at a street market in Florence.

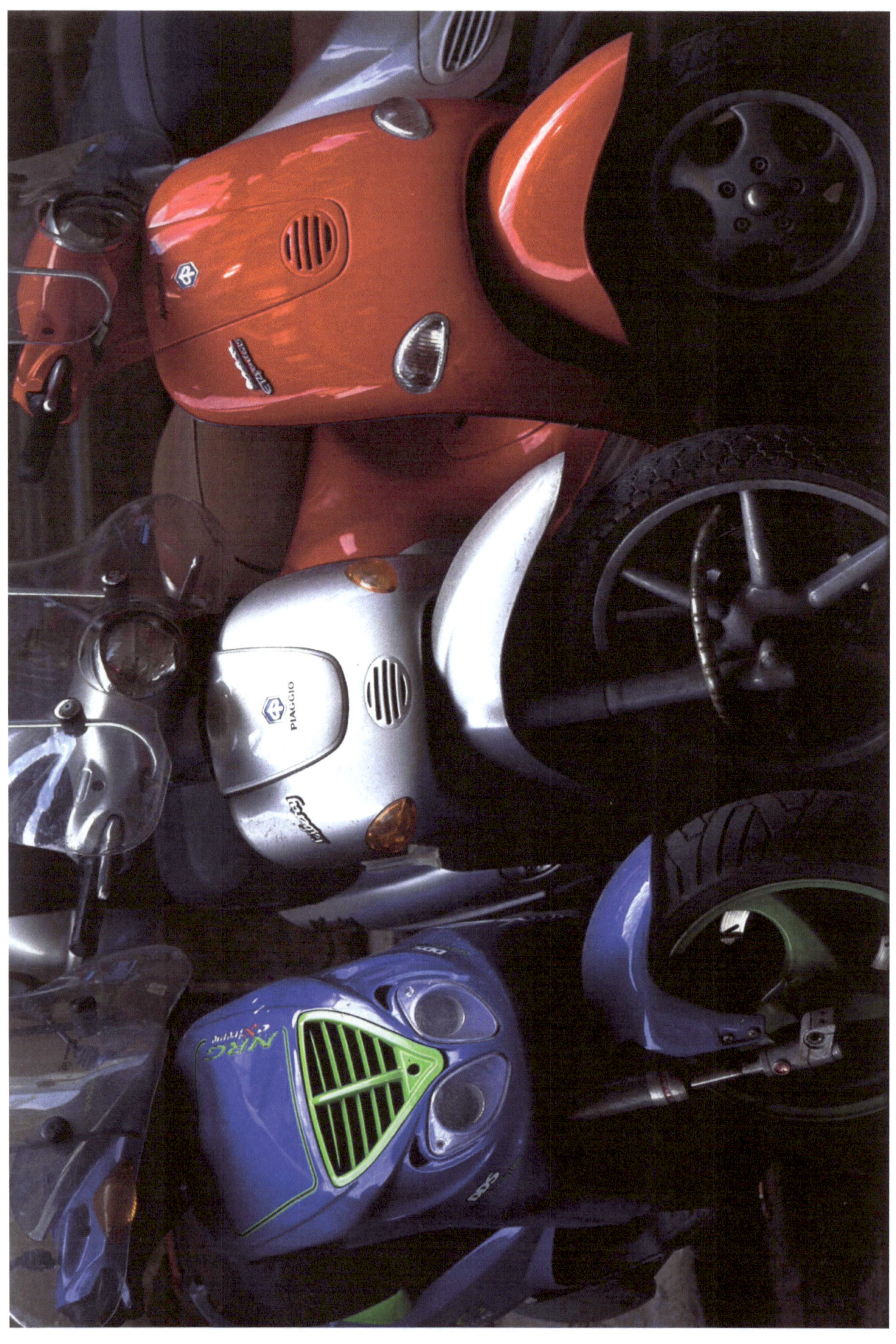

Very smart looking line-up of seemingly brand new mopeds in Florence.

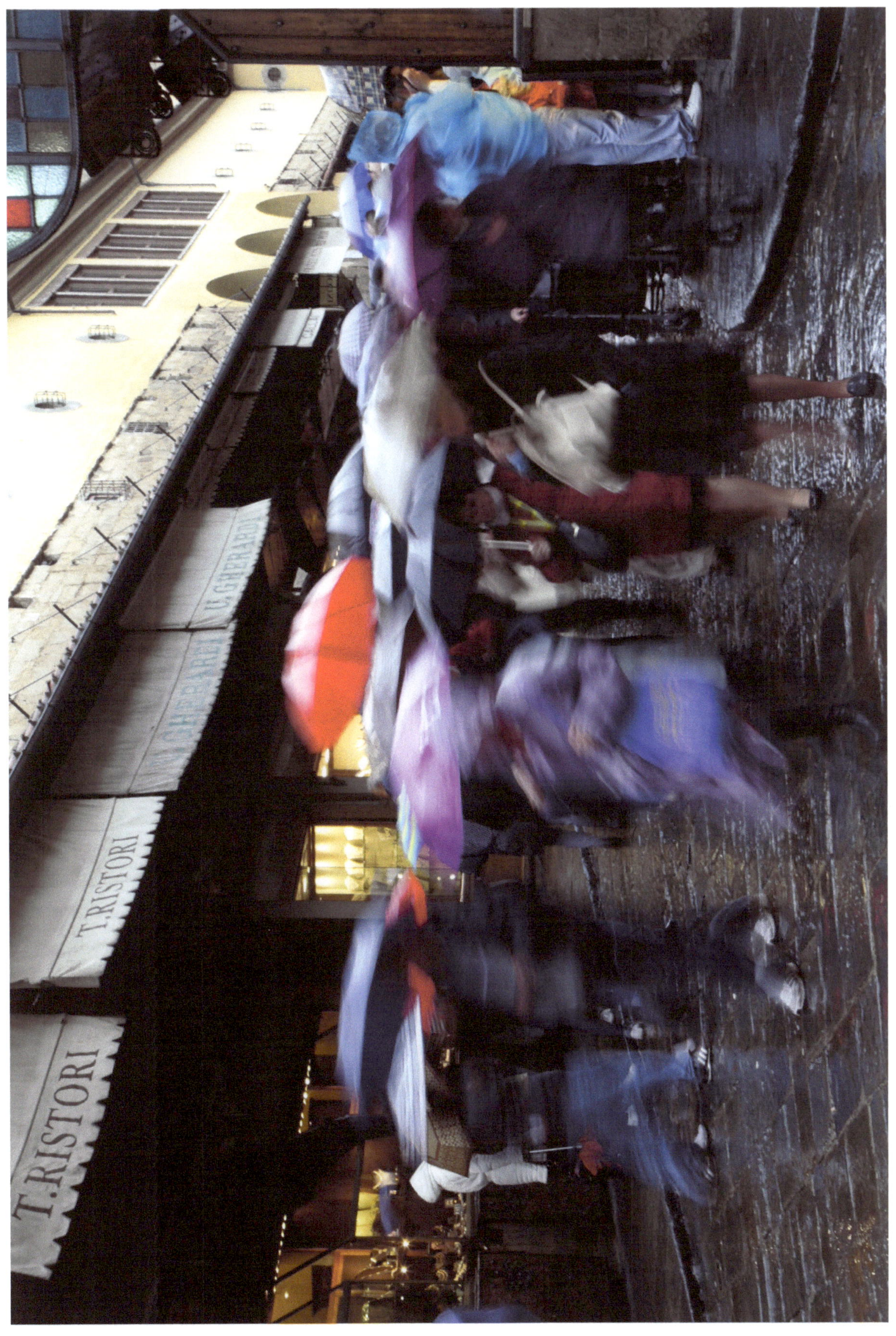

Very British weather on the Ponte Vecchio, Florence in autumn.

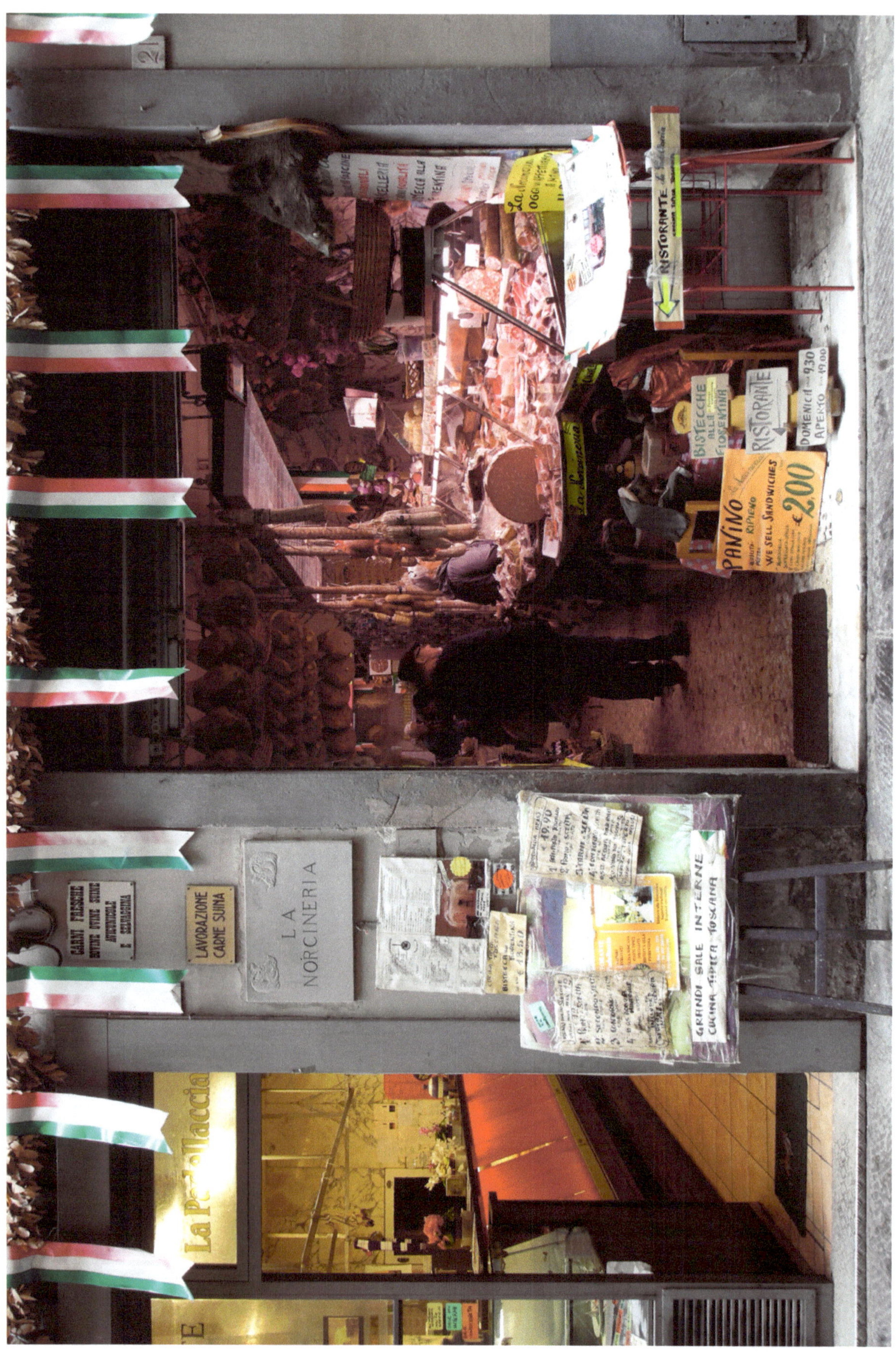

Just liked the contrast between these two shops in a quiet Florence back street.

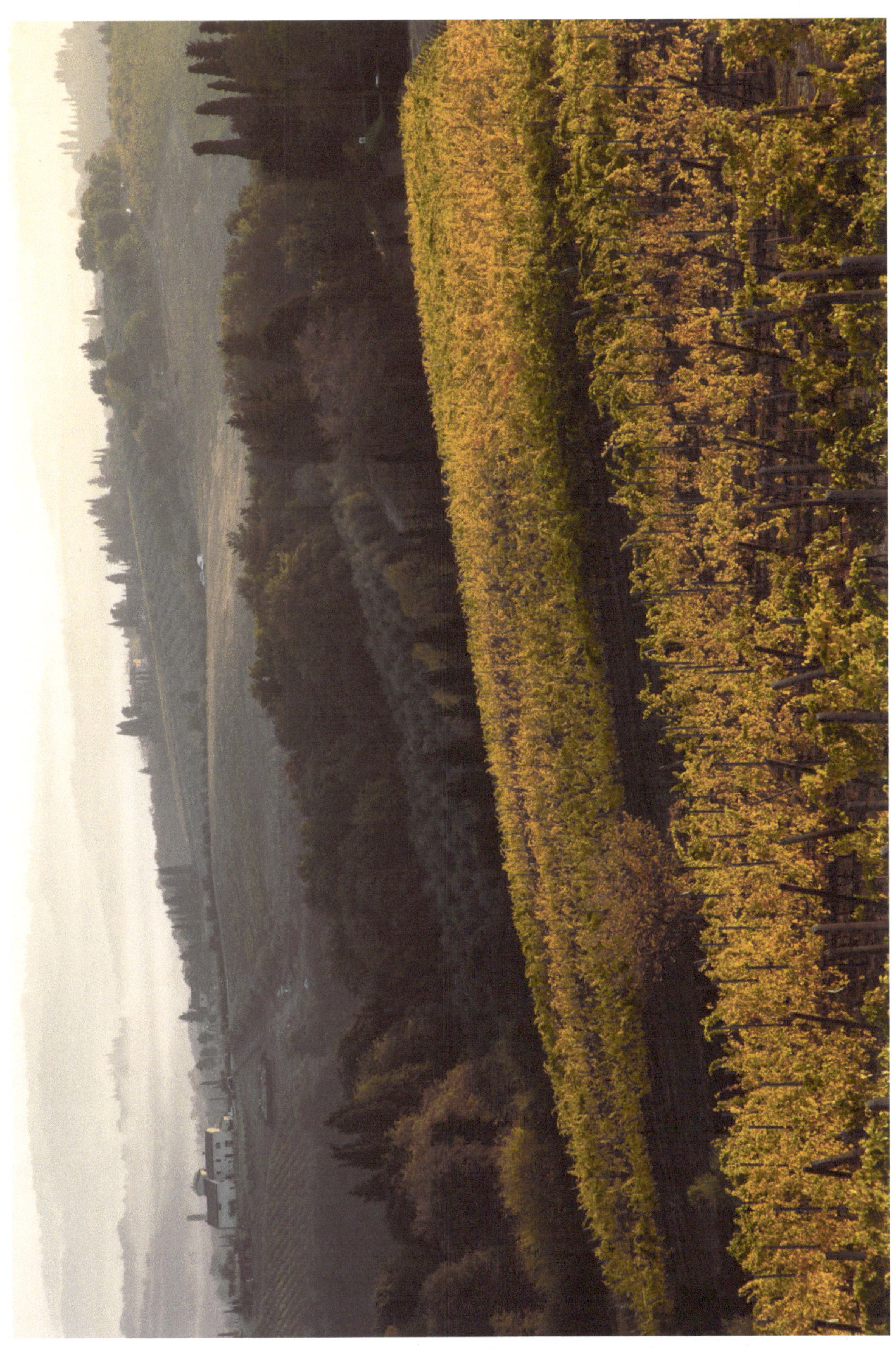

Beautiful early autumnal light in the country between Peccioli and Volterra.

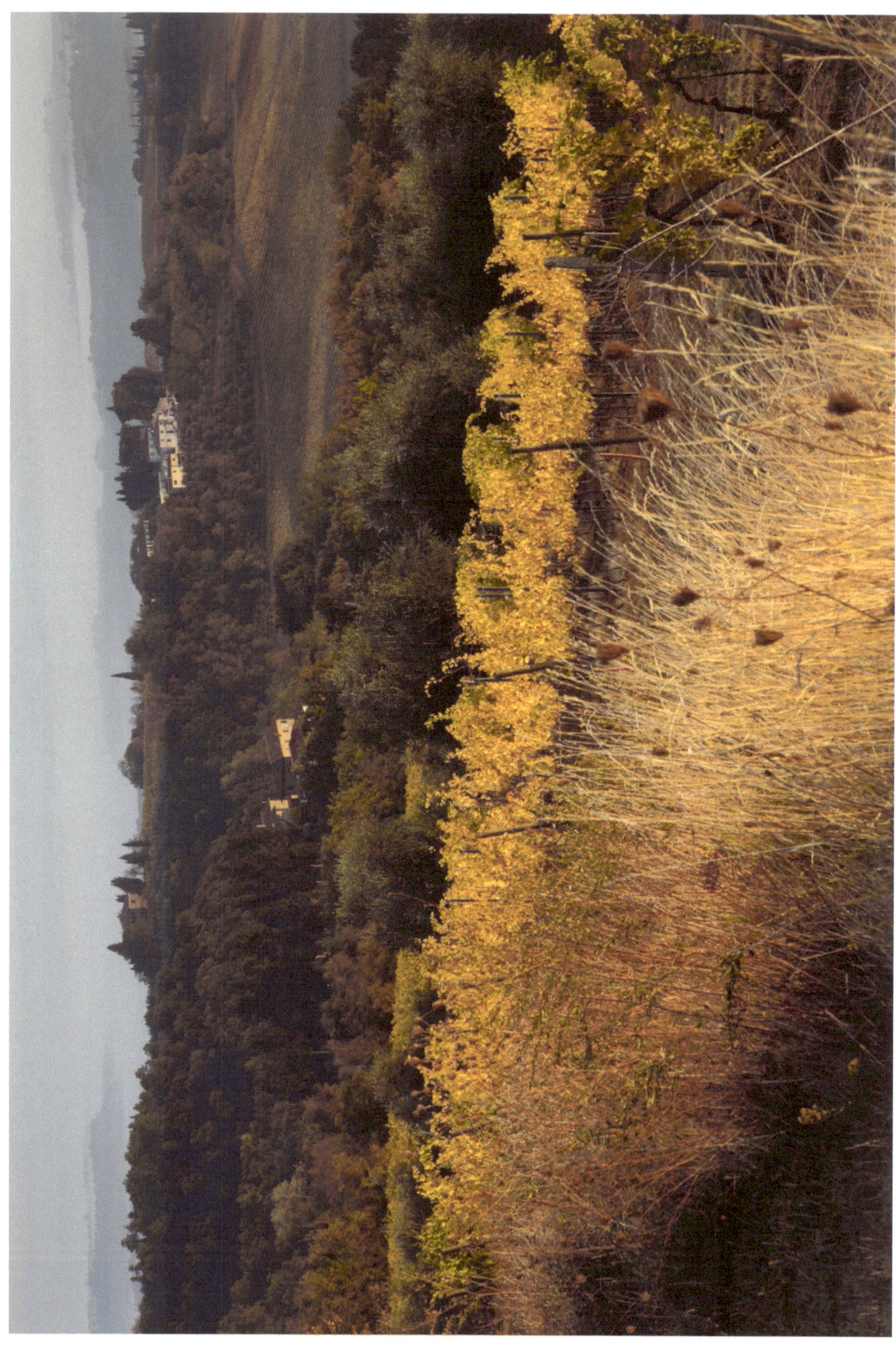

With light and colours like this it's just too difficult to stop taking shots.

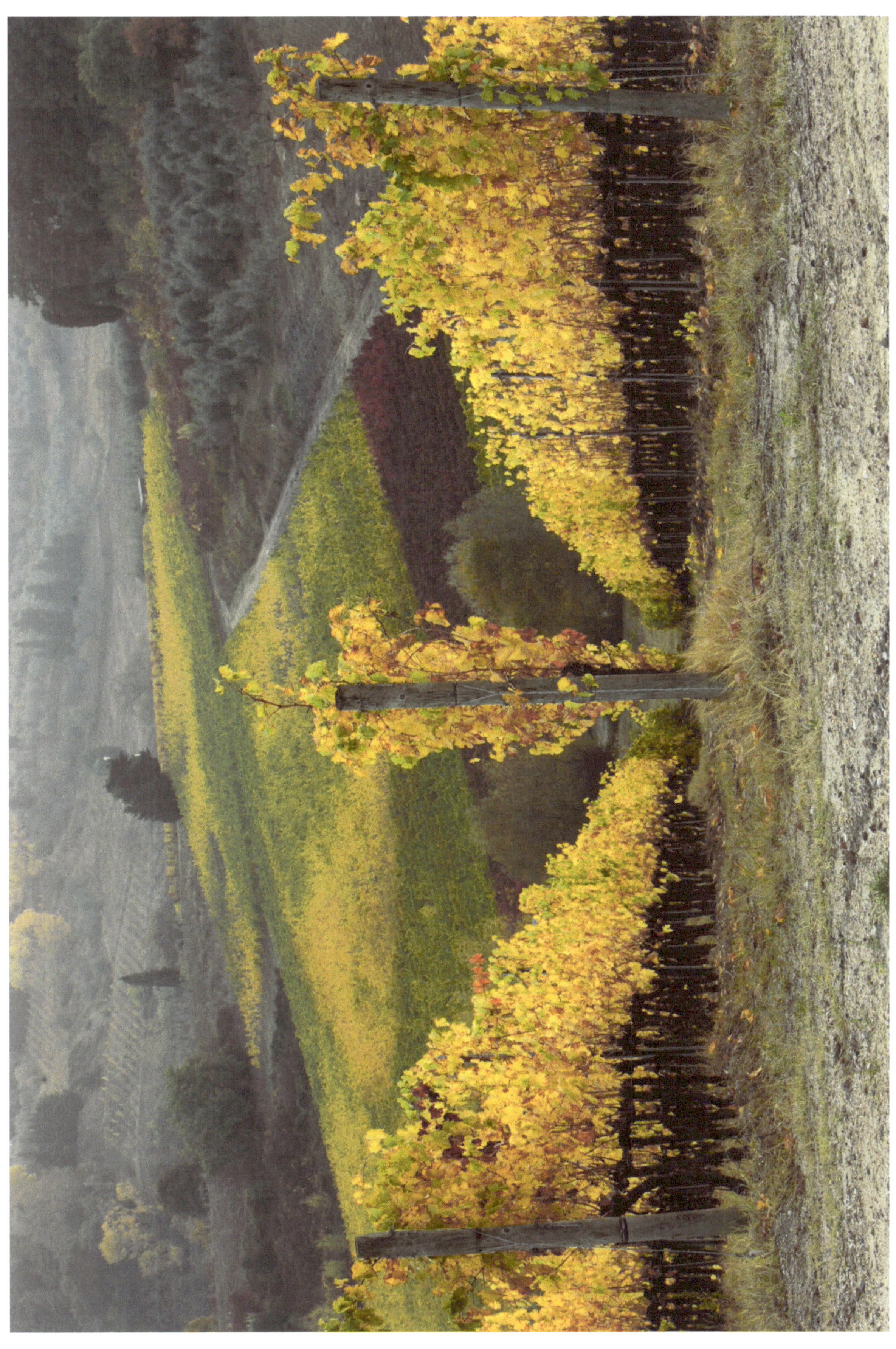

Autumn has to be my favourite time of year for landscape photography.

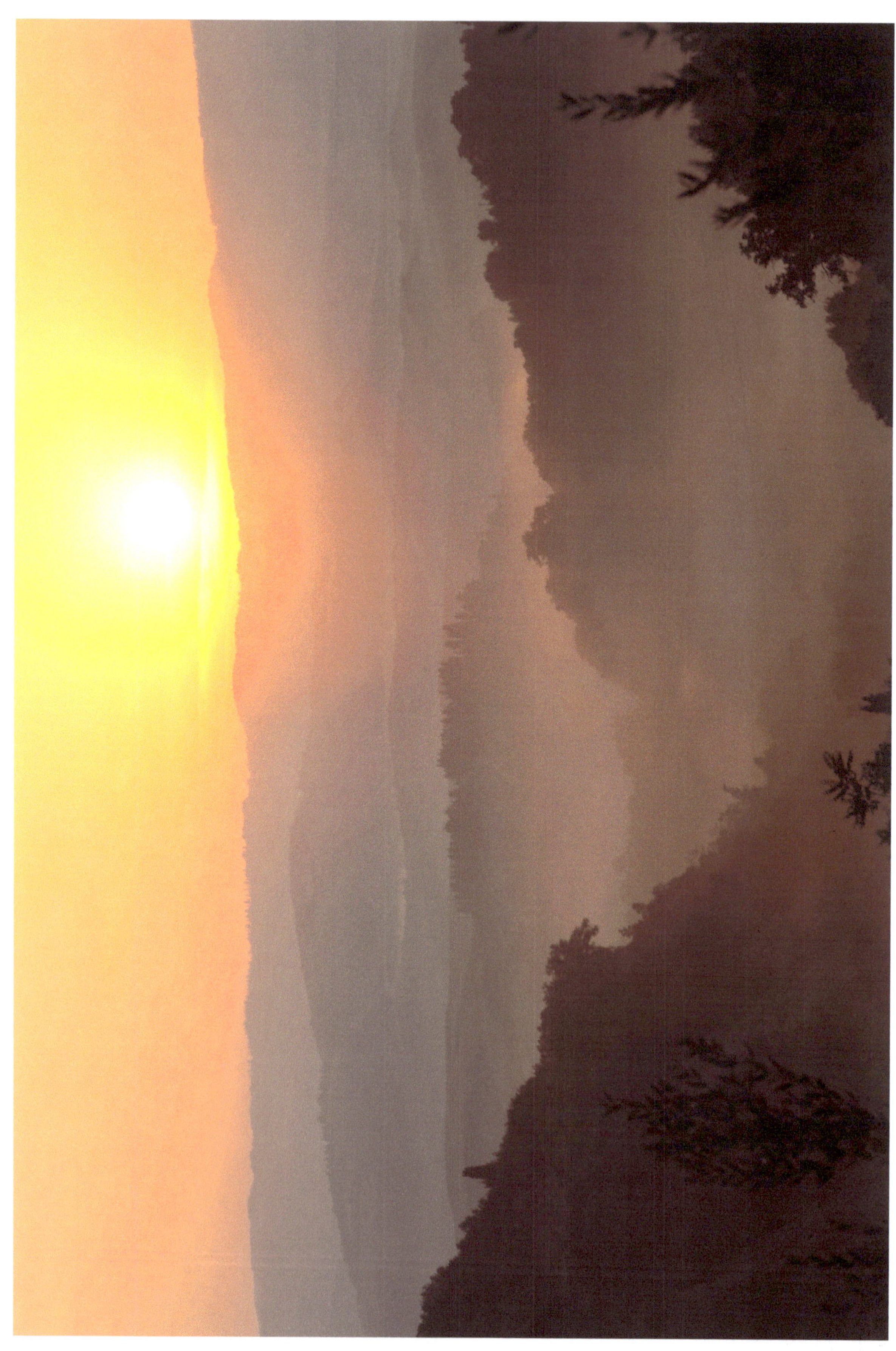

A roadside stop coming south into the outskirts of Volterra to catch sunrise.

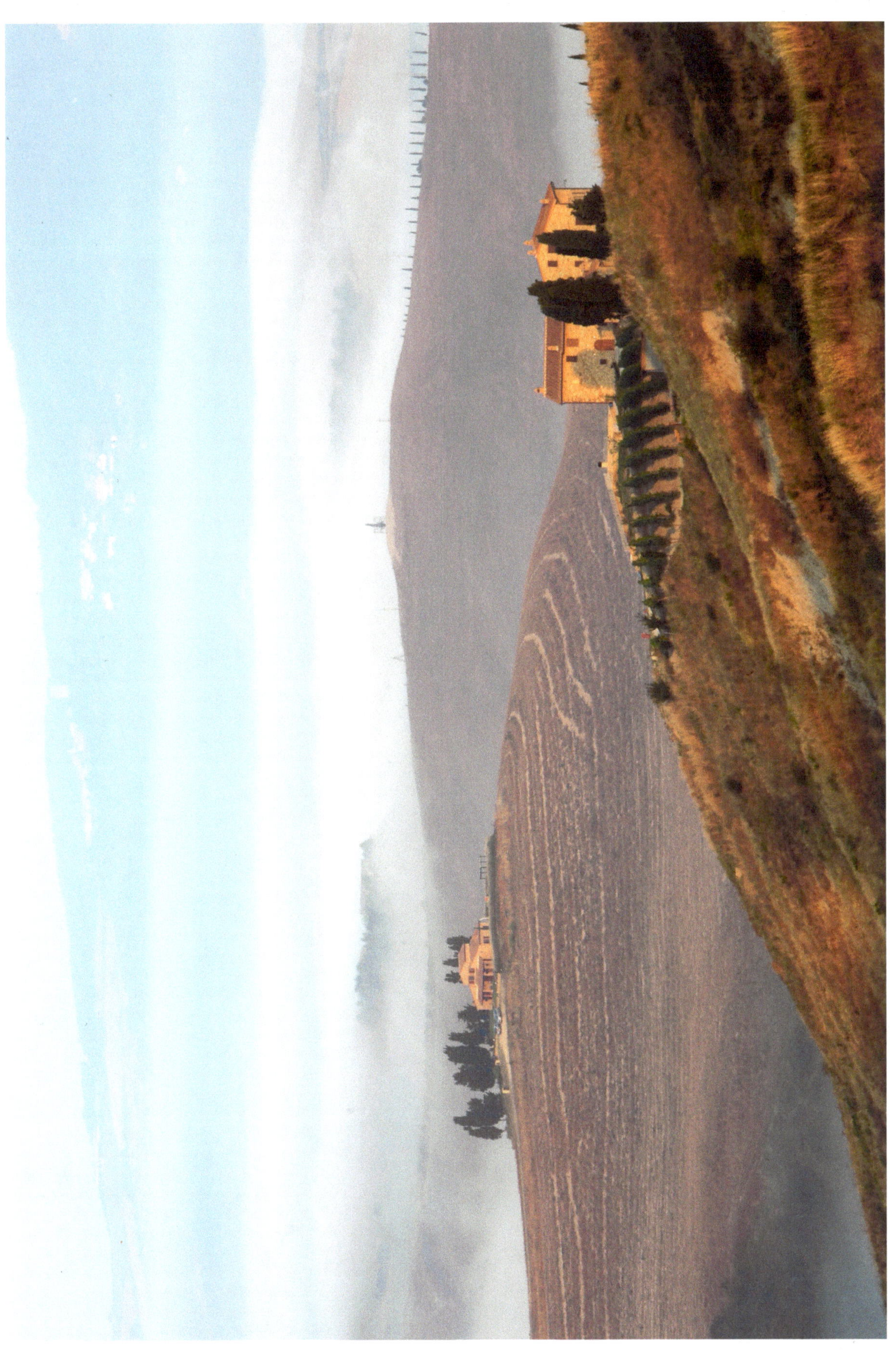

The other side of the road looking west a few minutes after the sun had risen.

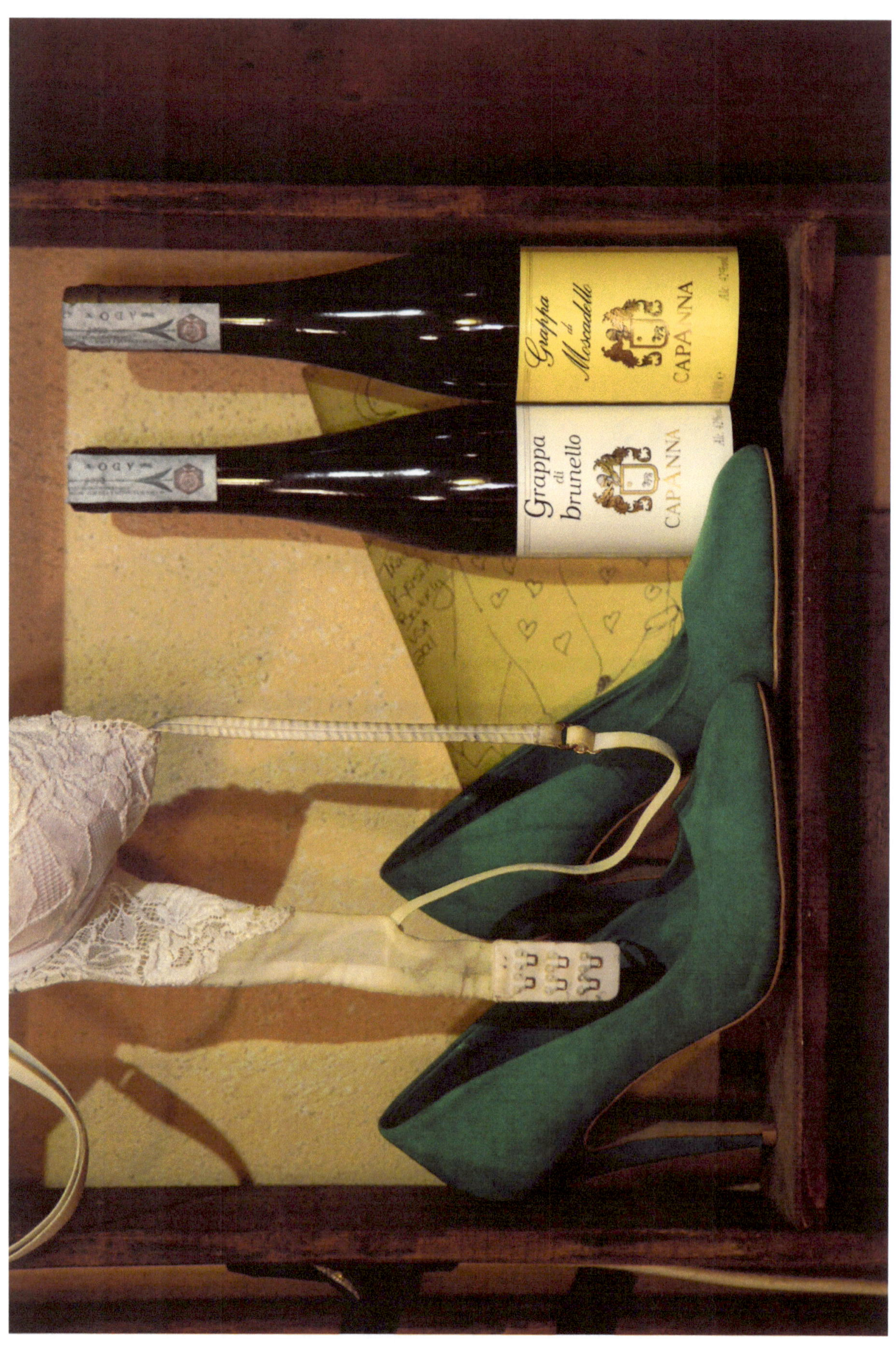

Curious wall art at La Vena di Vino bar in Volterra – well worth a visit.

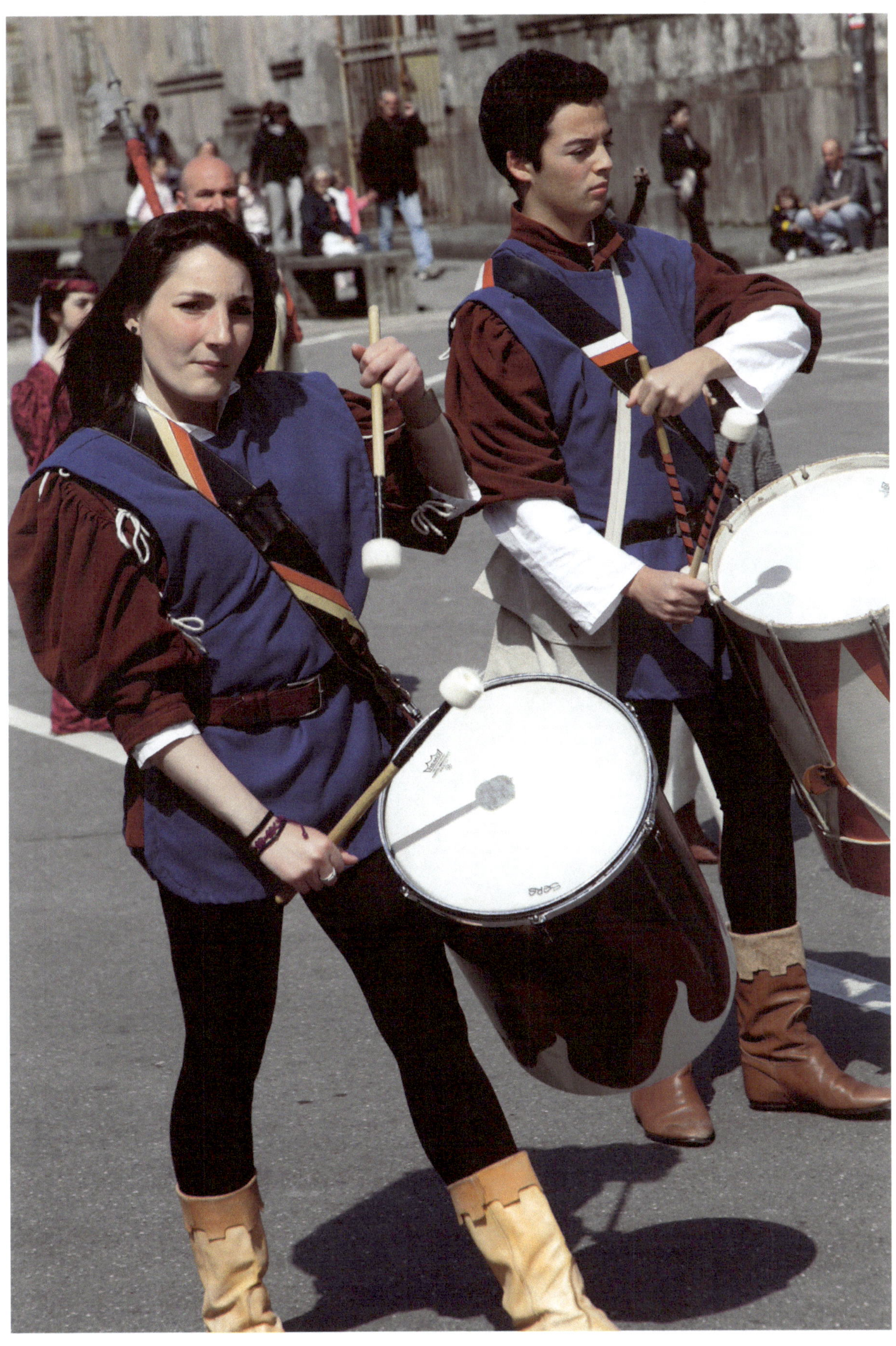

One of many traditional ceremonies in Tuscany, this being in Montalchino.

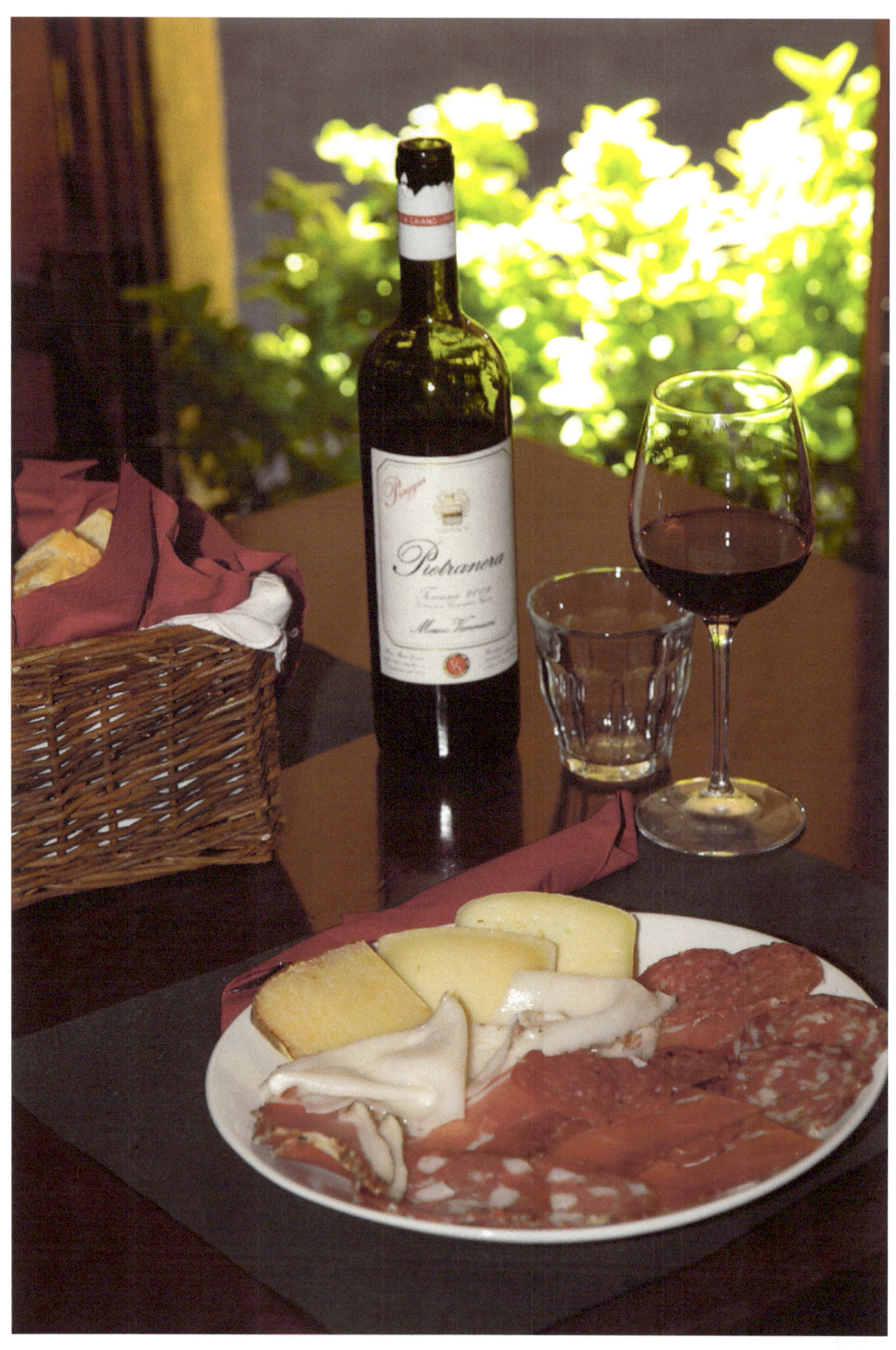

Inside Enoteca Scali in Volterra, a must-stop if you like your wine as the owner is incredibly knowledgeable and really helpful.

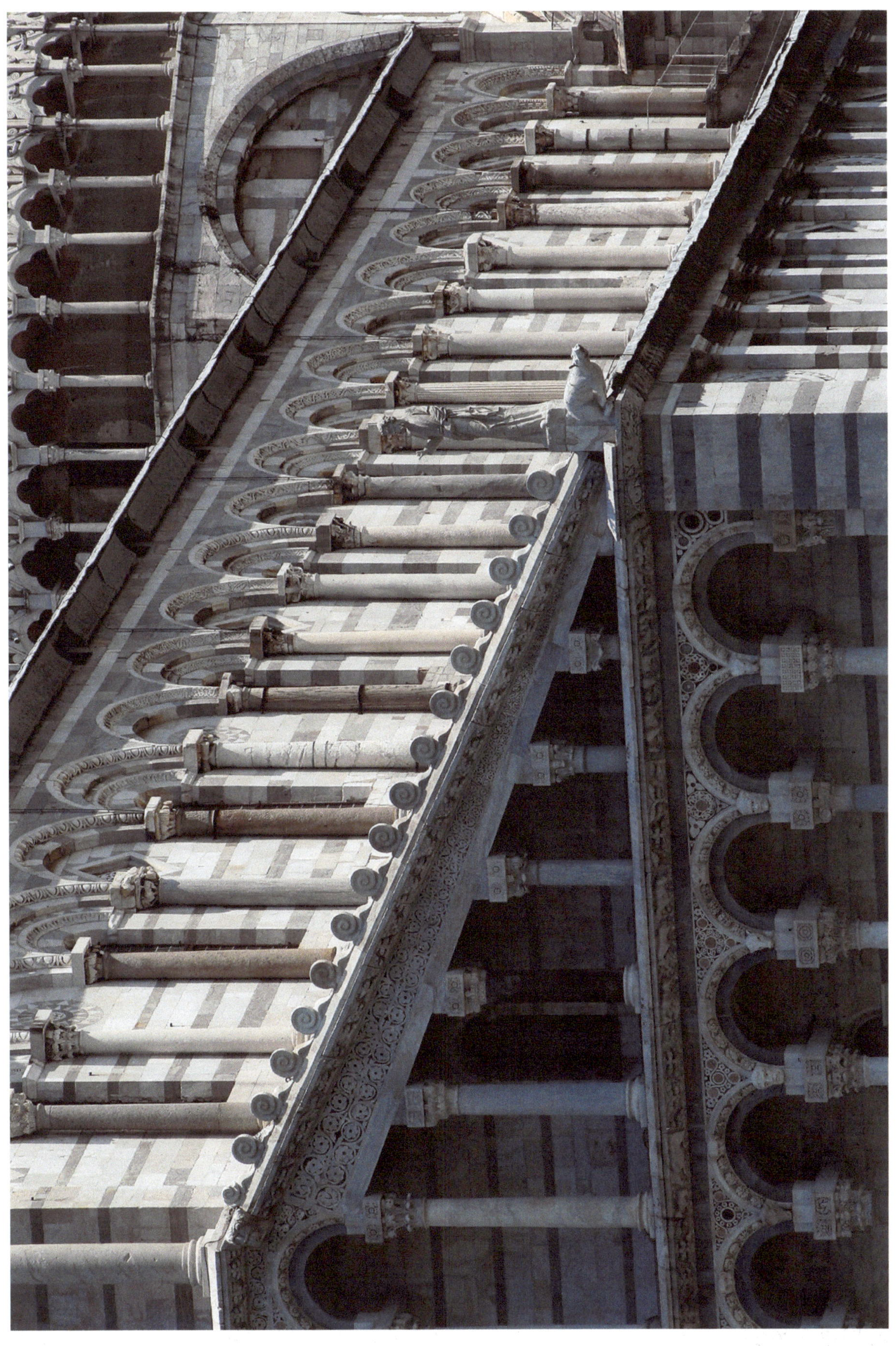

Taken by the lines on this zoom shot of the Duomo in Pisa.

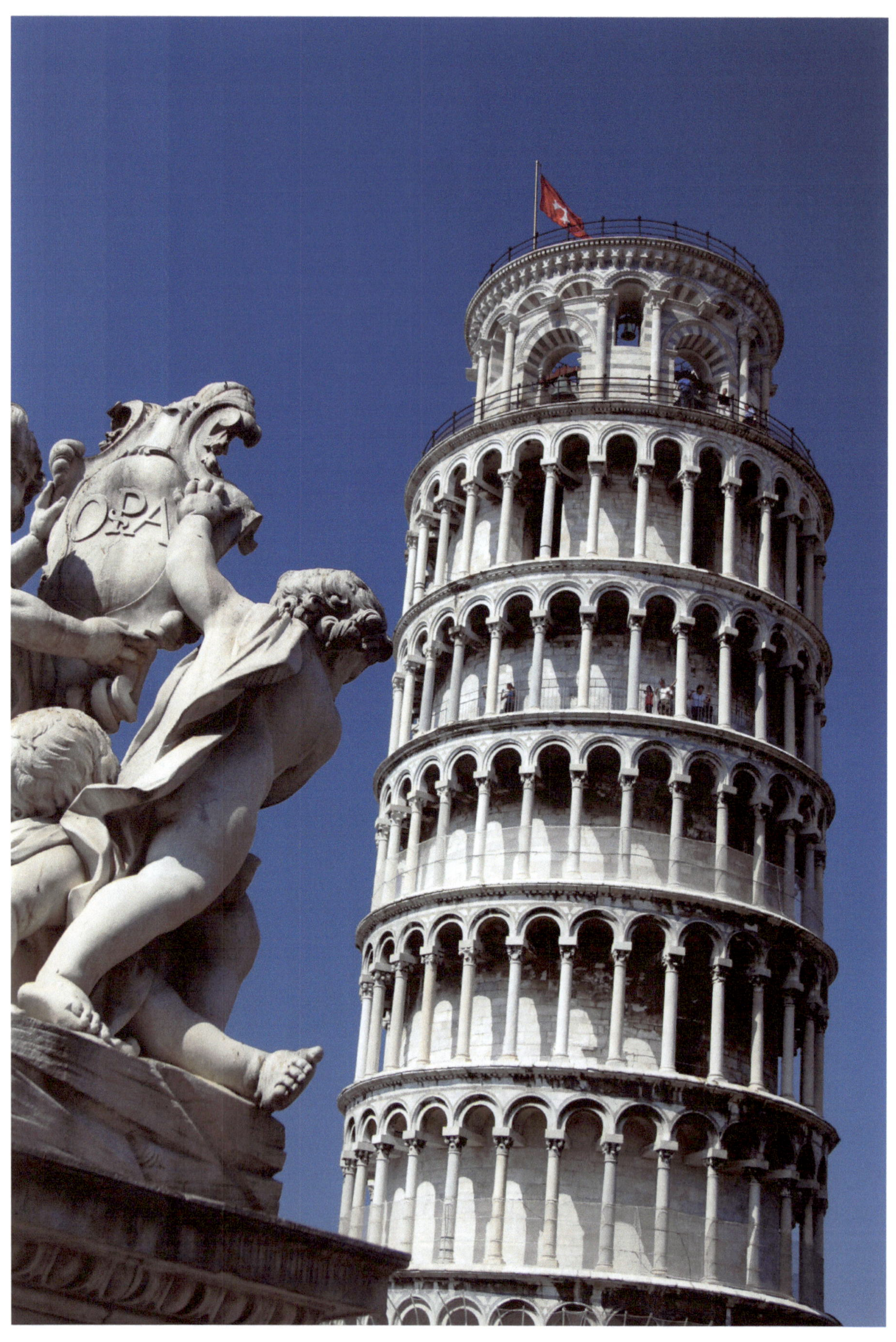

What makes this shot to me is the contrast between the red flag and the blue sky – little things that make a big difference even at the Leaning Tower.

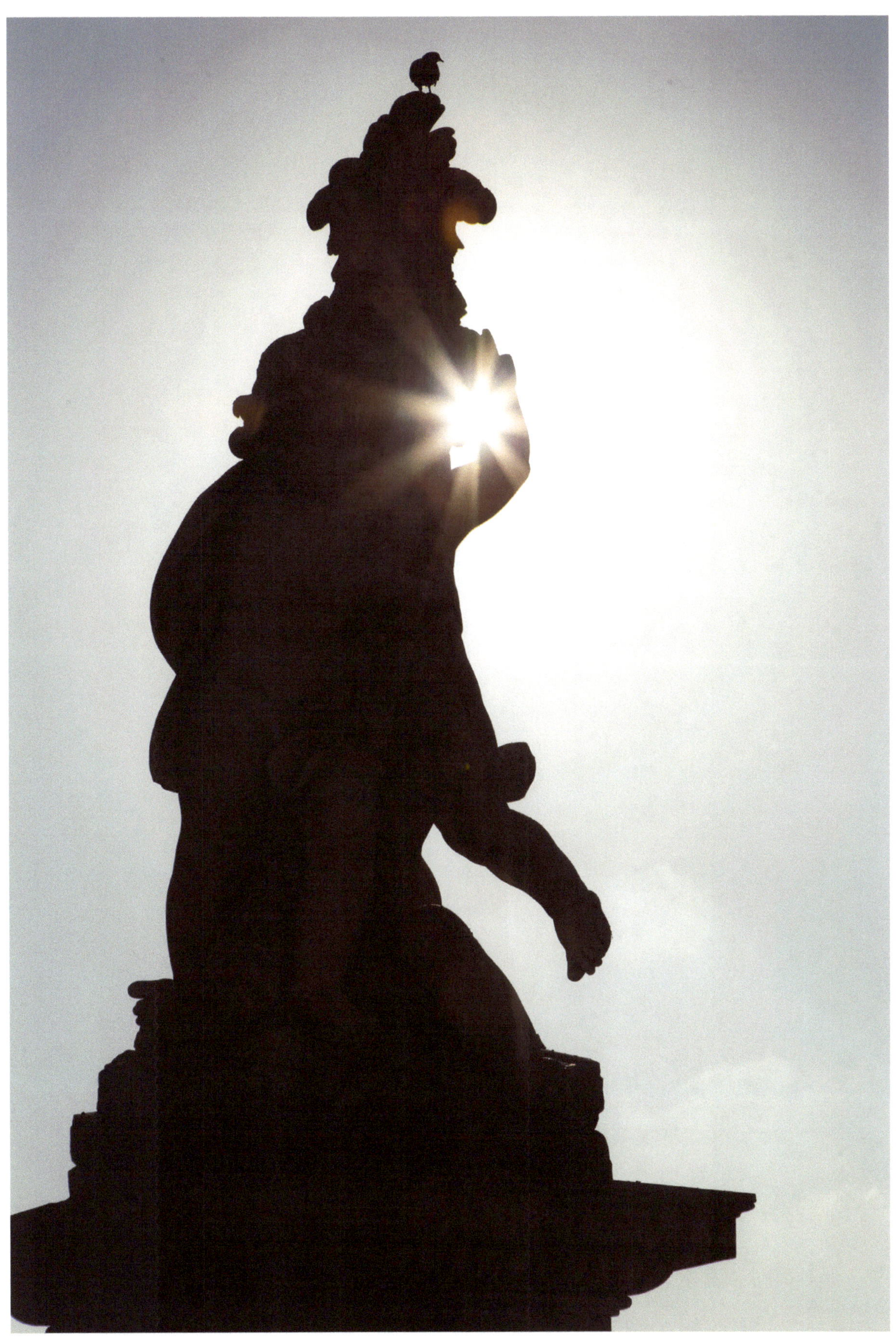

Using a statue near El Torre Pendente di Pisa to shoot into the sun and avoid flare.

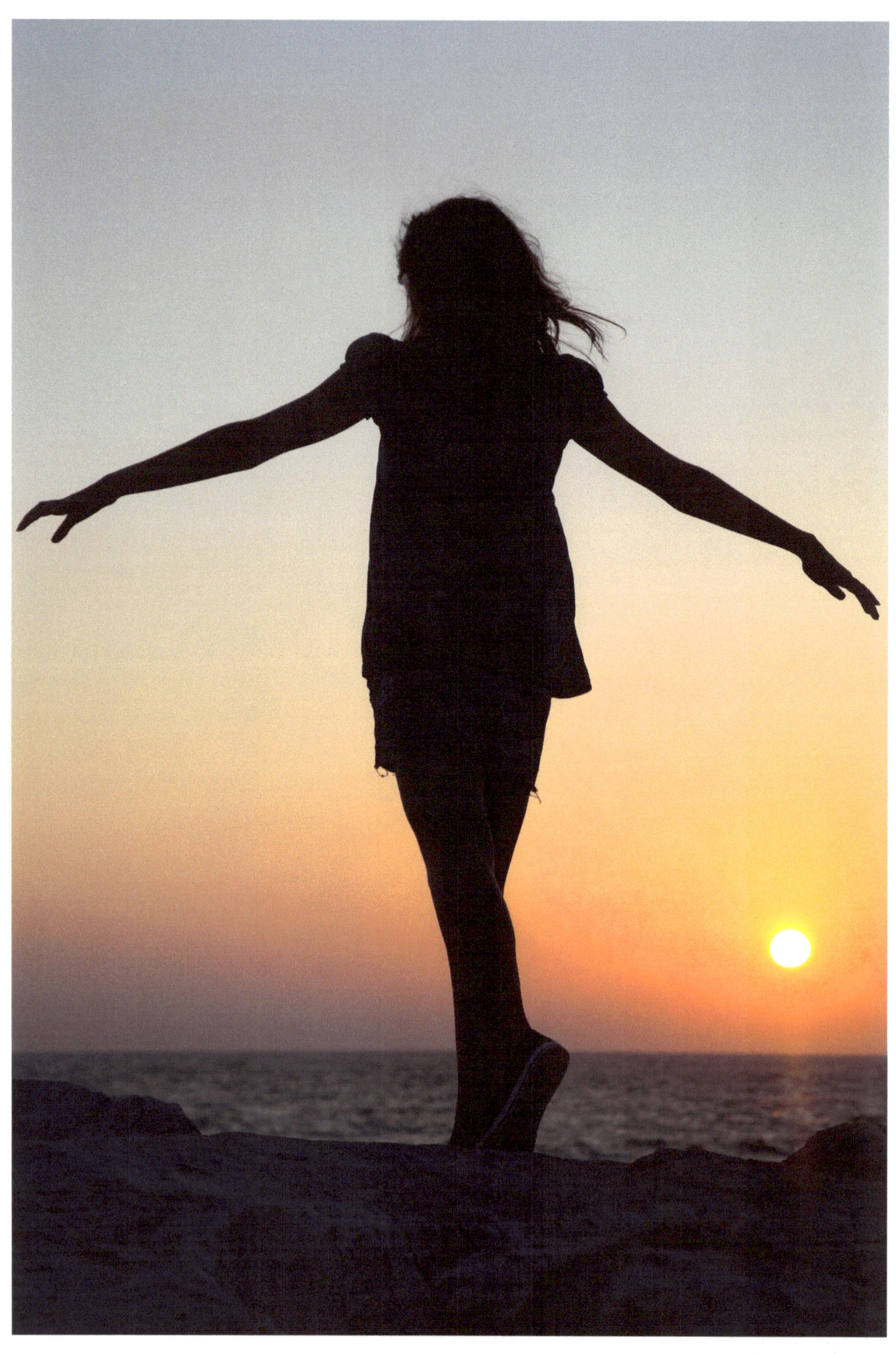

Sunset down on the waterfront at Marina di Pisa.

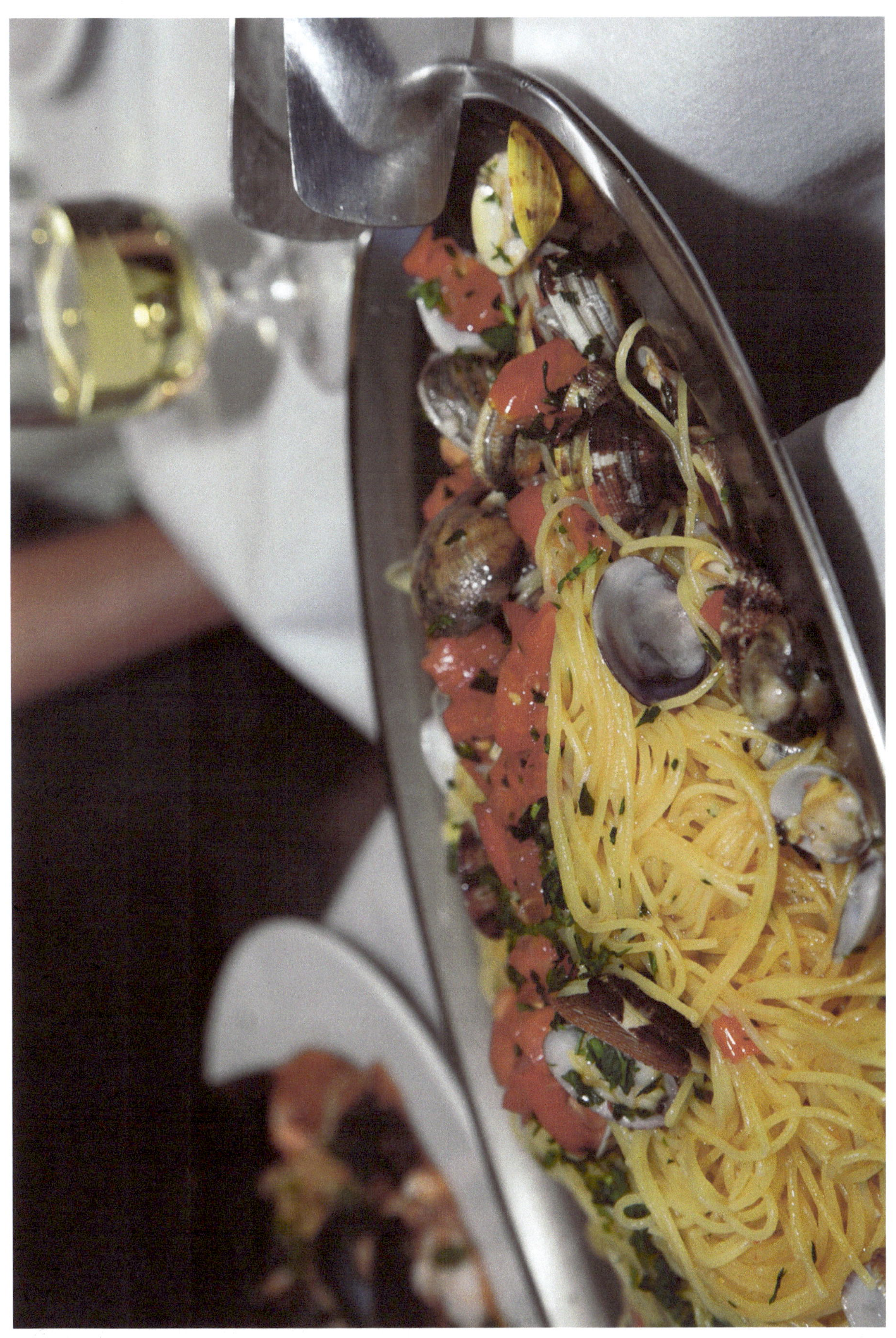

The best spaghetti vongole I've ever tasted at a roadside restaurant by a roundabout between Pisa and Marina di Pisa.

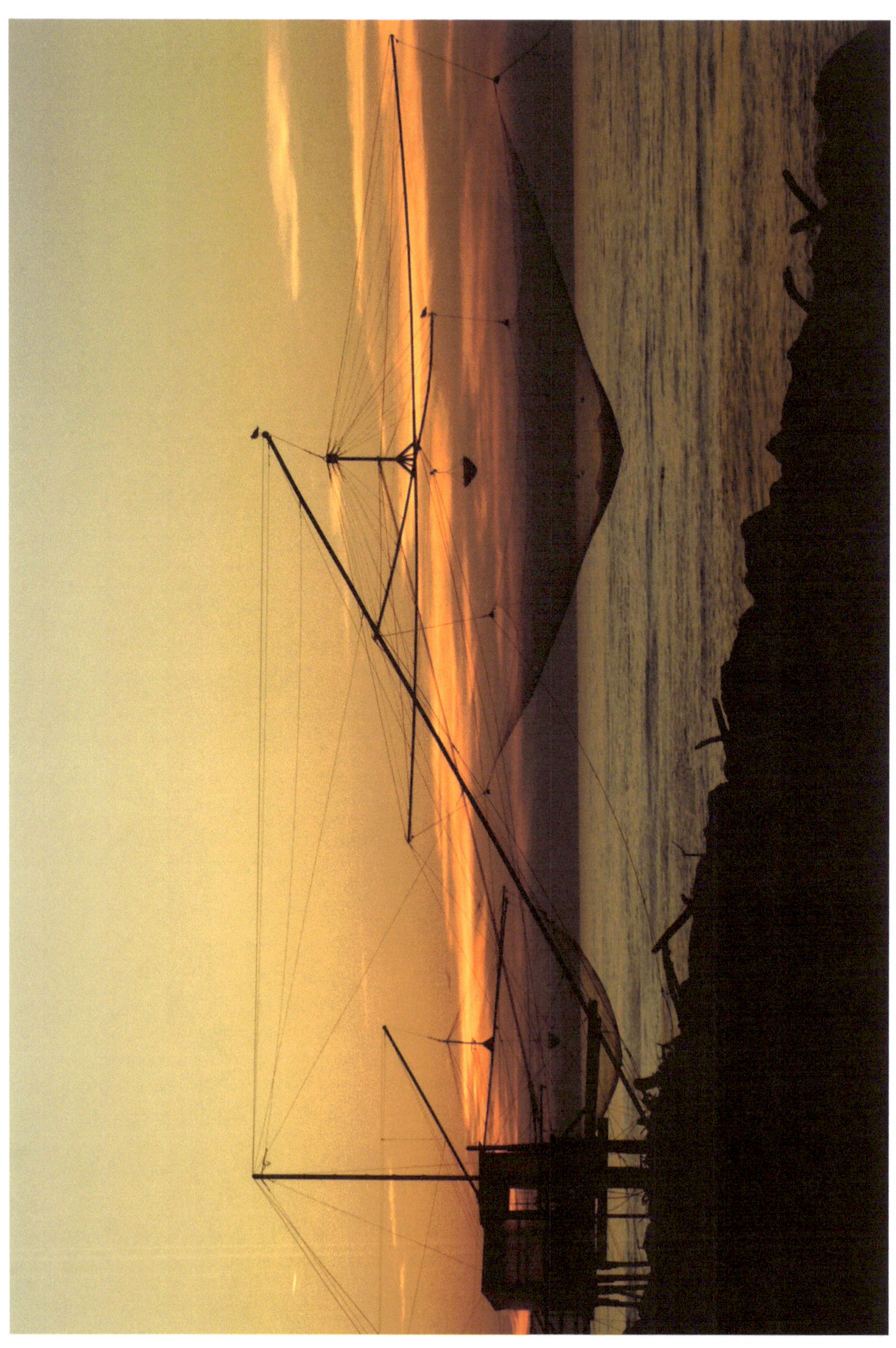

Fishing activity all quiet as the sun goes down over the Arno River, Marina di Pisa.

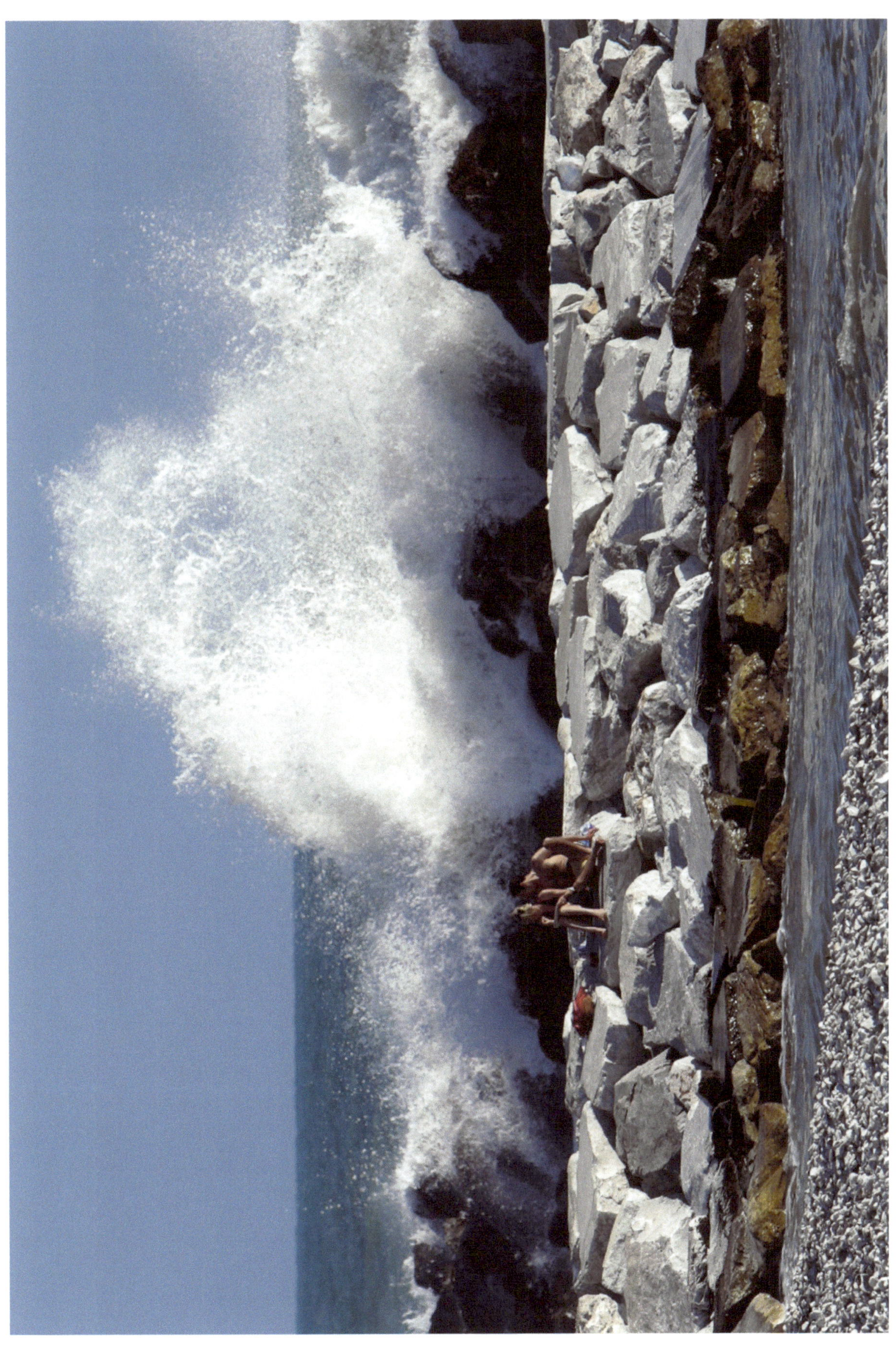

Sunbathers on the Marina di Pisa water front in danger of getting very wet!

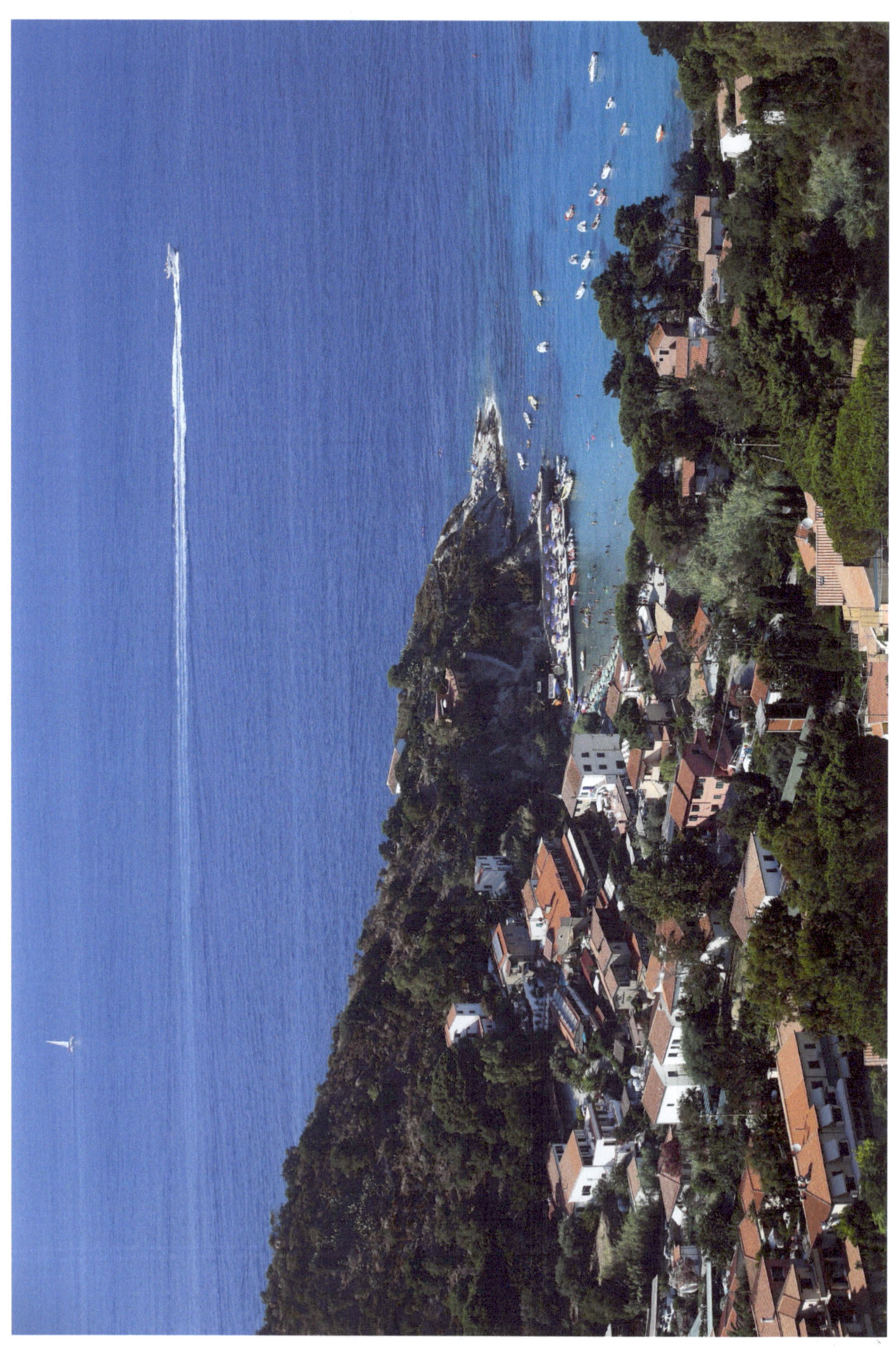

Looking down from the hill road to Marciana Marina on the coast of Elba.

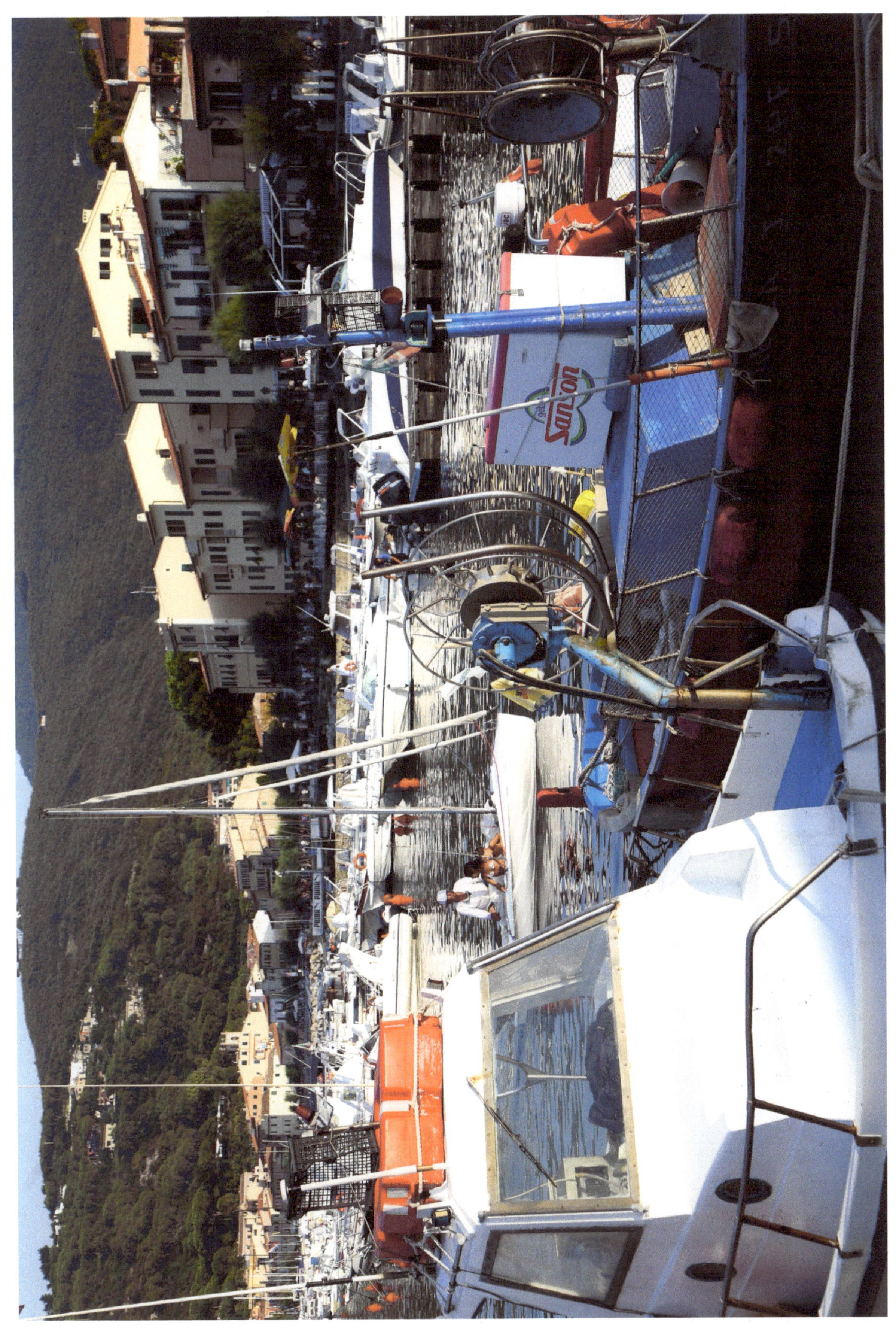

Busy, yet somehow peaceful waterfront at Marciana Marina.

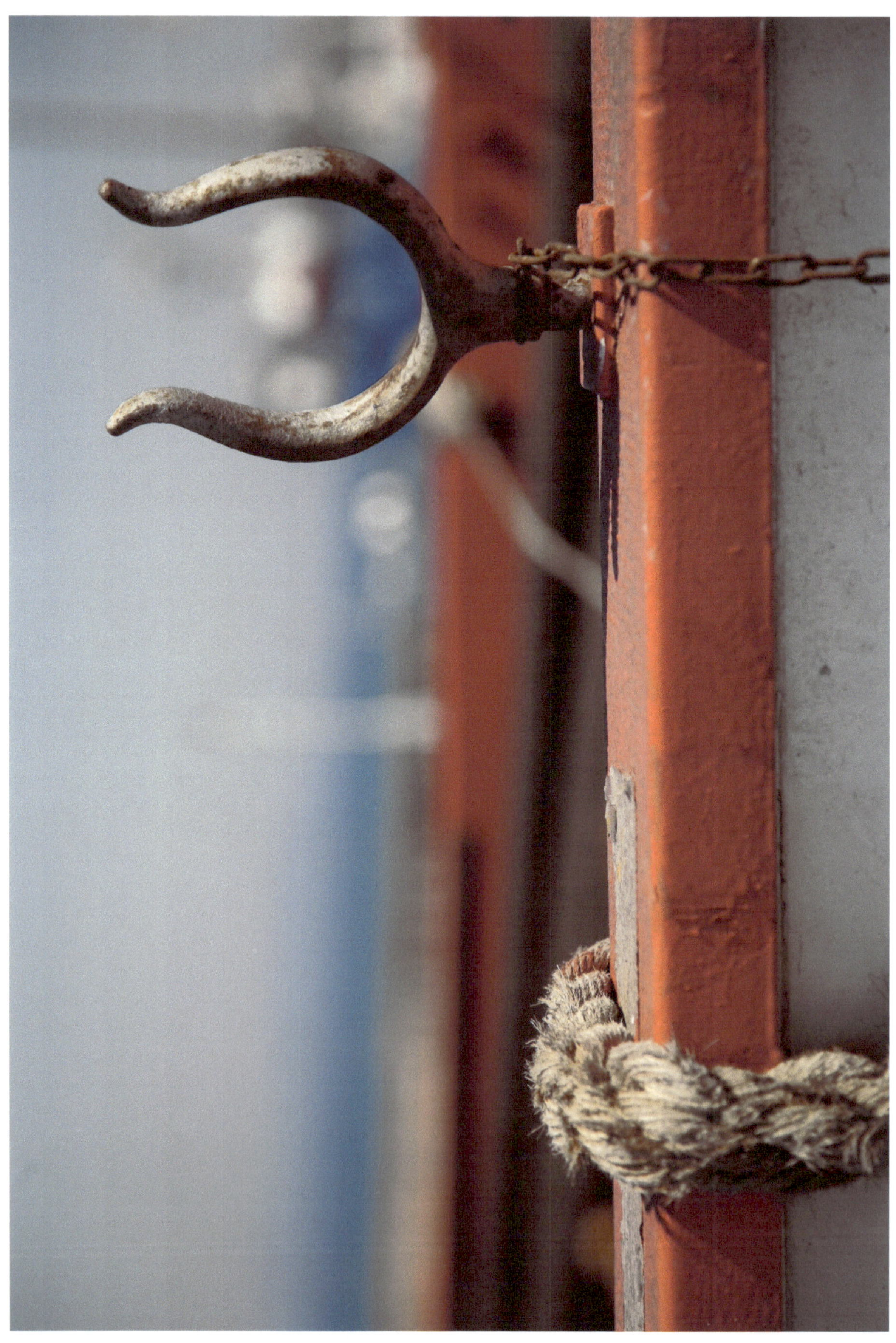

Quirky close-up among the fishing boats at Marciana Marina.

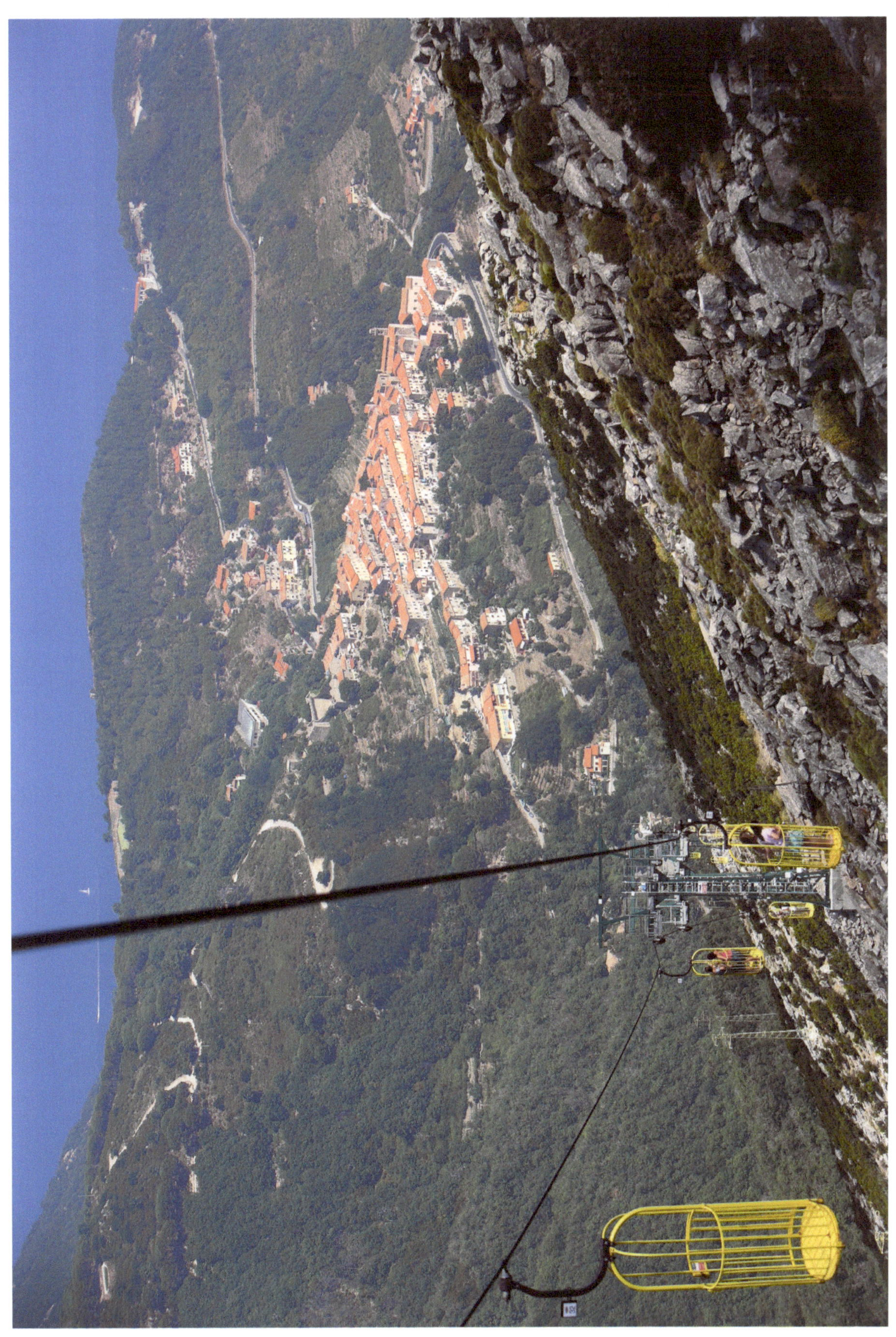

Unusual method of transport to the high point in Elba.

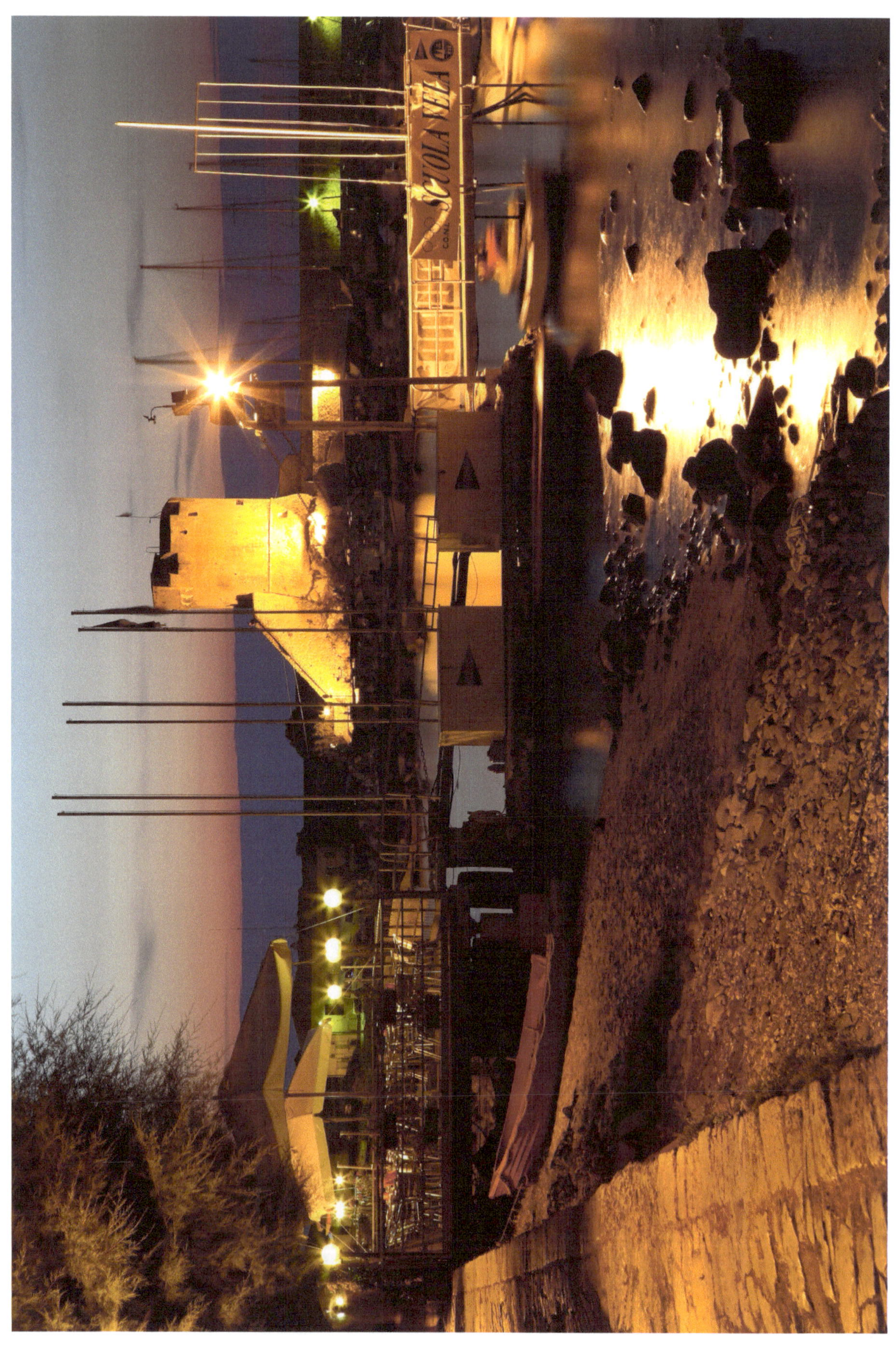

Tranquil early evening waterfront at Marciana Marina, before the evening rush.

Long exposure to get the movement at this lively evening street market in Marciana Marina.

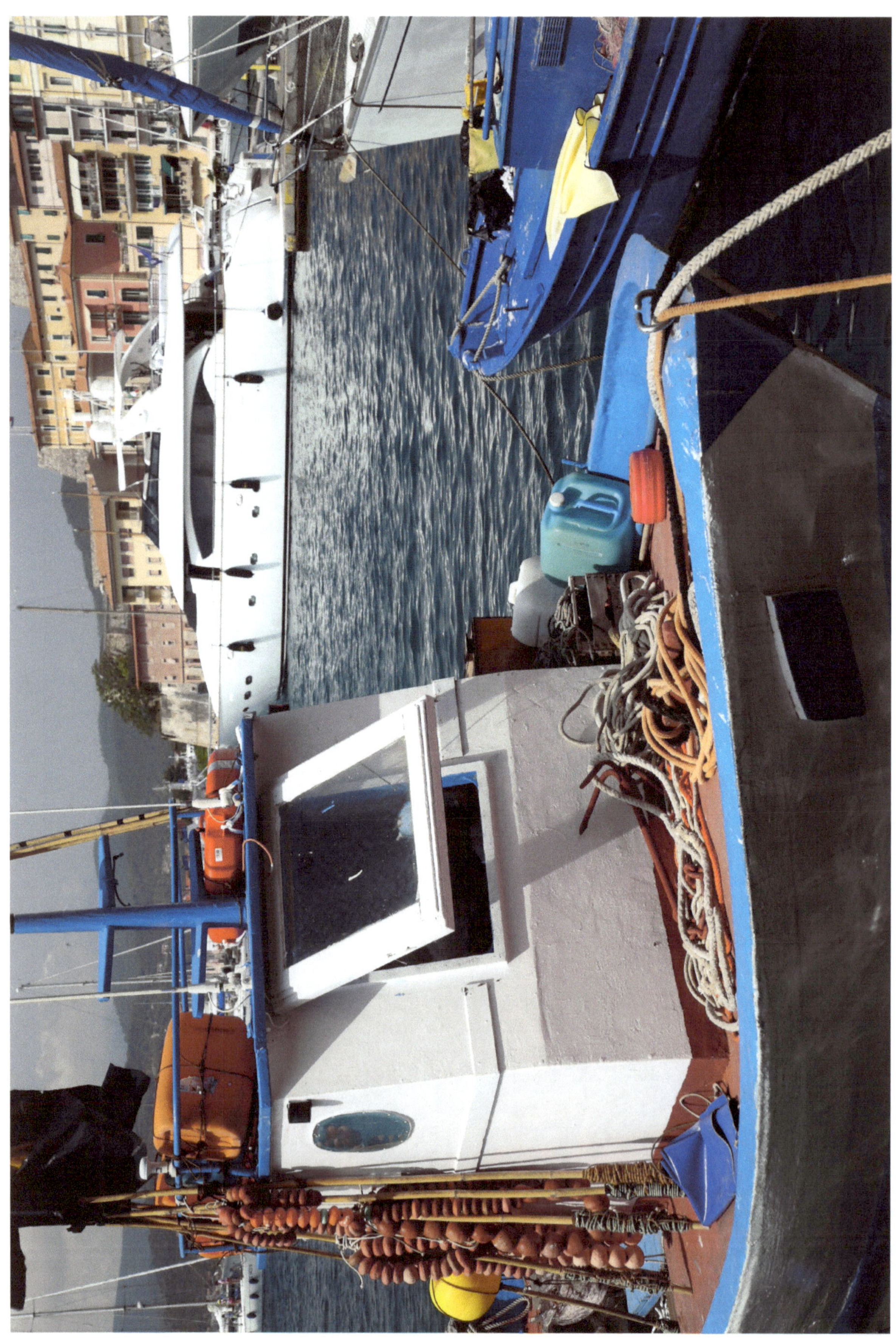

Loved the contrast between the humble fishing boat and the millionaire's 'gin palace' behind at Portoferraio, Elba.

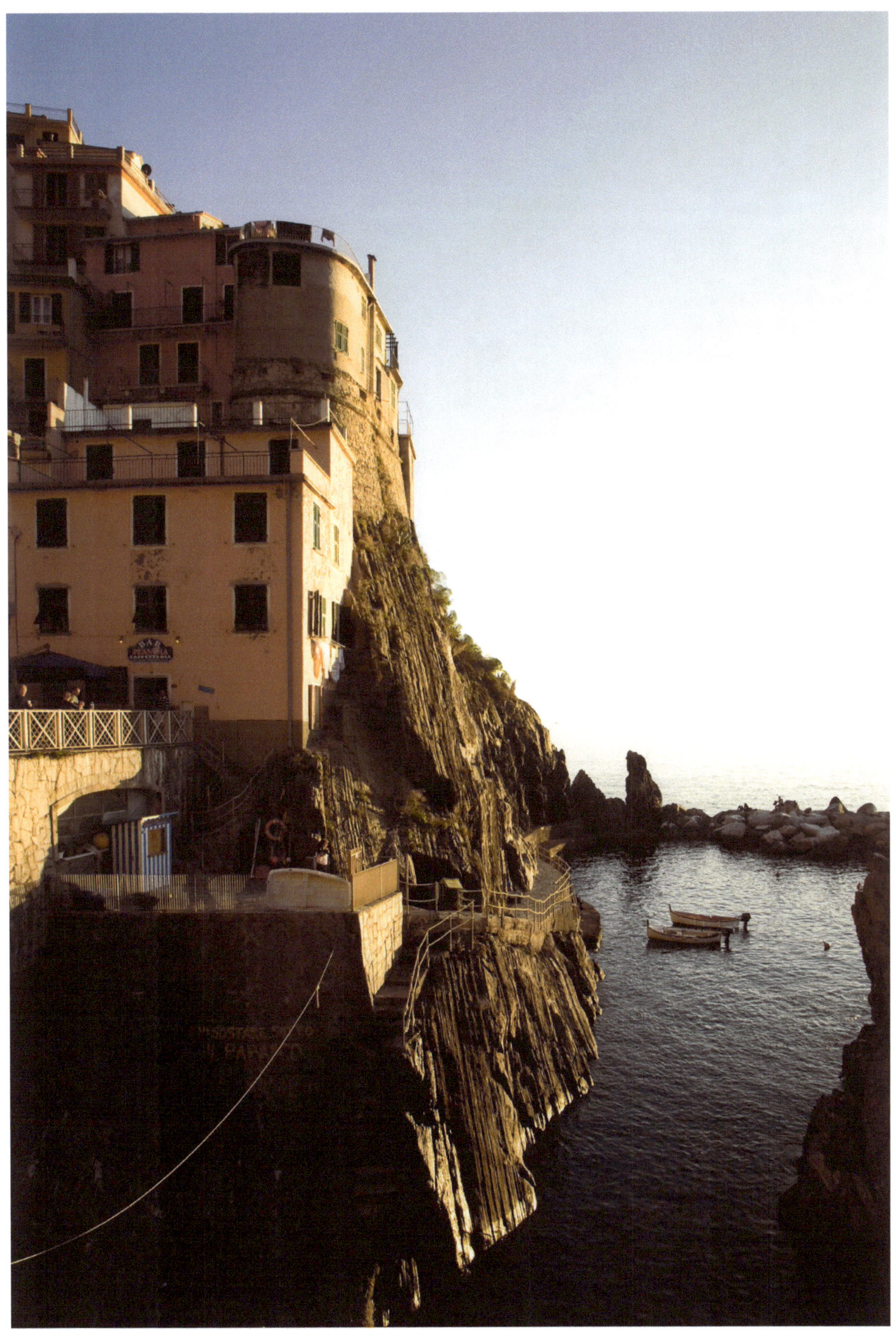

Manarola waterfront in Cinque Terre.

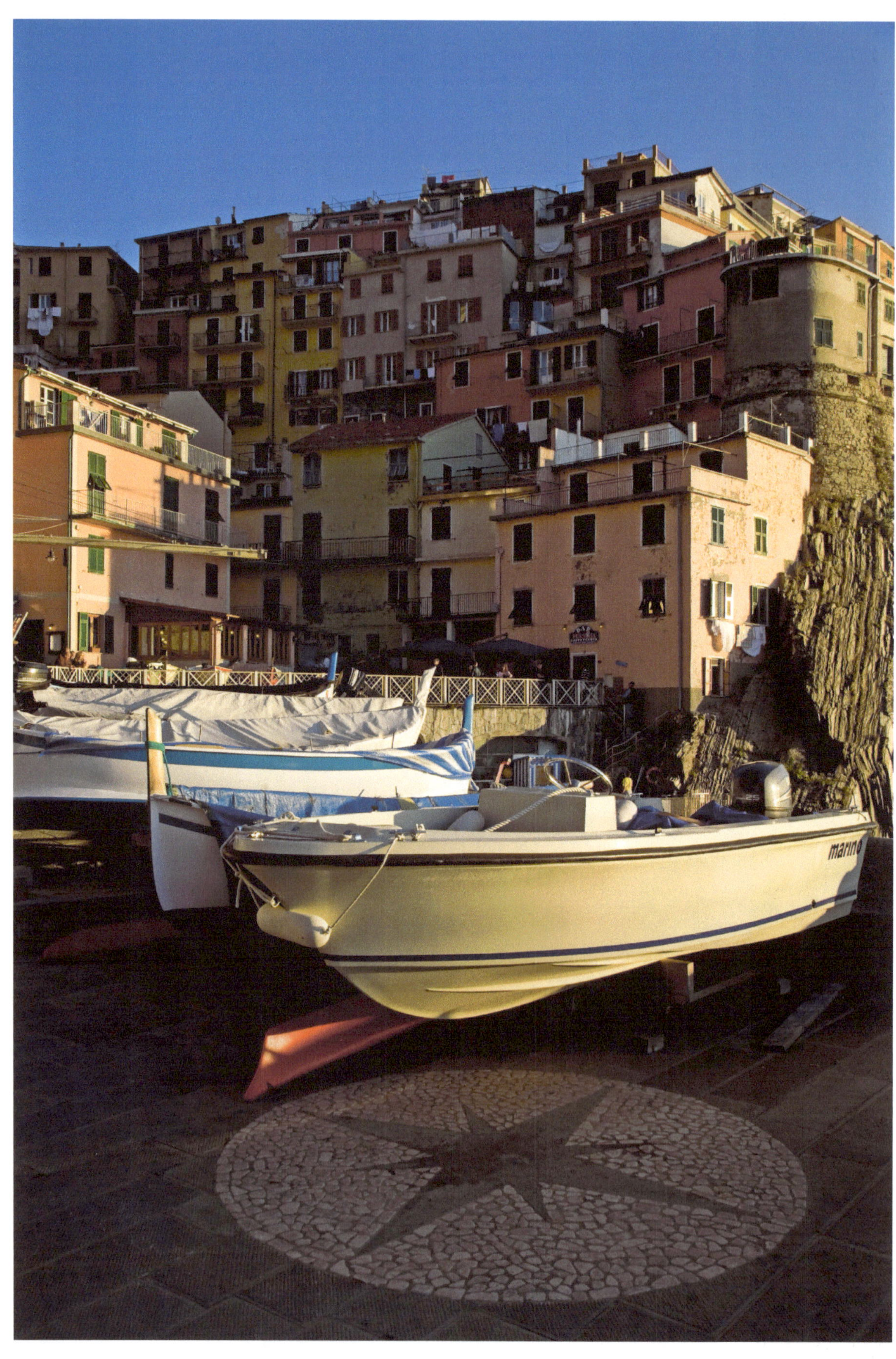

Warm evening light on the picturesque town of Manarola.

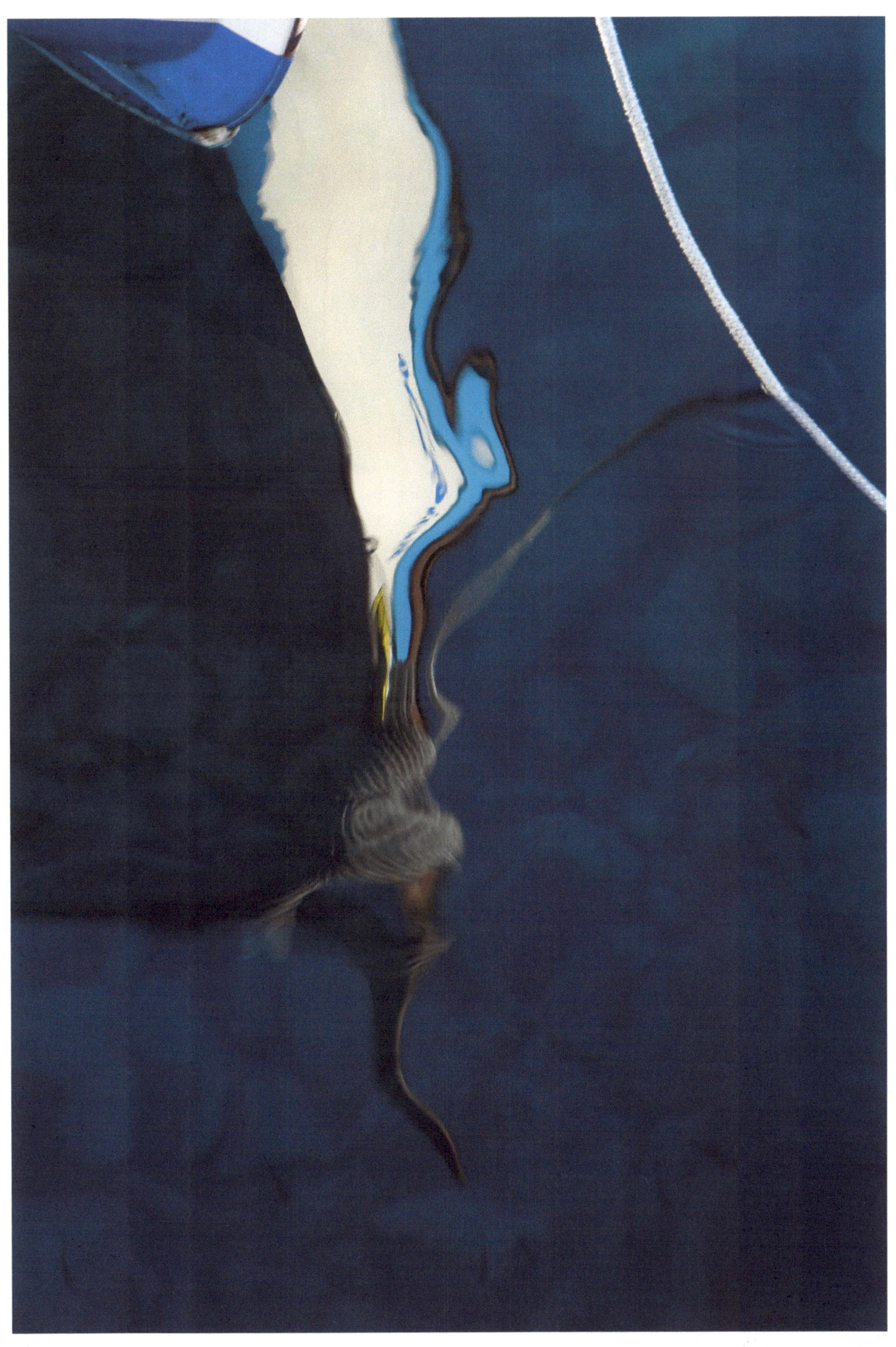

Abstract reflections in Vernazza harbour, Cinque Terre.

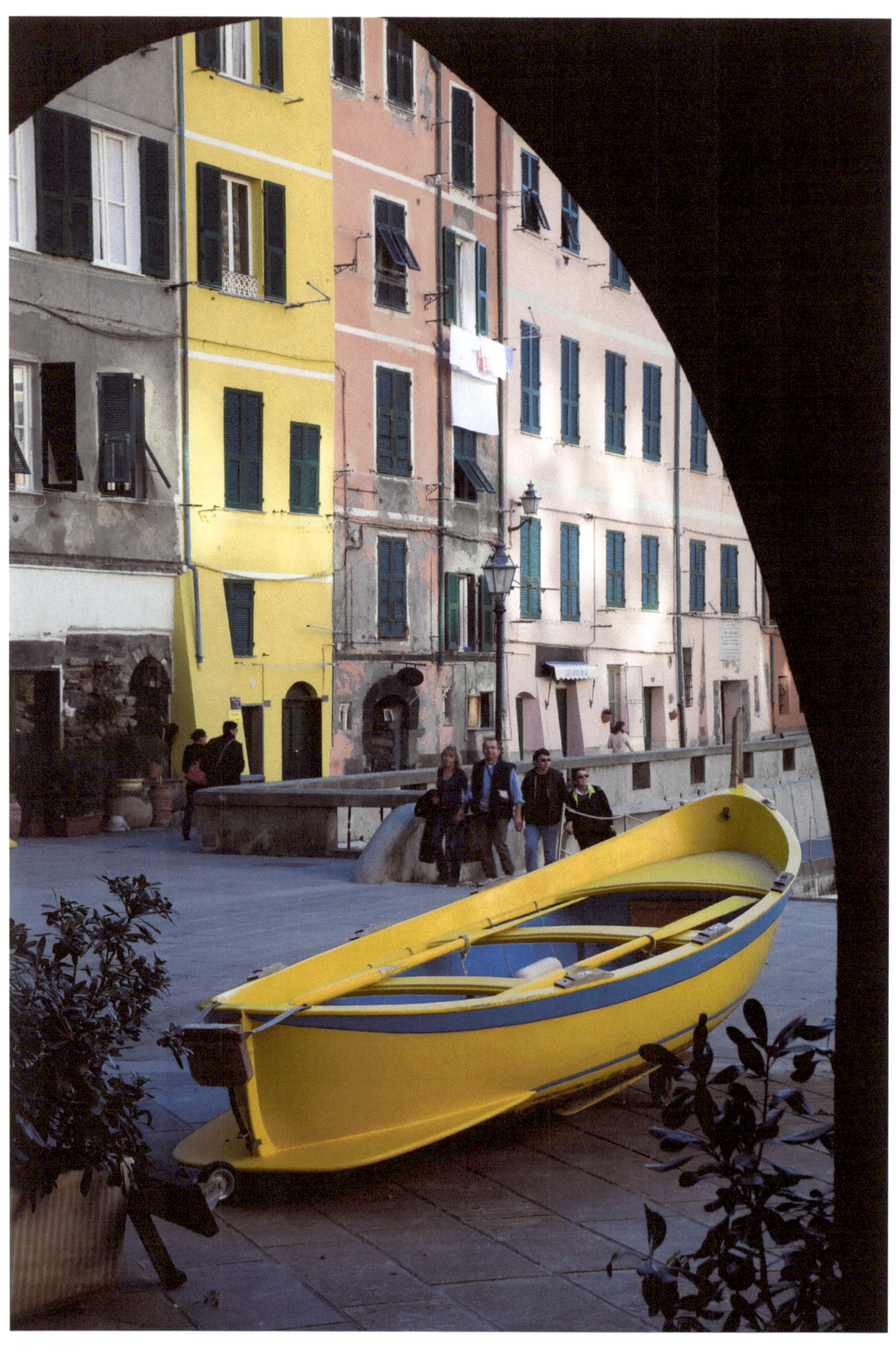

Off season November shot at Riomaggiore, Cinque Terre.

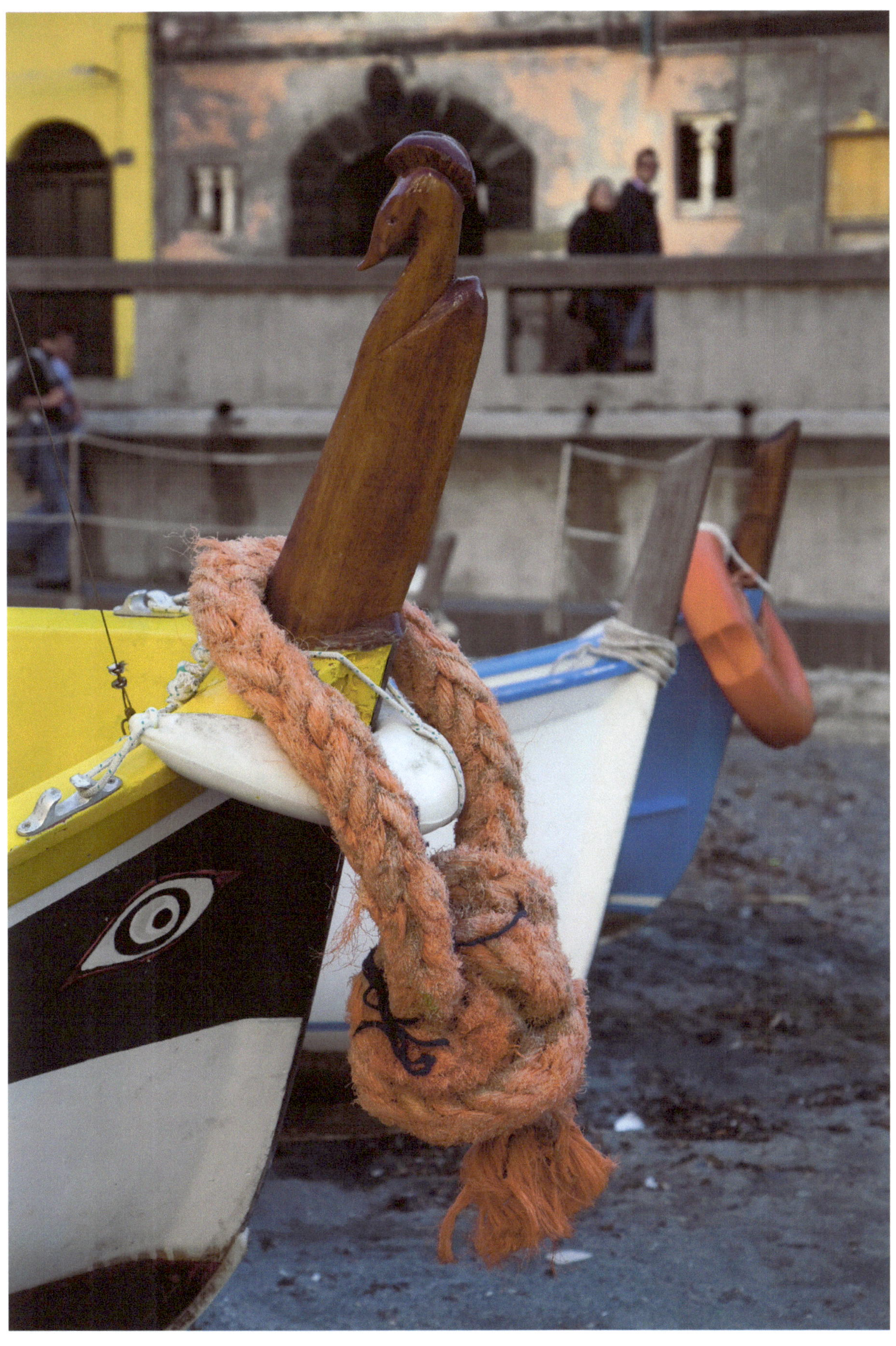

The eye on the boat front just caught my attention for a shallow depth of field shot.

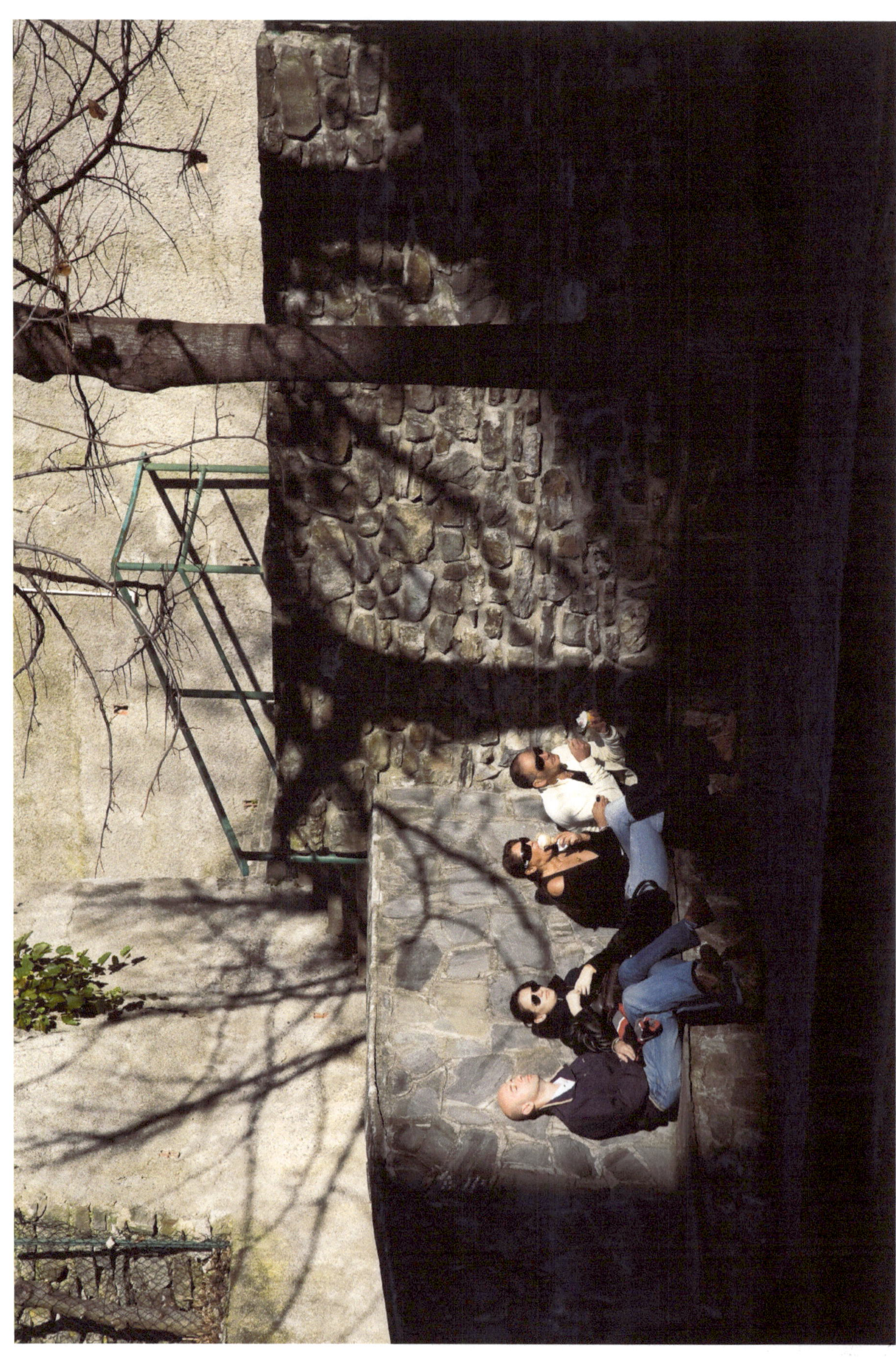

Catching the warm autumnal sun in Cinque Terre.

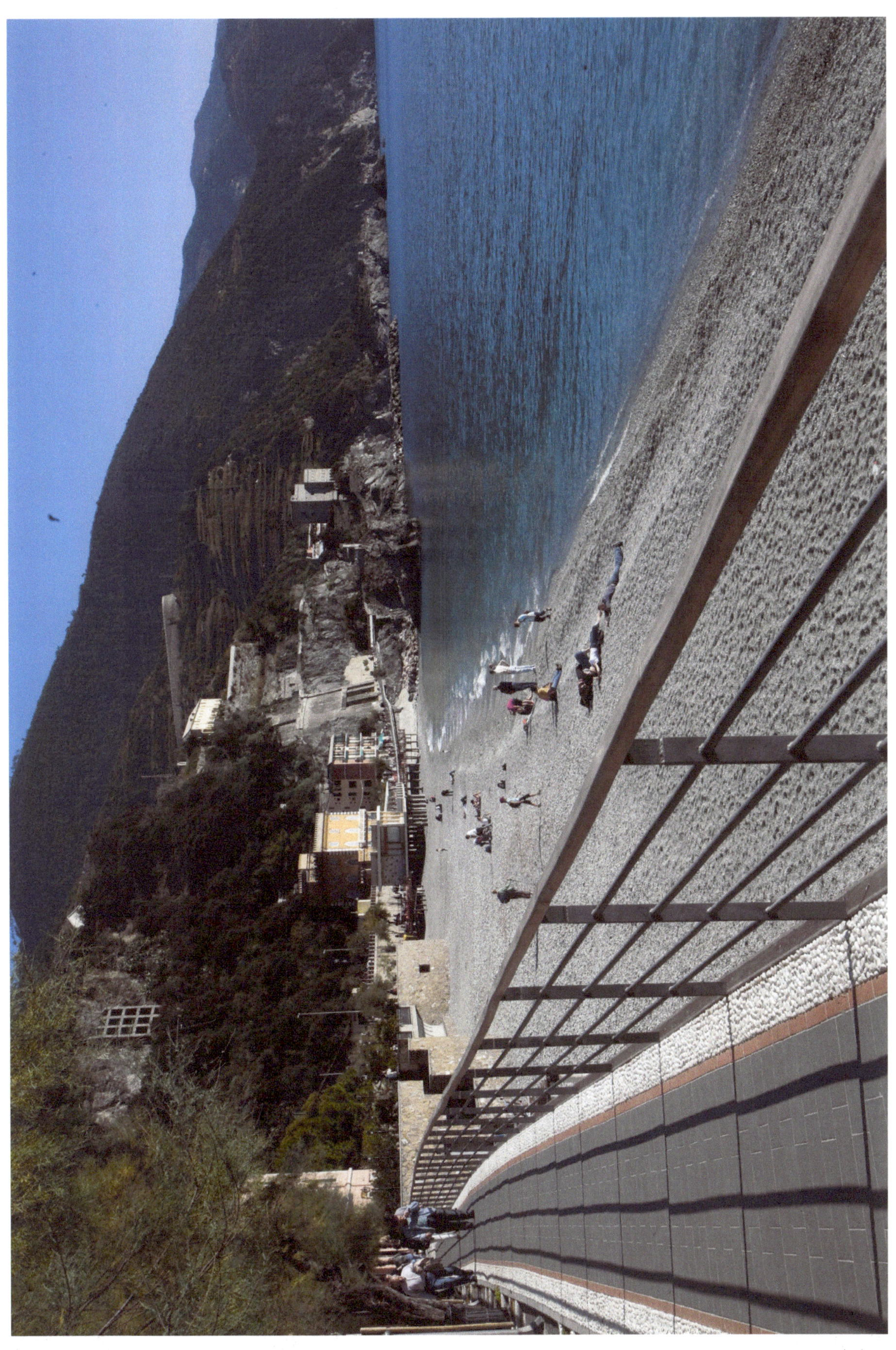

The quiet beachfront of Vernazza in November.

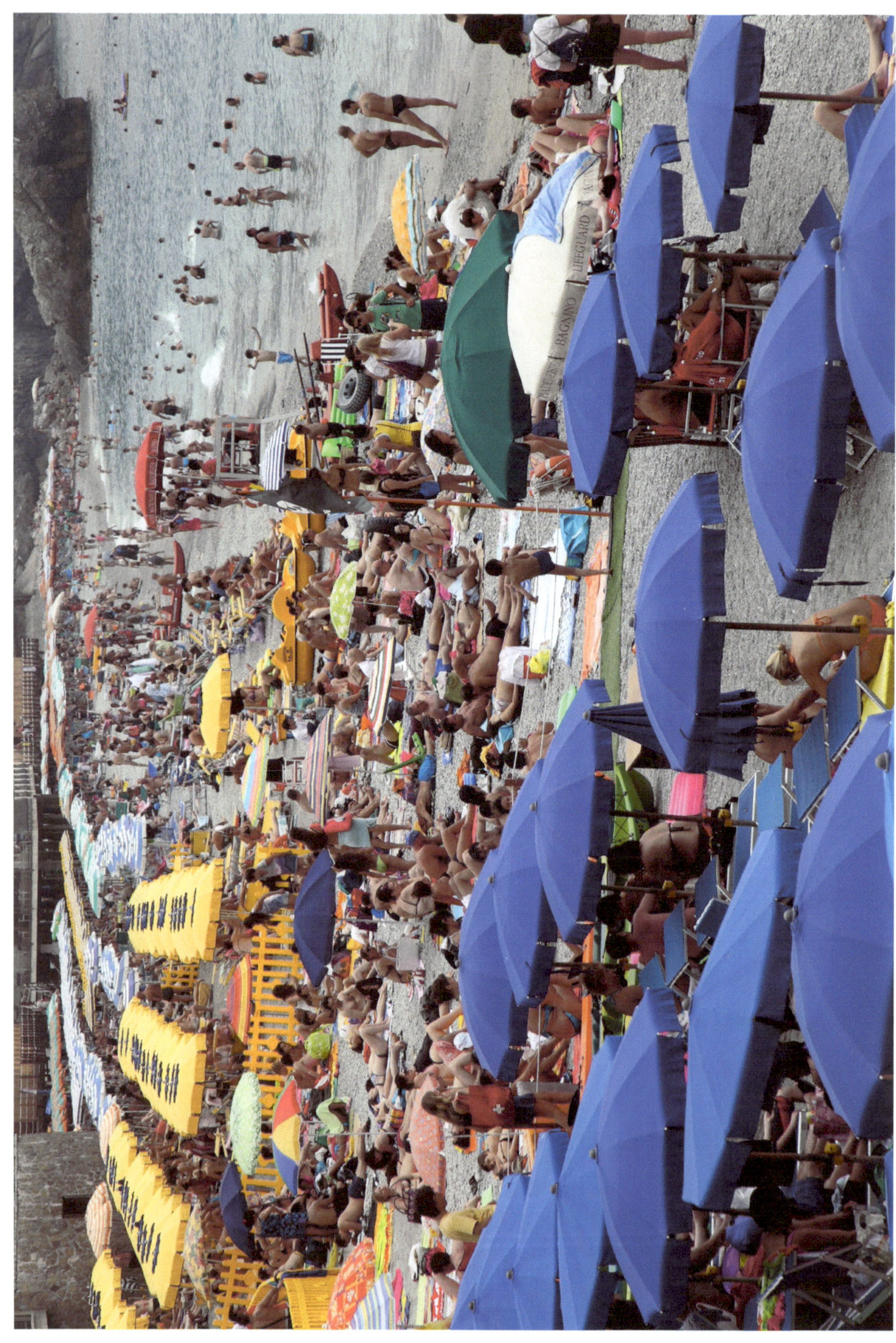

The same beachfront in July, proving slightly more popular!

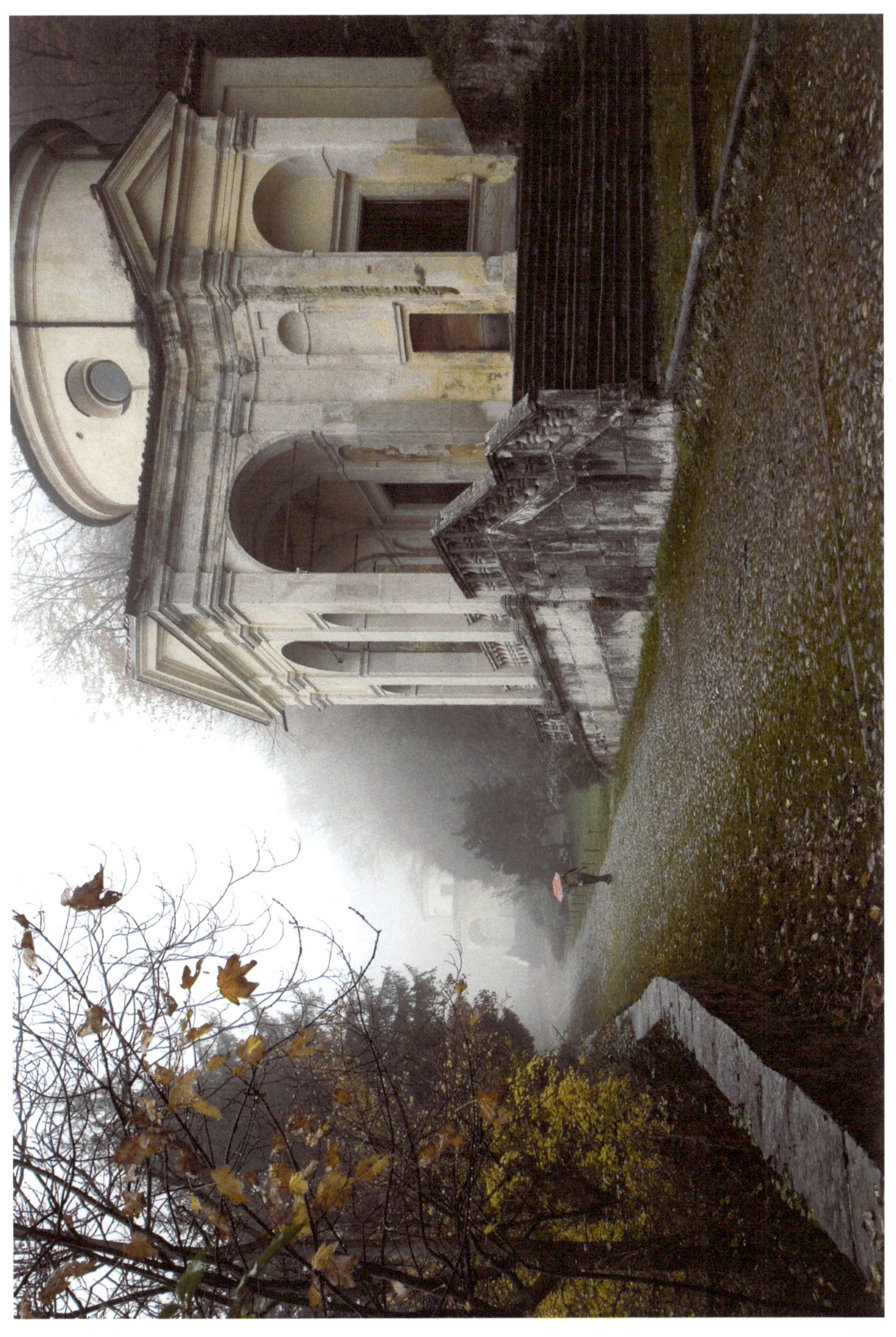

Sacre Monte Di Orta on a wet, cold December day, but a walk well worth taking.

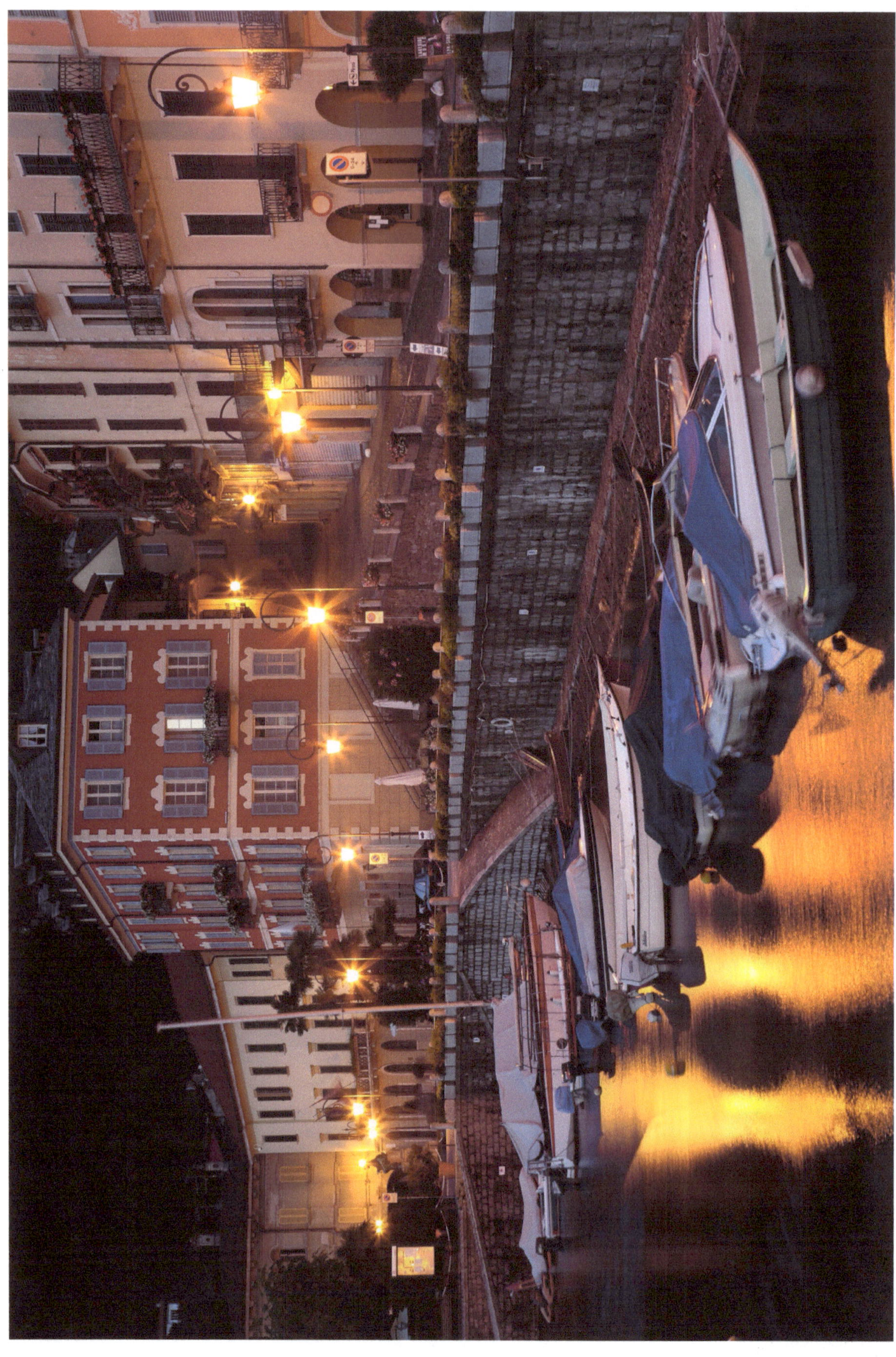

Night time, long exposure shot of the Cannobio waterfront on Lake Maggiore.

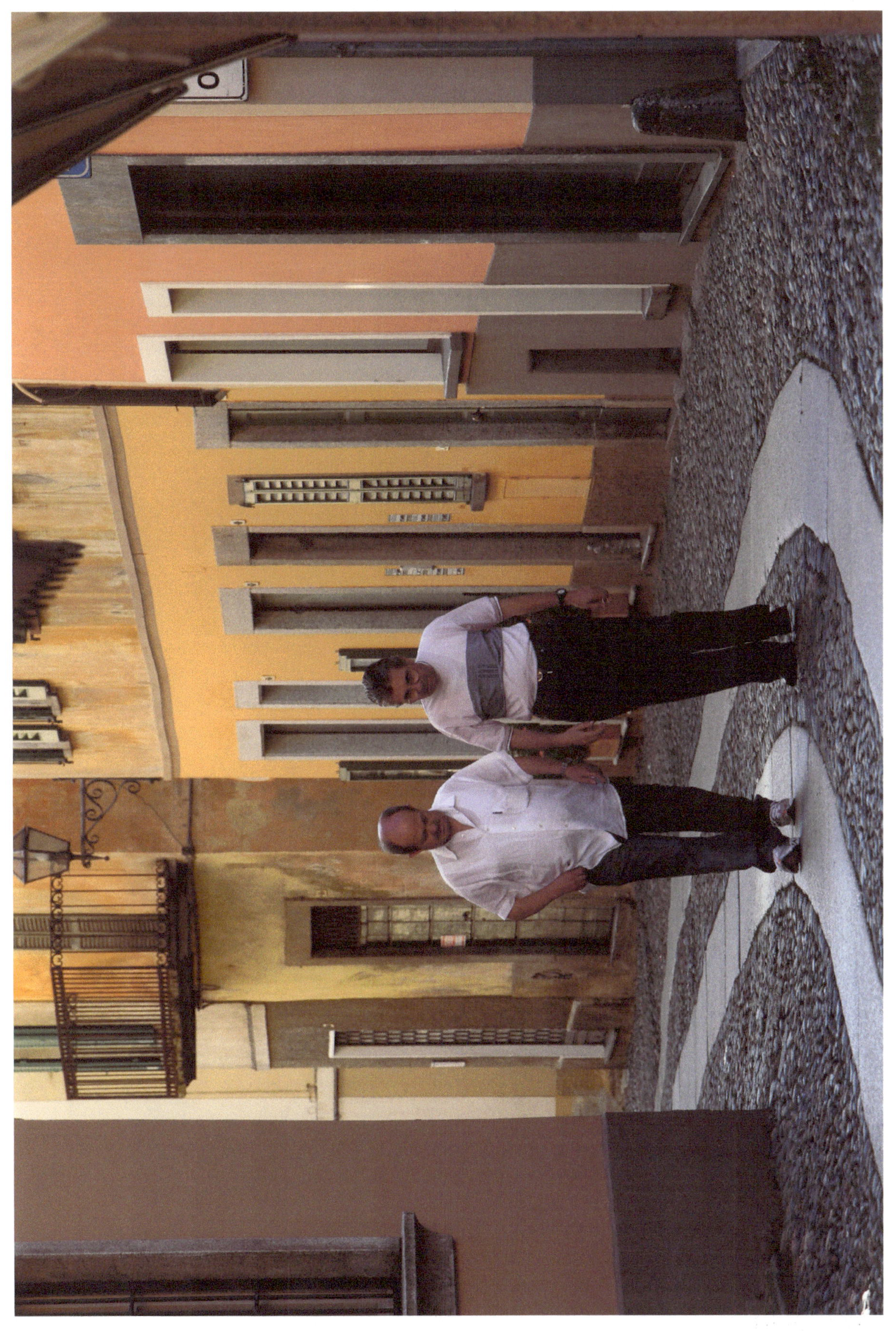

Gentle stroll through the quiet side streets of Cannobio.

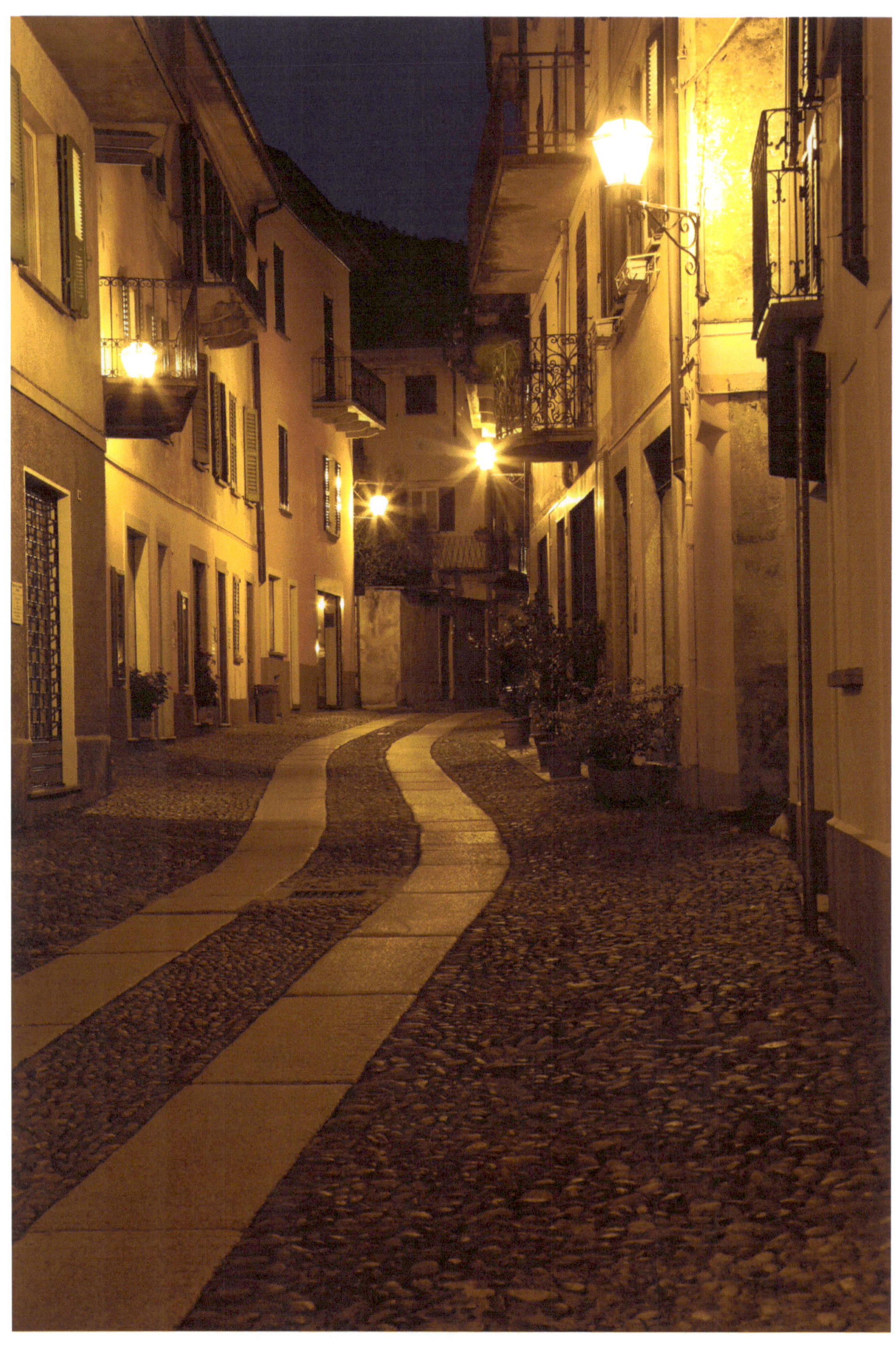

Winding cobblestone streets of Cannabio at some ungodly hour in the morning!

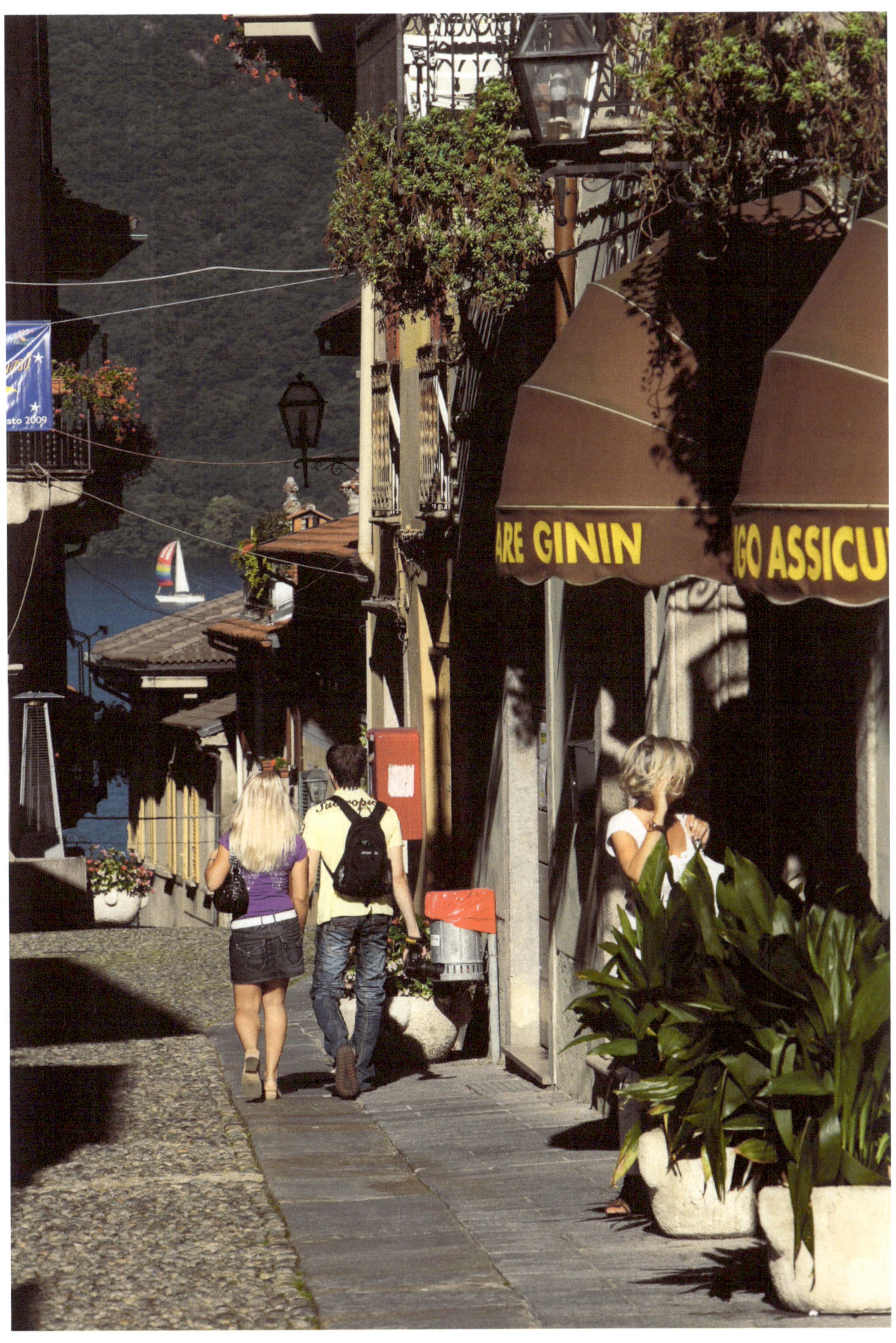

Short late afternoon walk down to the waters' edge in Cannobio.

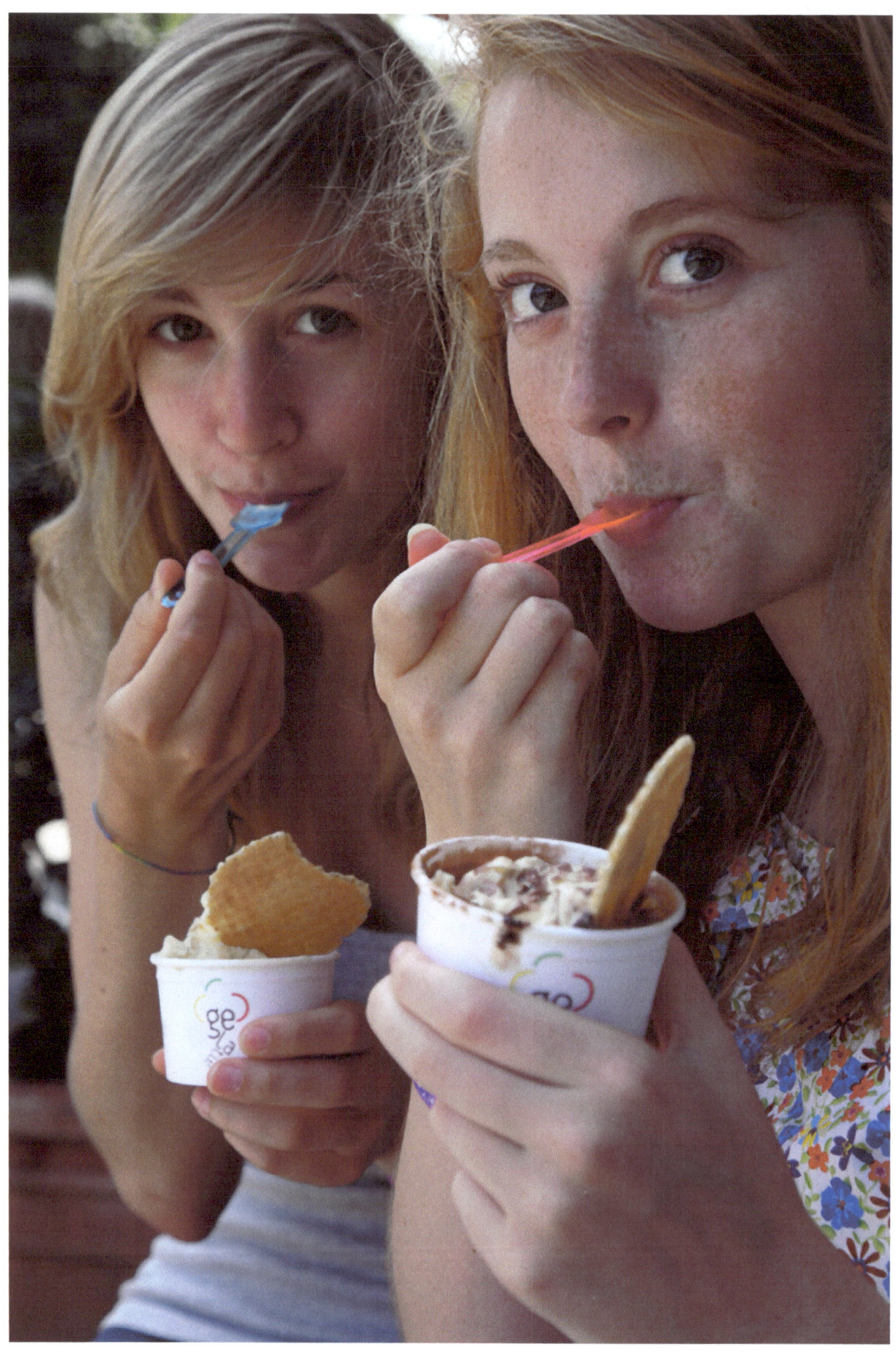

Is Italian gelato the best there is? These two wouldn't disagree.

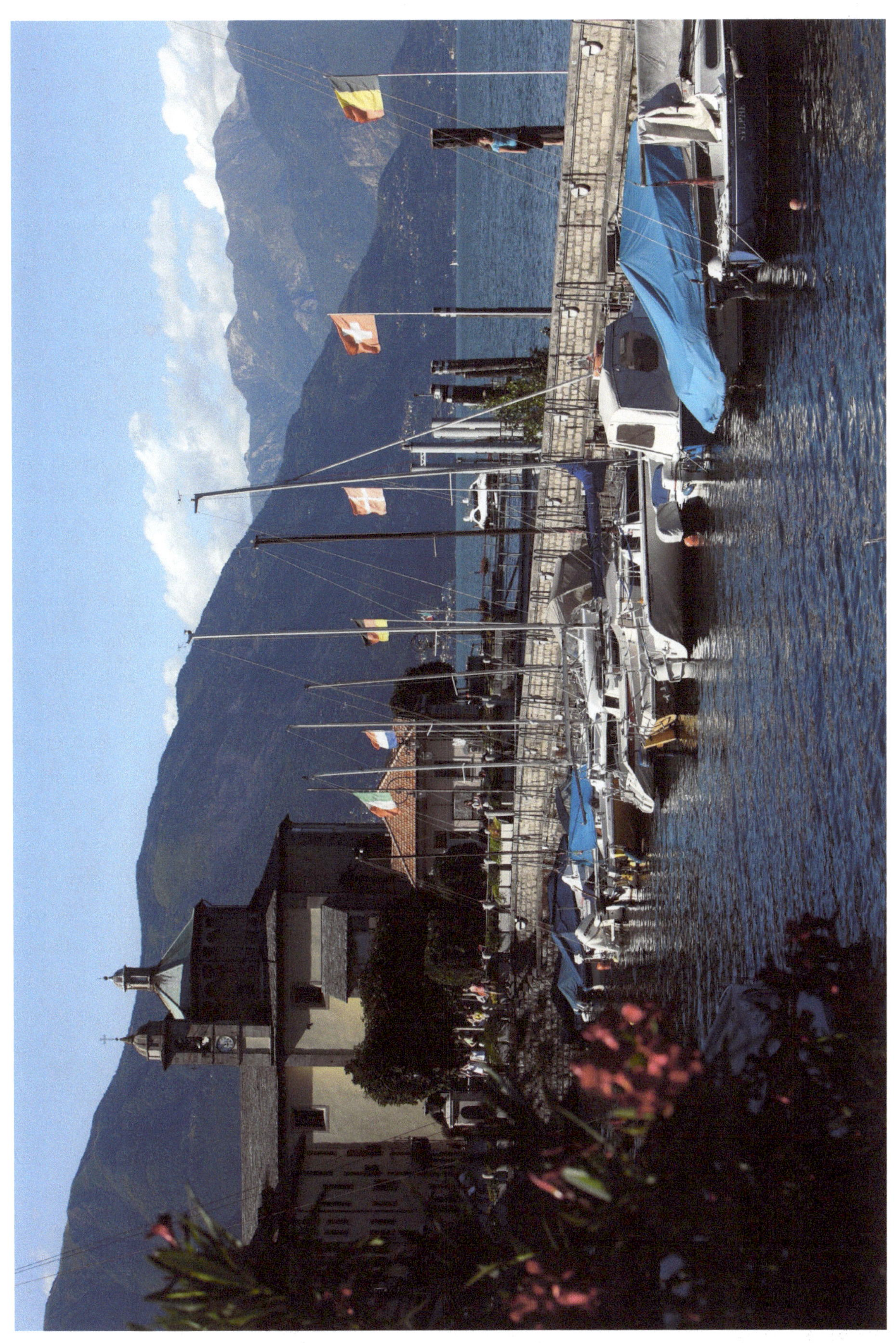

Locarno waterfront on Lake Maggiore in Switzerland.

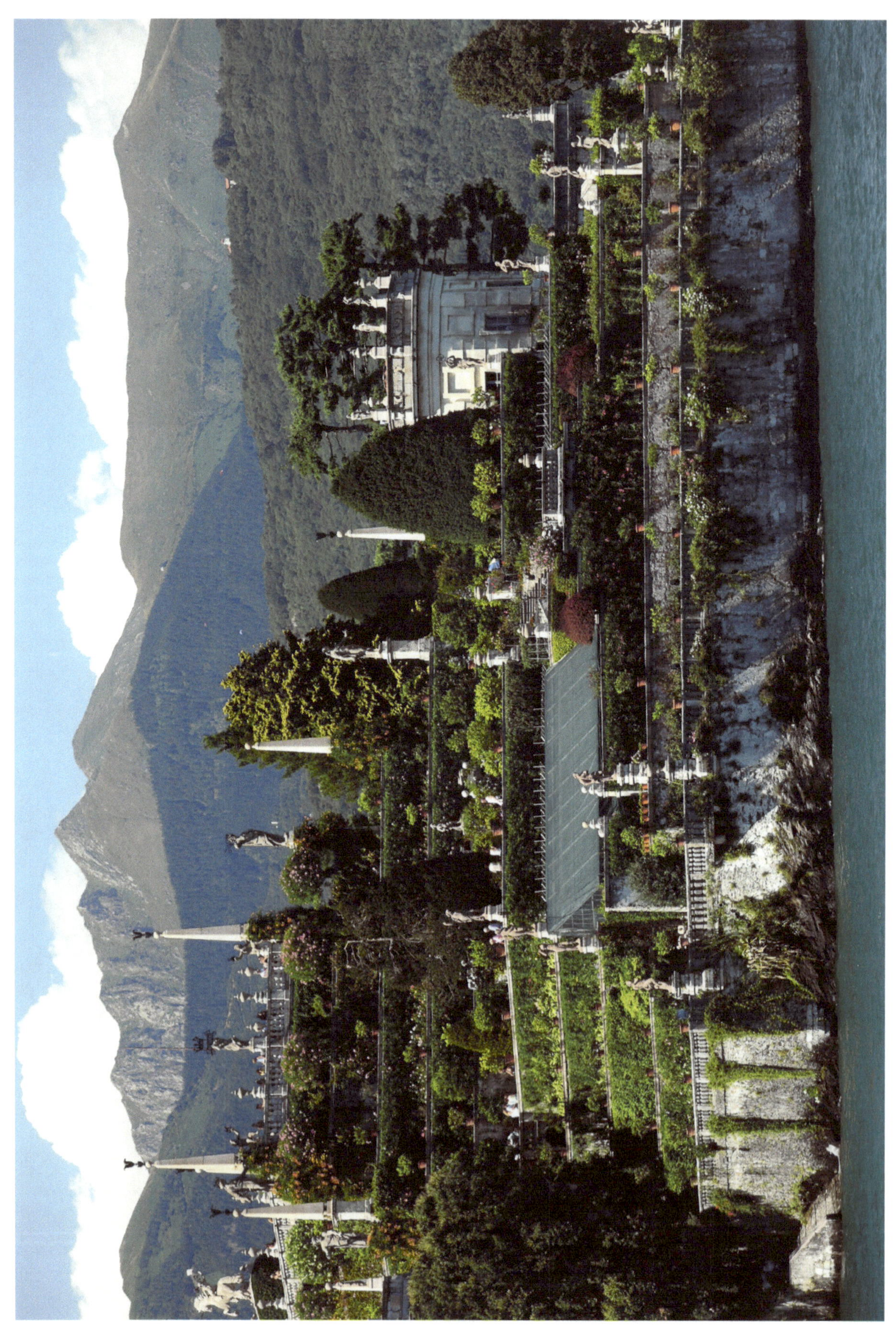

Isola Madre in the Borromean Islands, Lake Maggiore.

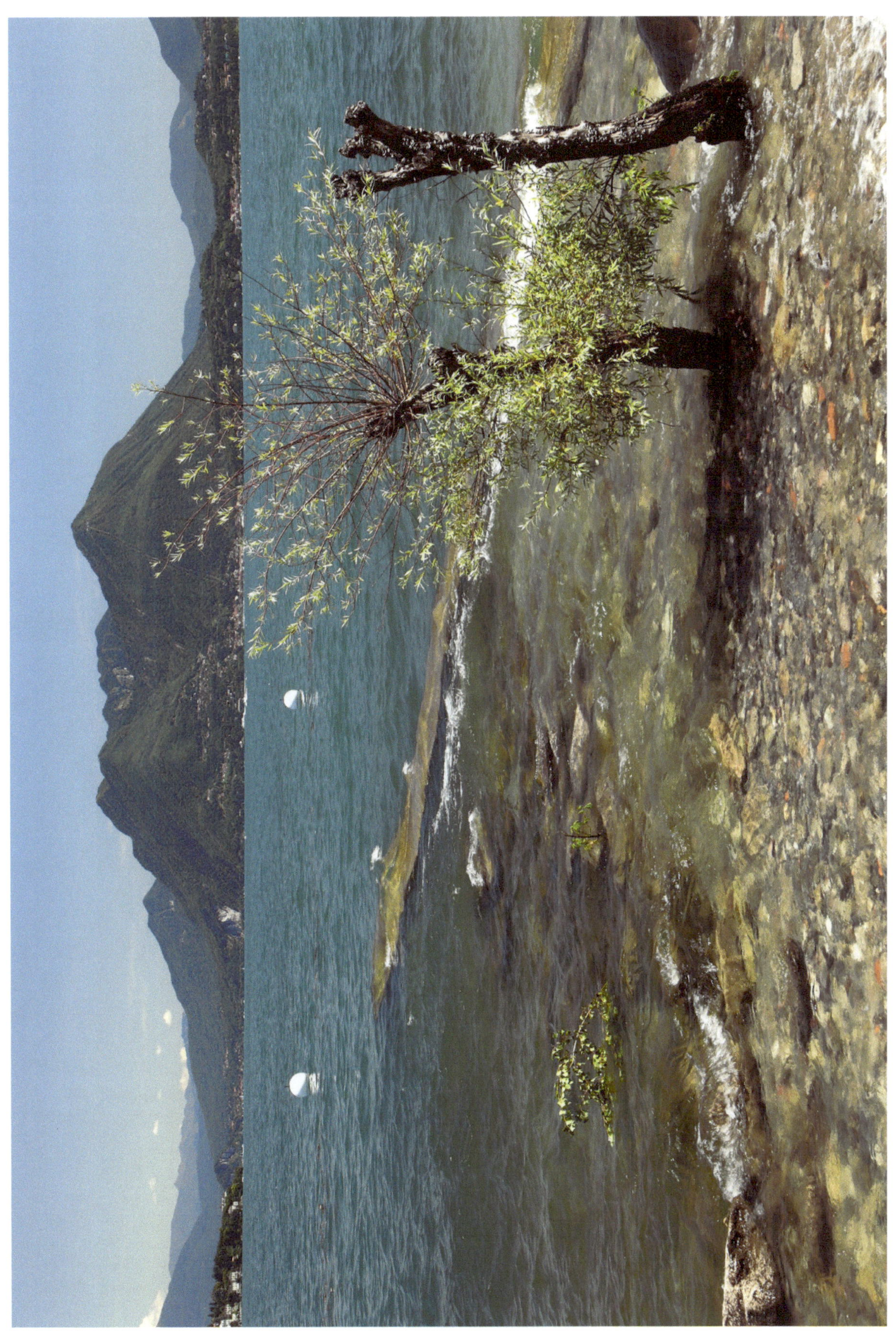

Isola Pescatori, Borromean Islands, Lake Maggiore.

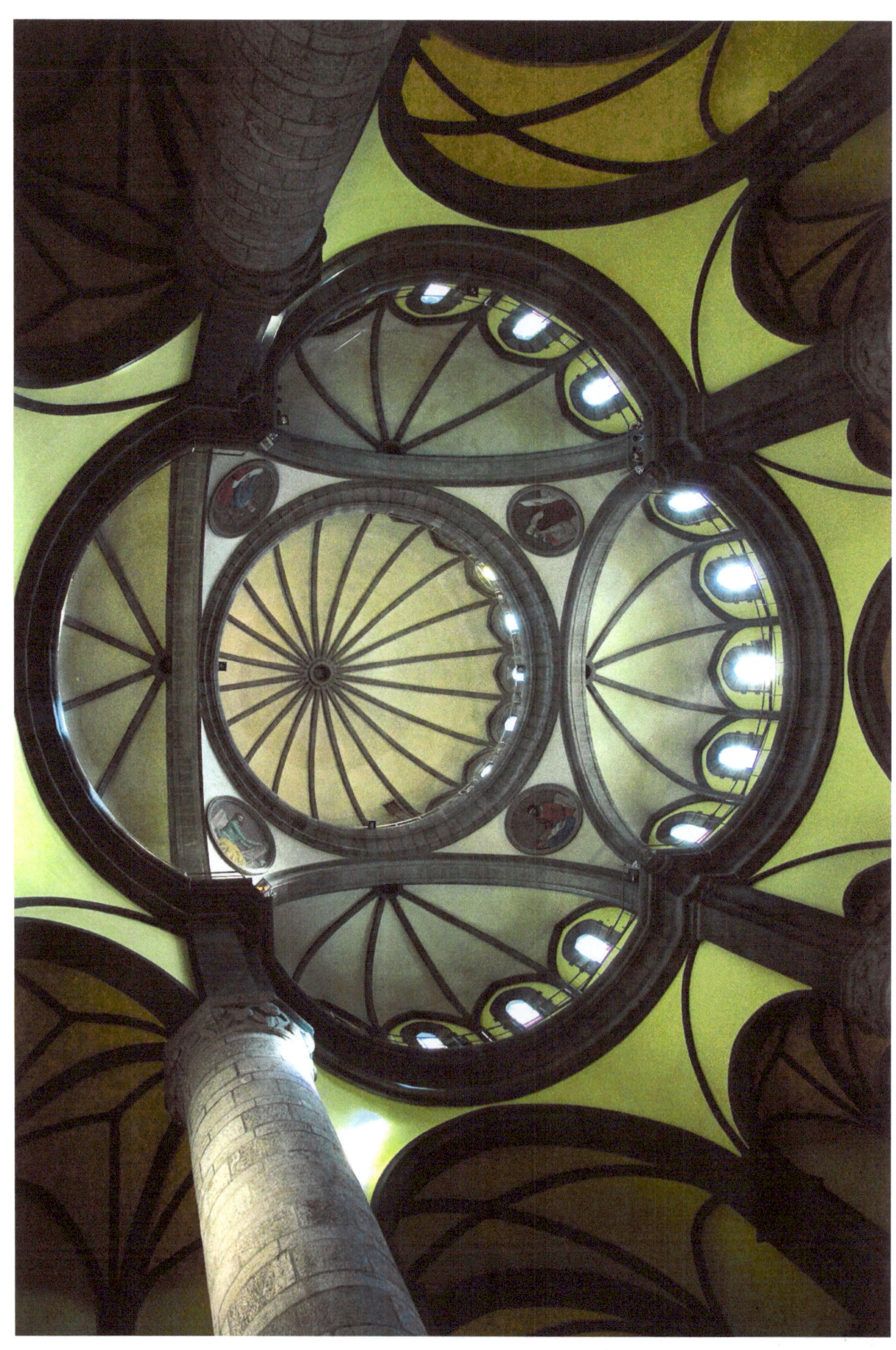

Ornate ceiling work inside the cathedral at Ré.

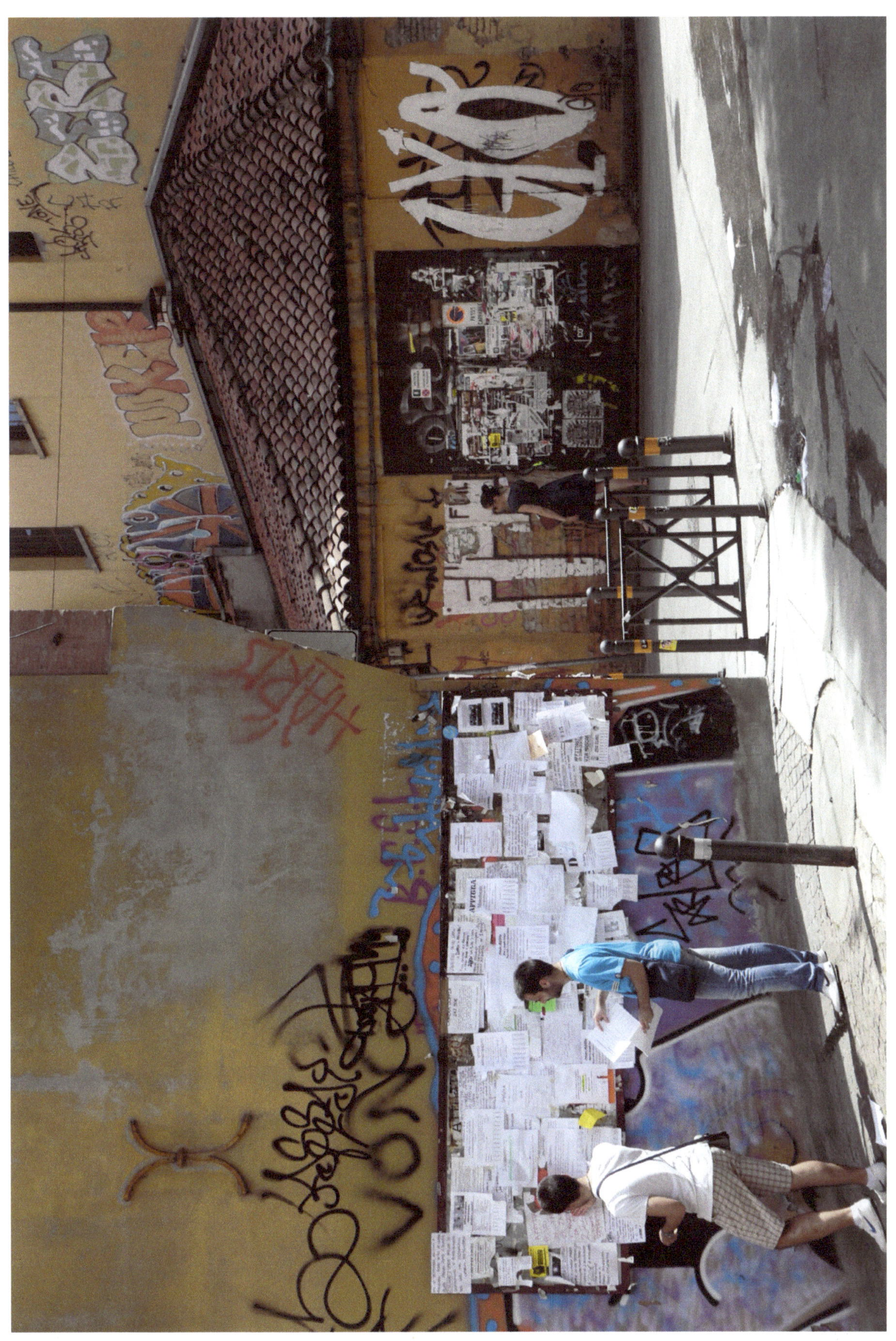

Where to leave messages in Bologna.

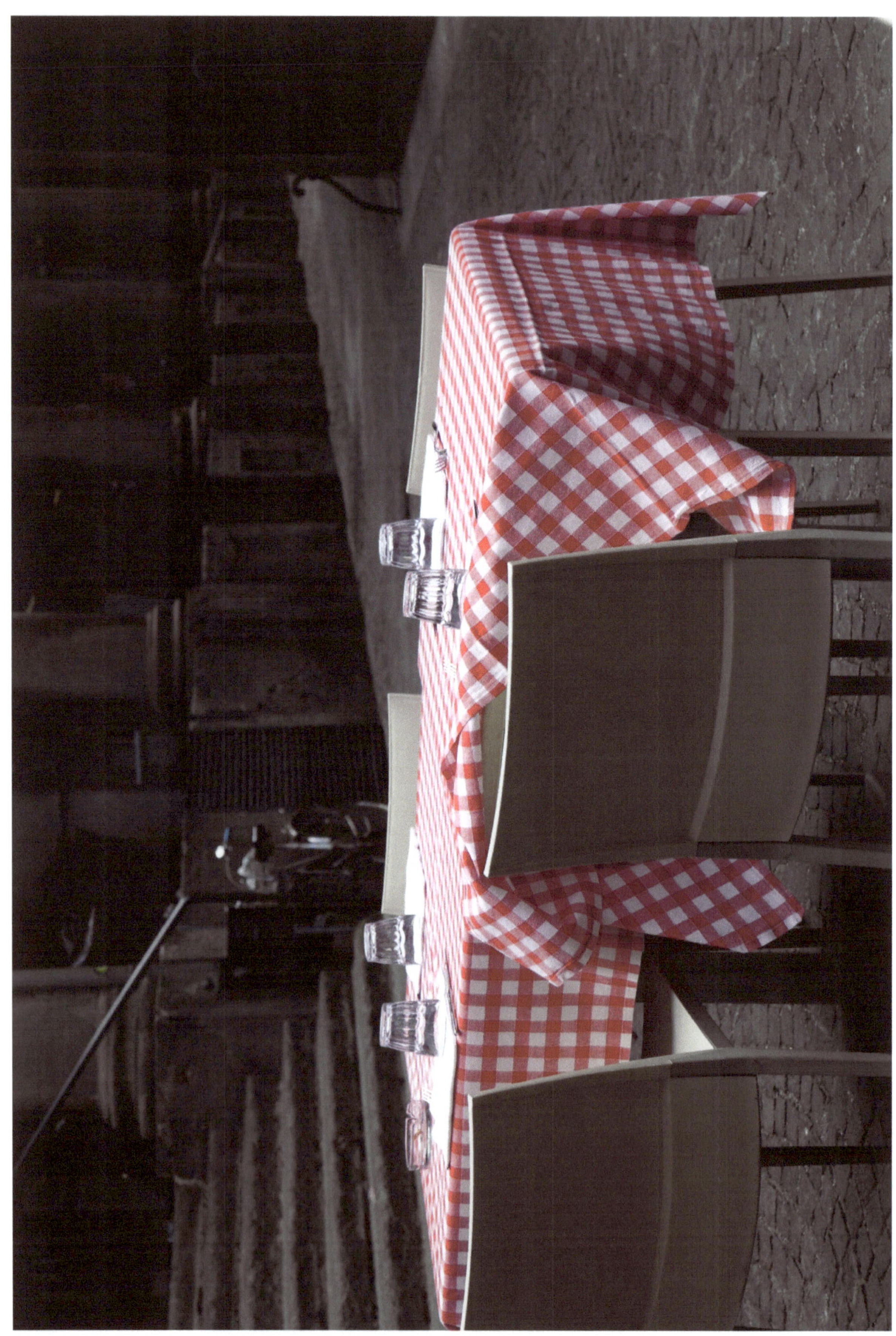

Was taken by the ruffled tablecloth at this side street cafe in Bologna.

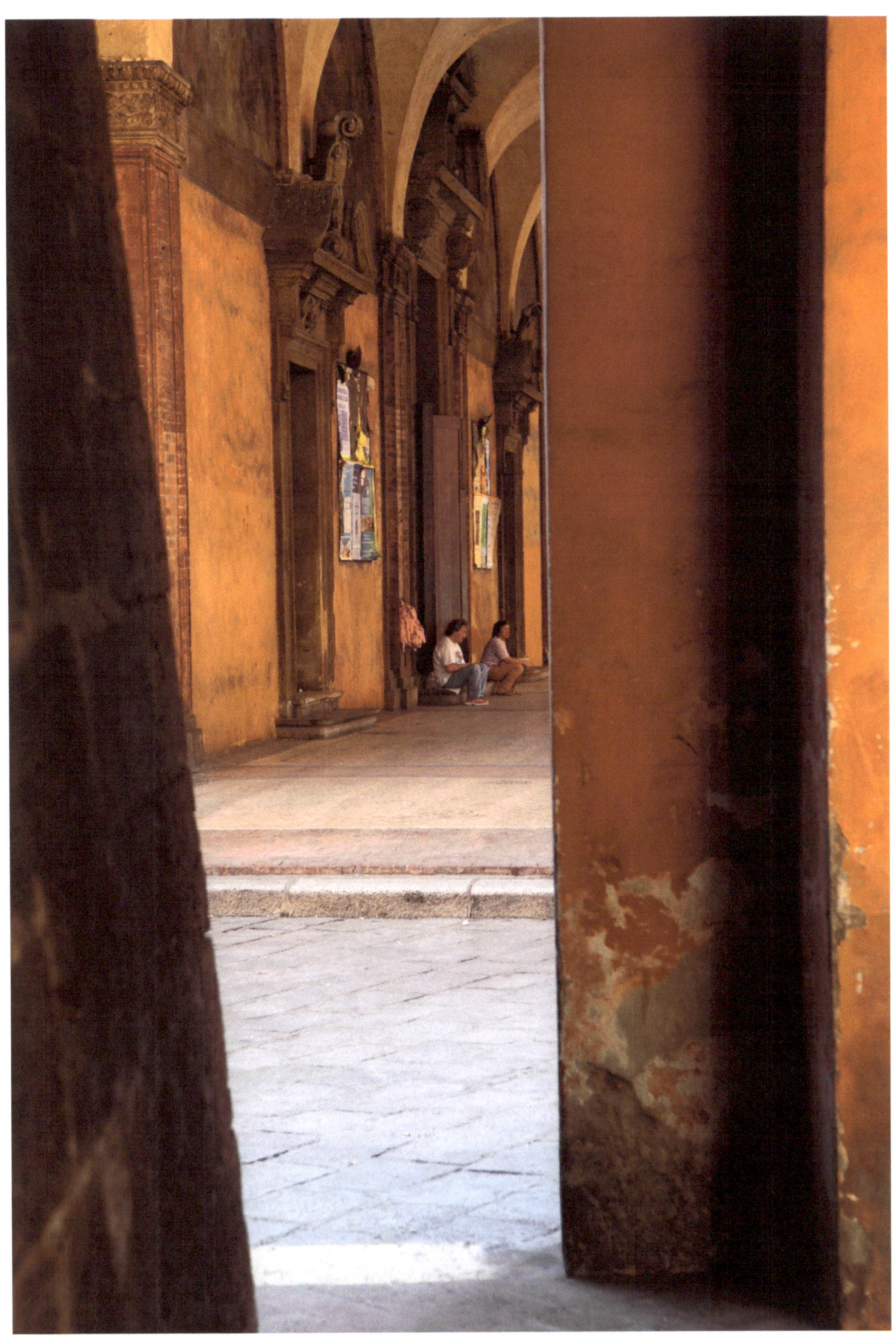

People watching underneath the two towers in Bologna.

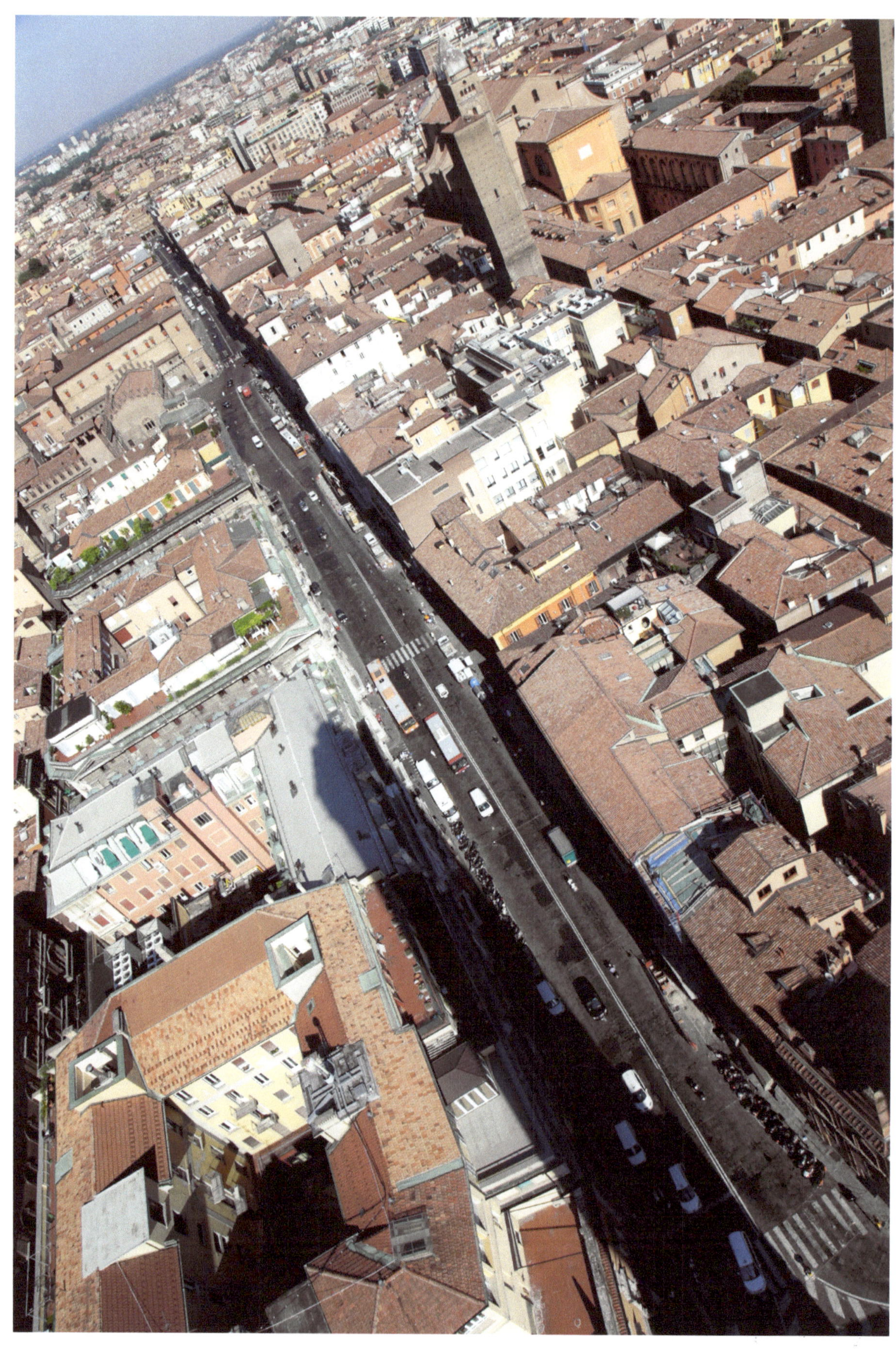

View from the top of the Asinelli Tower, Bologna, after just the 498 steps!

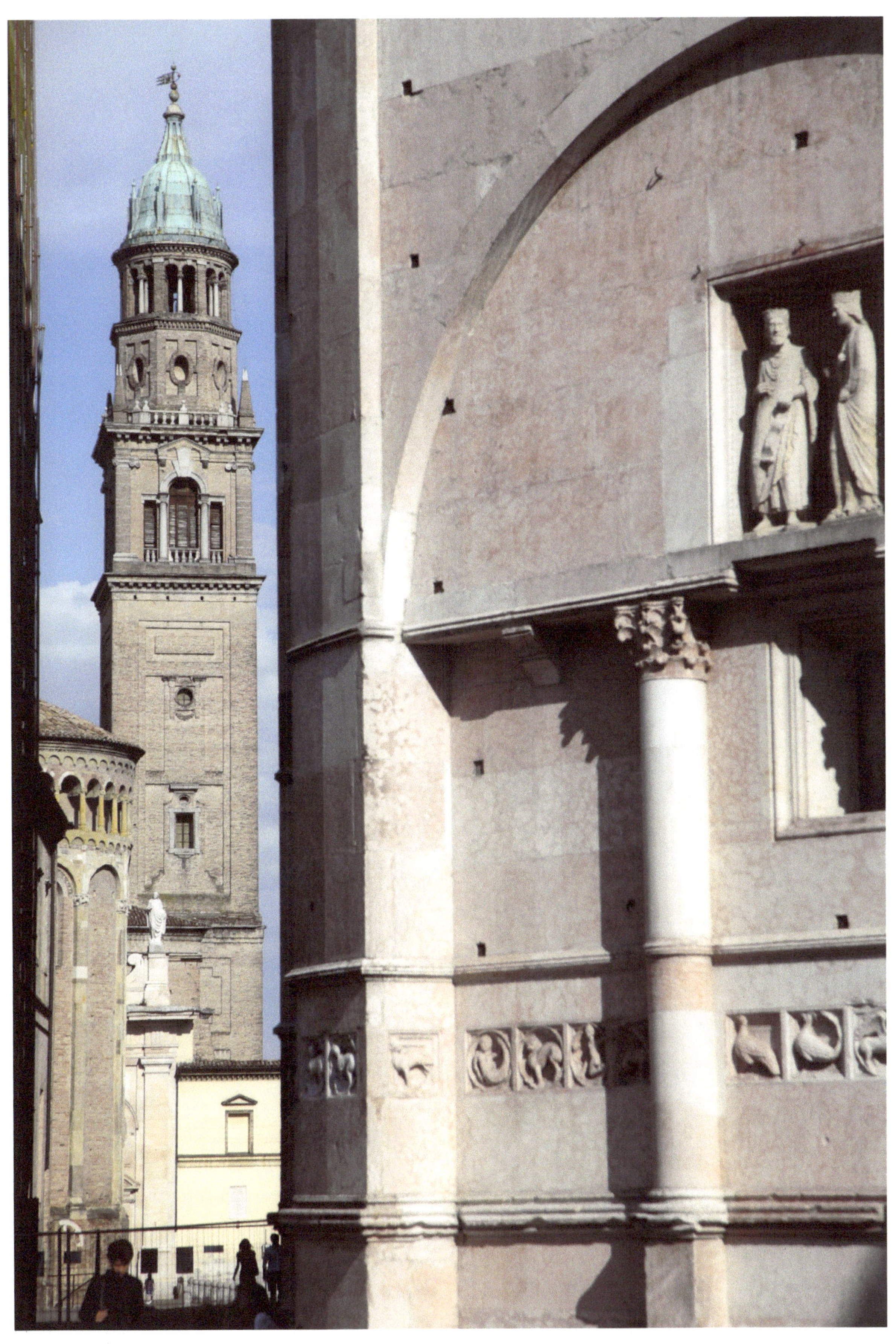

Using shallow depth of field to blur the foreground.

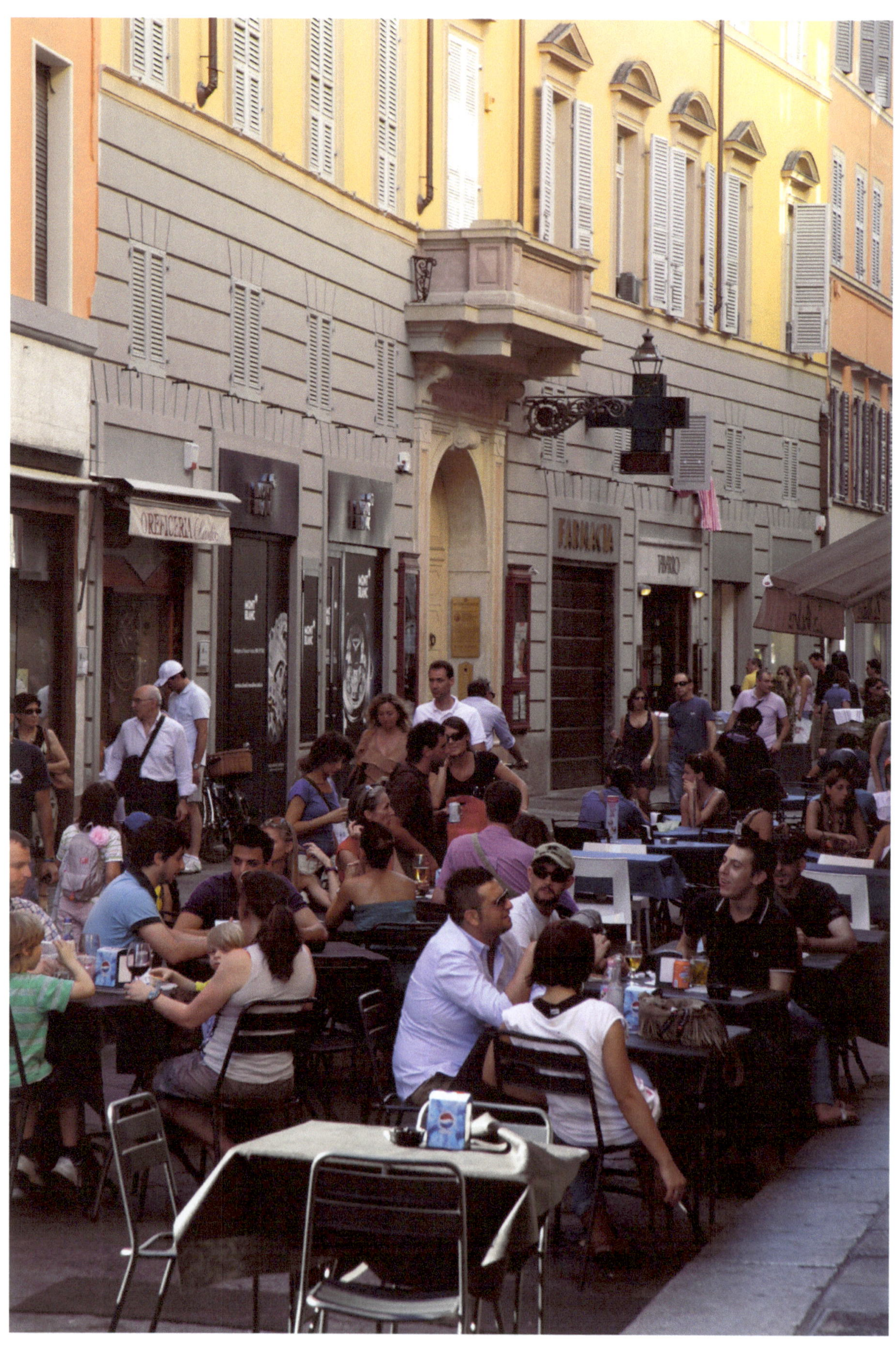

Summer street scene in Parma.

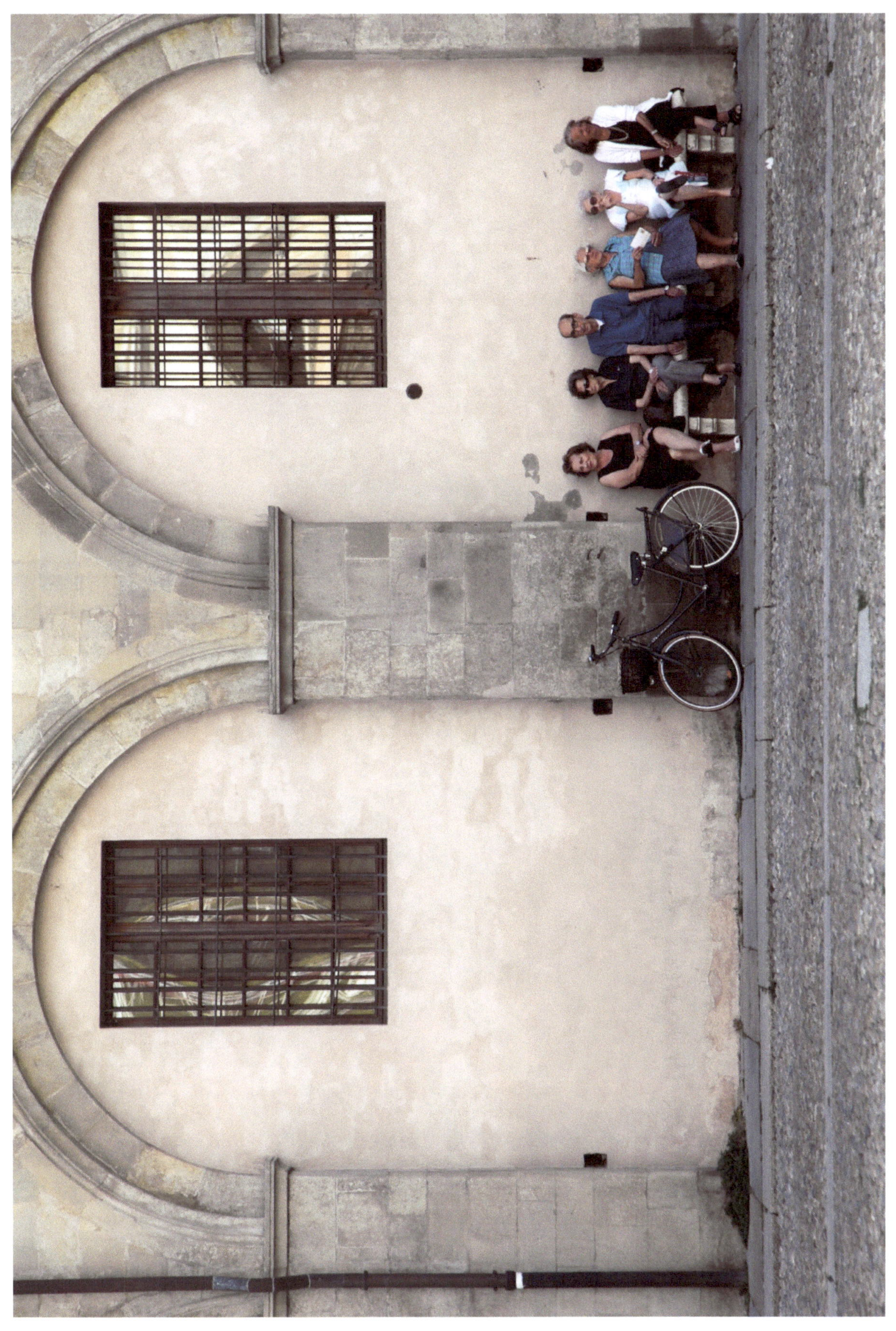

Just liked the way there was no seat on the left of the picture, leaving a pleasantly unbalanced shot.

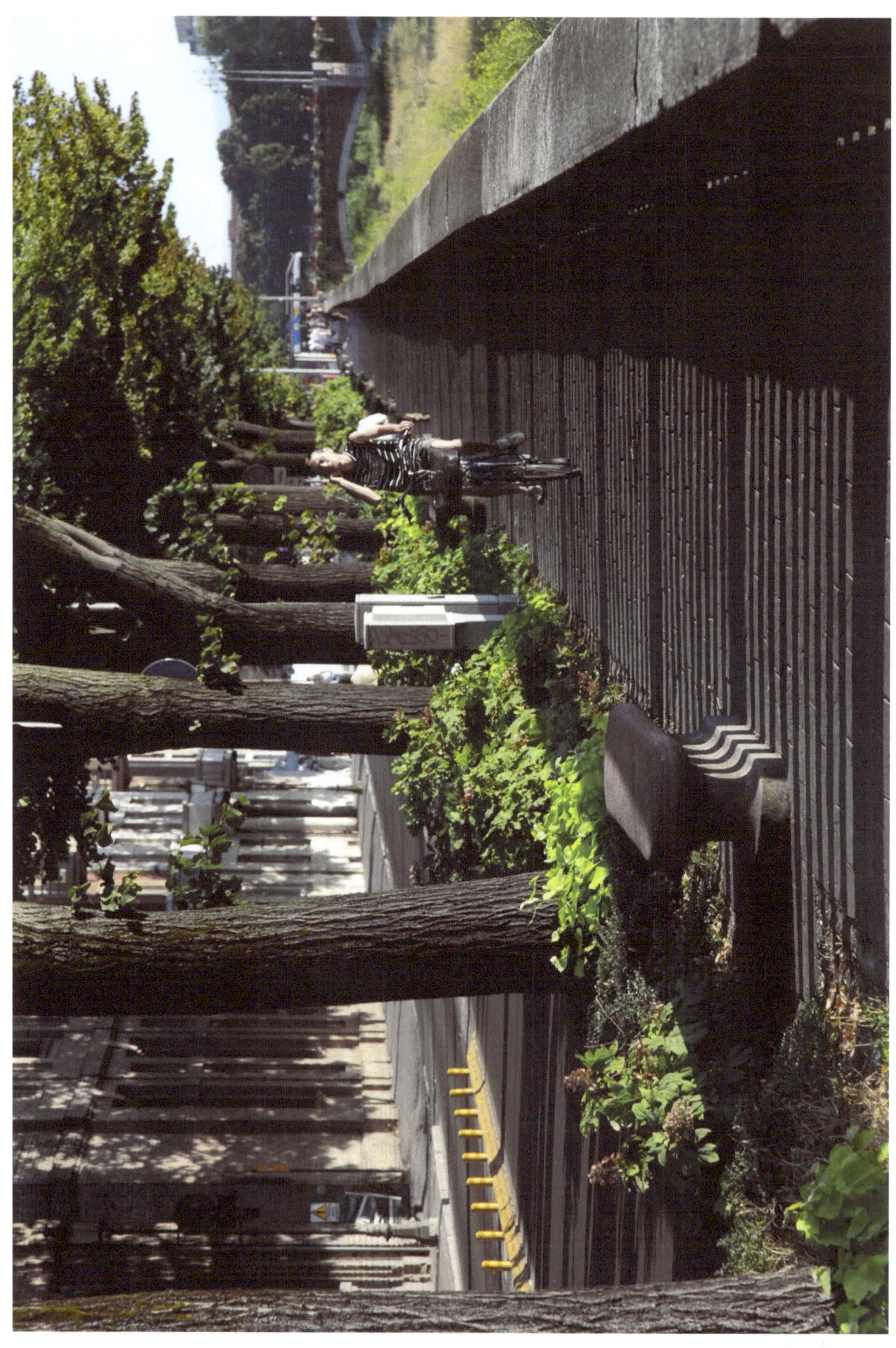

Relaxing way to get around Parma in summer.

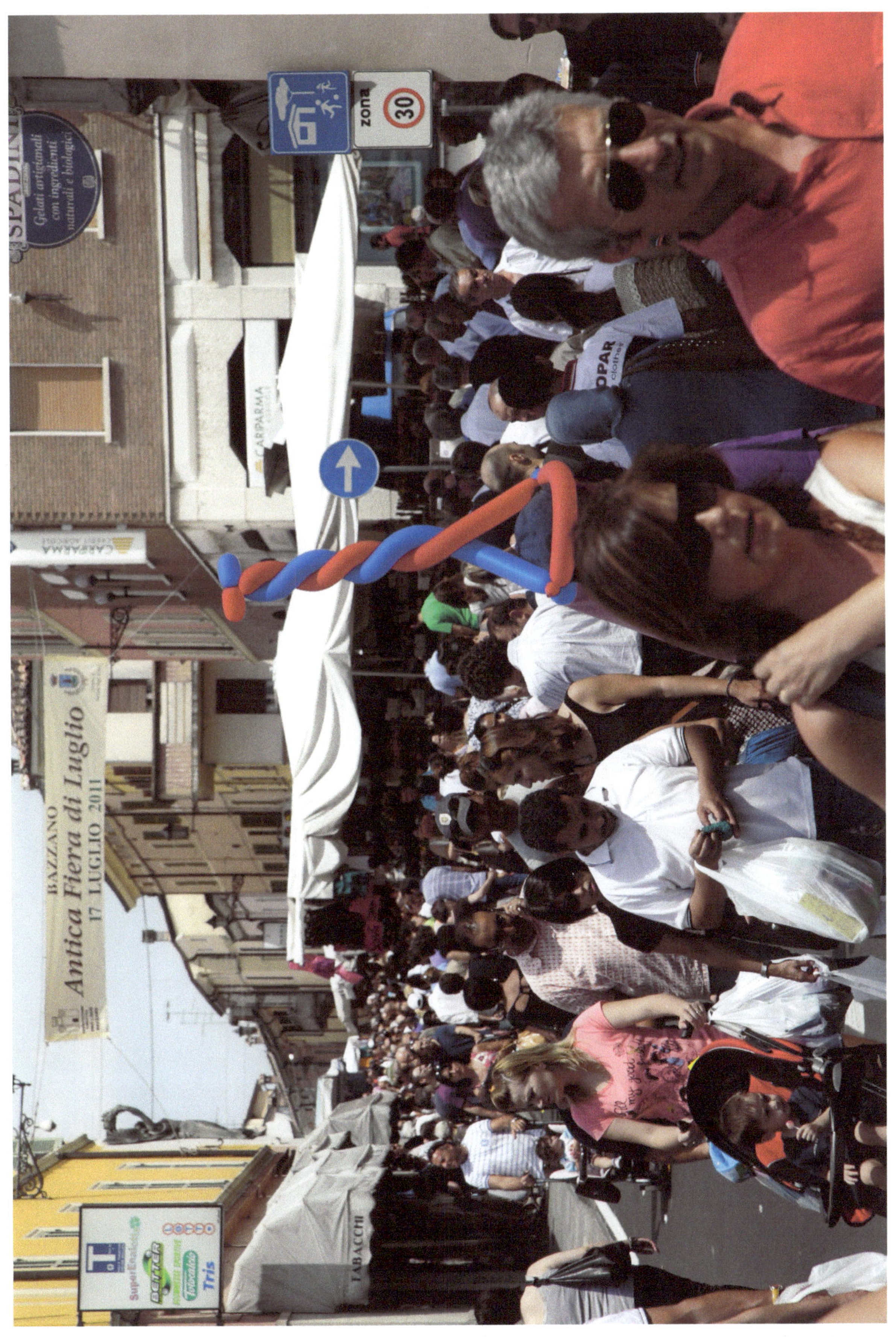

Busy street market scene in Bazzano.

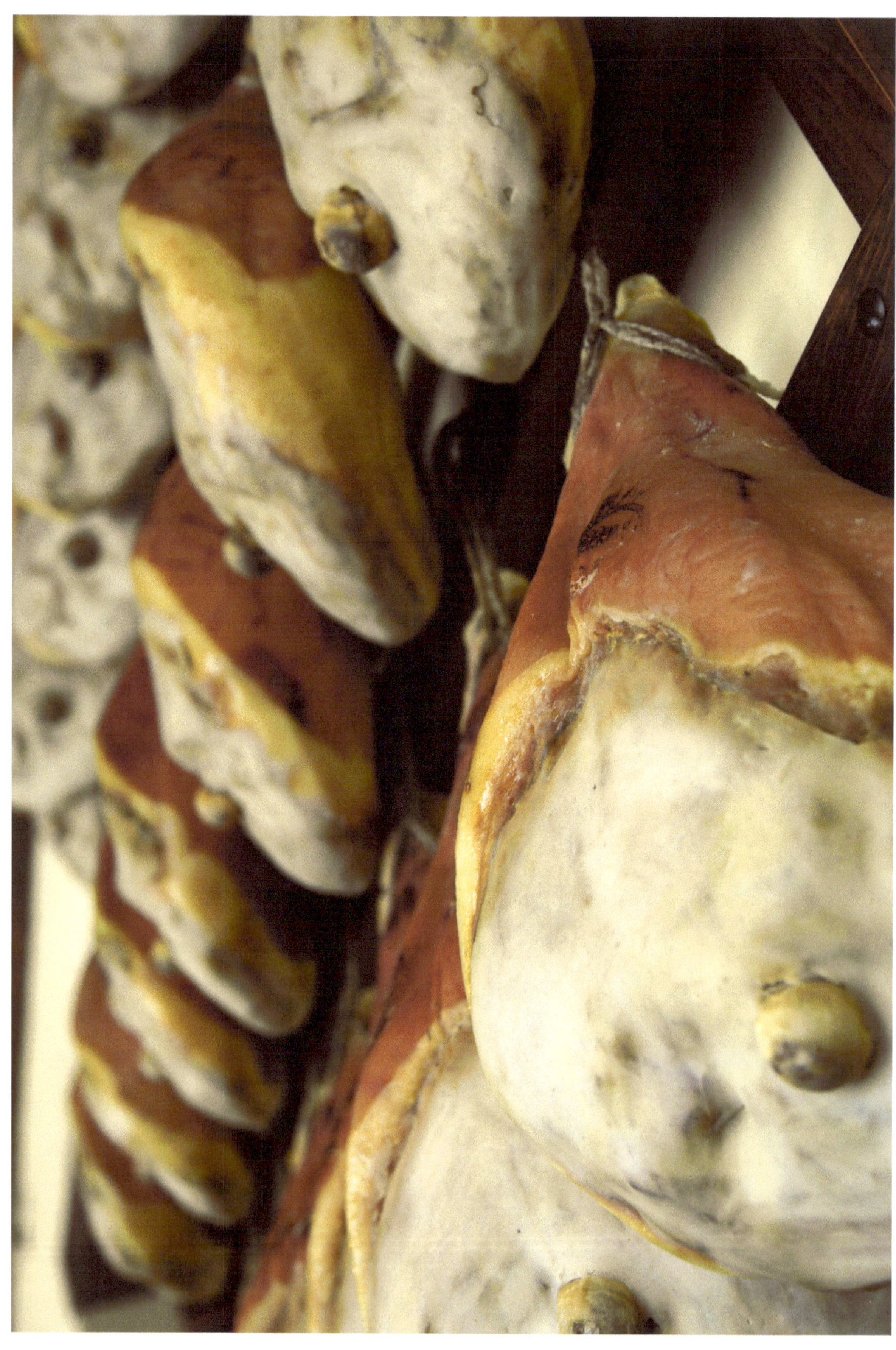

Plenty of sampling was done at this Parma ham factory.

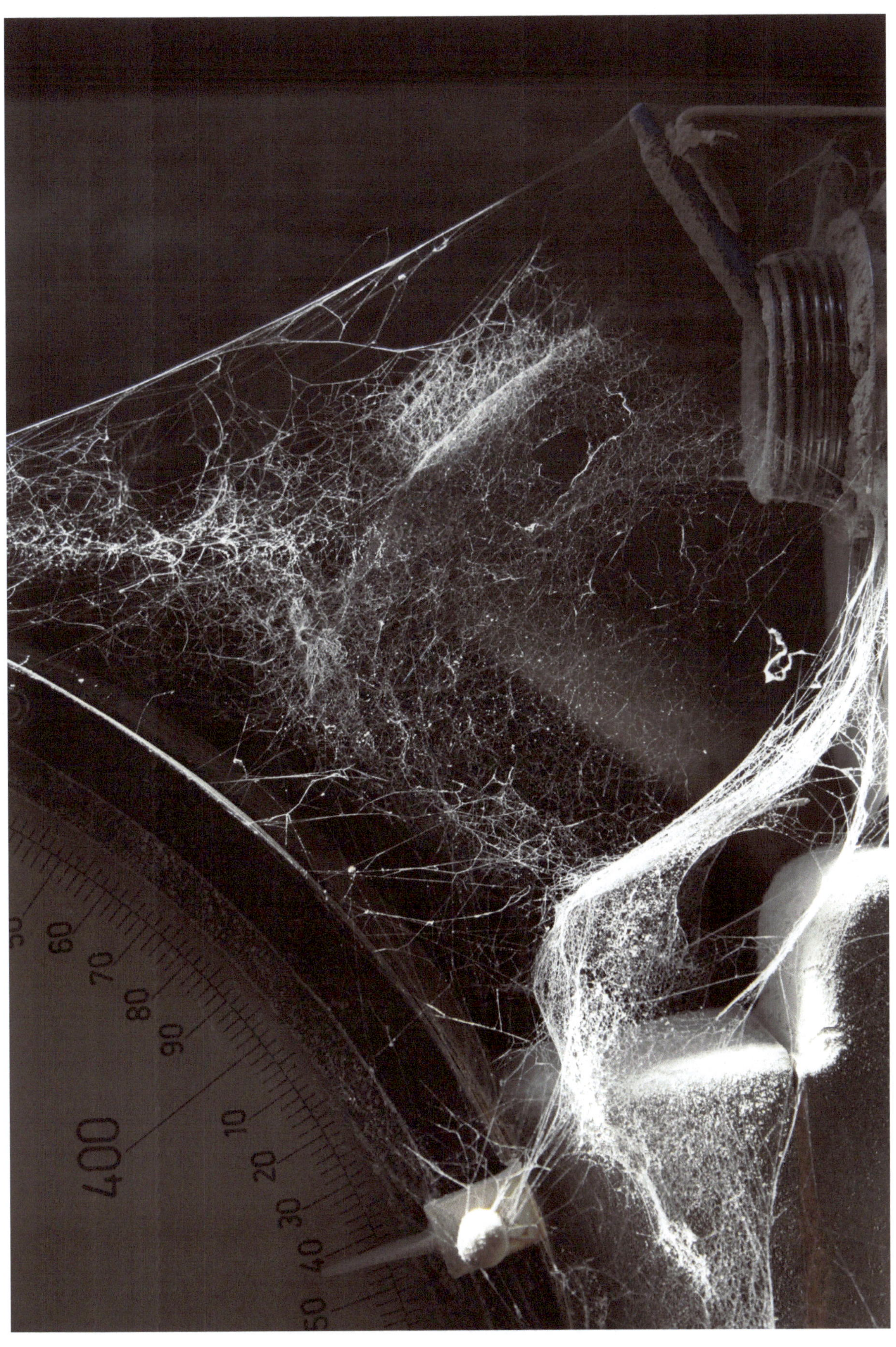

Amazing ray of light picking out the cobwebs in this animal feed factory behind the parmesan cheese making centre, Parma.

Making Parmesan Cheese

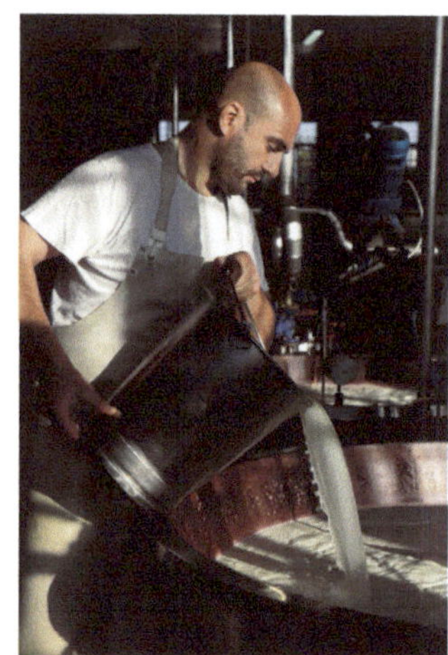
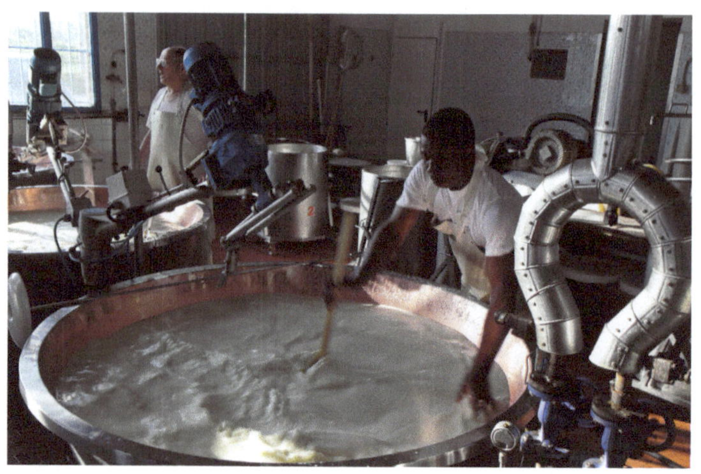
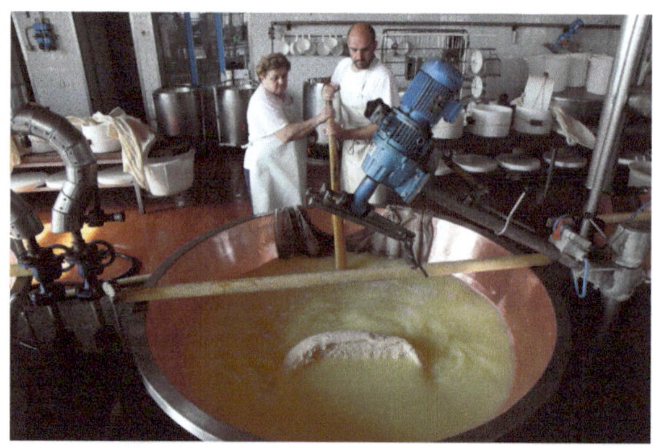
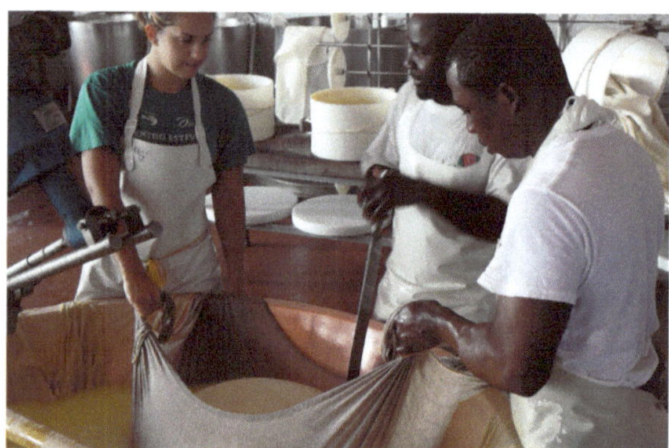
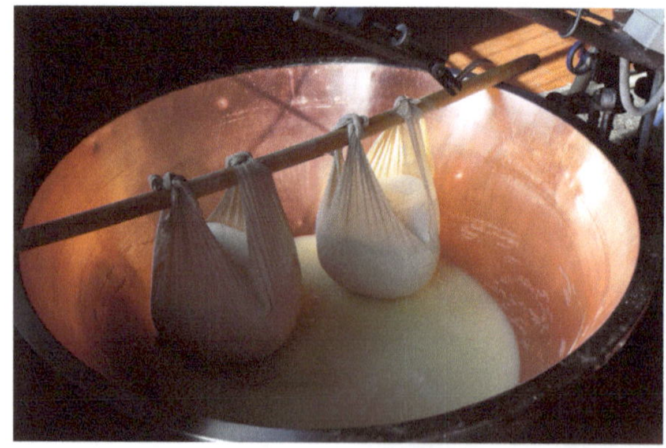
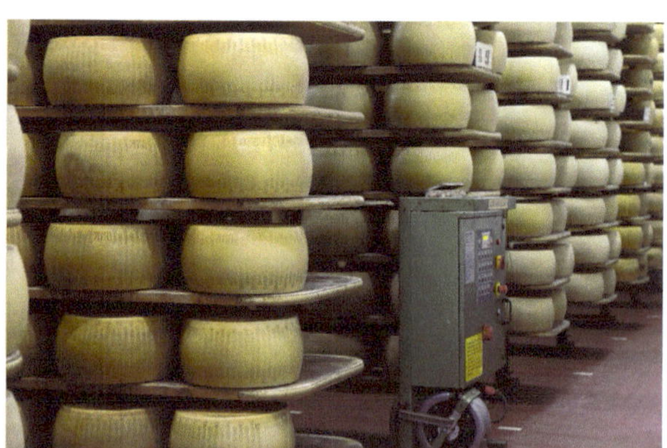
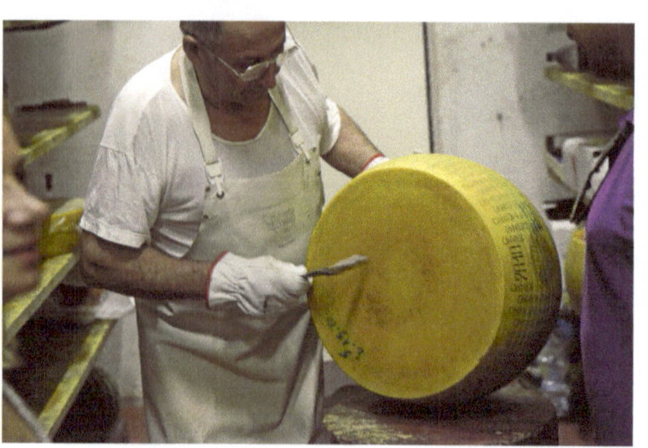

Also from Keith Hern

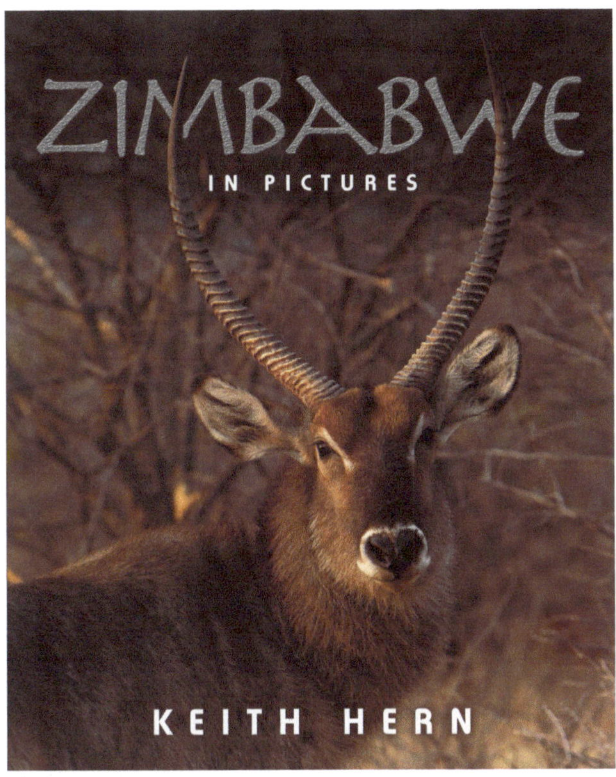

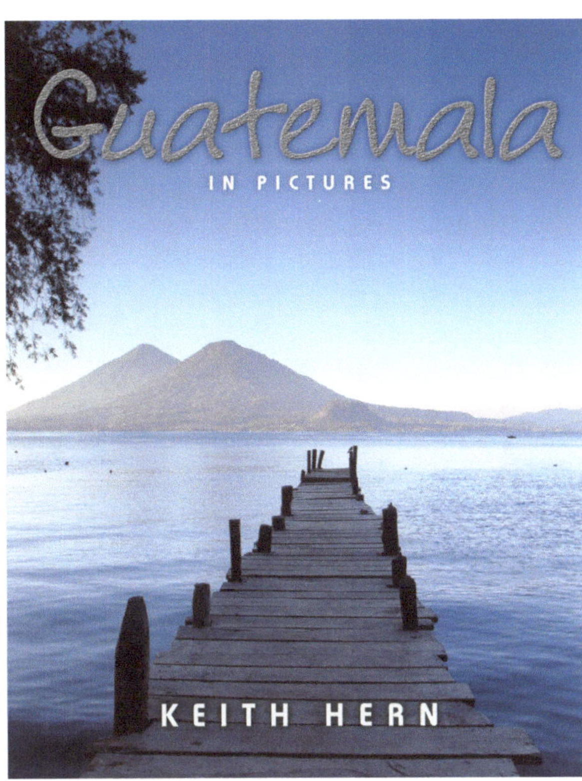

"In my experience of working with photo journalists on Zimbabwe, the images you have produced are outstanding and second to none. The photographs of people, animals and scenery bring out the reality and beauty of Zimbabwe. We treasure your work in showcasing Zimbabwe internationally".

Zimbabwe Tourist Office

www.ingramcontent.com/pod-product-compliance
Lightning Source LLC
LaVergne TN
LVHW070127110826
845147LV00002B/202